D1265860

MIAMI FLAVORS

MIAMI FLAVORS

OUR CITY'S CULINARY POINT OF VIEW

MIAMI
CHILDREN'S
HOSPITAL.
FOUNDATION

DEDICATION

This cookbook is dedicated to children everywhere, especially those who have been and will be helped at Miami Children's Hospital.

Thanks to a generous contribution by Cargill, Inc., through its Grain & Oilseed Supply Chain, Americas Marketing Group business based in Coral Gables, Florida, all proceeds from the sale of this book will be donated to Miami Children's Hospital.

Copyright © 2008 by Miami Children's Hospital Foundation

All rights reserved. No part of this publication may be reproduced, stored
in a retrieval system, or transmitted in any form or by any means, electronic,
mechanical, photocopying, recording or otherwise, without prior permission
in writing from the publisher, except in the case of brief quotations in critical
articles and reviews.

Project Management: form & funktion
Design & Layout: doink, inc., Coral Gables, Florida
Executive Editor: James Connolly
Art Director: Charlie Calderin
Editors: Community Council Members of Miami Children's Hospital Foundation
Design & Production: Melissa Blanco Silva at doink, inc.

Library of Congress Cataloging-in-Publication
Data on file with the Publisher

ISBN: 978-0-615-24638-3

Printed and Bound by Global Printing Services, Inc.
www.globalprintservicesinc.com
USA: 786.242.4393
Printed in Korea
10 9 8 7 6 5 4 3 2 1

All information is accurate at the time of production.
Recipes are the sole origin of the contributor.

TABLE of CONTENTS

CONTRIBUTORS

Alonzo Mourning

Alvah H. Chapman, Jr.

Arthur Agatston, M.D.

Arturo Sandoval

Arva Moore Parks

Audrey Bowers

Becky Roper Matkov

Belkys Nerey

Berta Blecke

Bill and Grace Nelson

Bob and Adele Graham

Brett and Ali Bibeau

Calvin Hughes

Carmenza Jaramillo

Charlie Crist

Cleveland Bell, III

Cliff Drysdale

Cristina Saralegui

Dan Le Batard

Dave Barry

David Lawrence, Jr.

Deborah Spiegelman

Diana Gonzalez

Don Noe

Donna Shalala

Dwight Lauderdale

Edward and Linda Villella

Elizabeth Plater-Zyberk

Evelyn Langlieb Greer

Frank Ravndal

Freda Coffing Tschumy

Gene Singletary

Glenna Milberg

Gloria Estefan and Gloria Fajardo, Gloria's Mother

Gwen Margolis

Harry and Susie Horgan

Humberto Calzada

Hunter Reno

Ileana Ros-Lehtinen

James Grippando and Mrs. Russell, James' Mother-in-Law

Jimmy Cefalo

Jodi Dickinson

Joel M. Hoffman, Ph.D.

Jon Secada

Jorge Estevez

Kristi Krueger

Laurie Jennings

Laurinda Spear

Lee Brian Schrager

Lili Estefan

Linda Gassenheimer

Lisa Petrillo

Louis Aguirre

Lucy Morillo

Lynn Martinez

Mary Cagle

Max Mayfield

Meg Green

Michael Bloise

Mike Maunder, Ph.D.

Michele Oka Doner and Mitchell Wolfson, Jr.

Narendra Kini, M.D. and Rekha Kini, M.D.

Nestor Torres and Provi F. Torres, Nestor's Mother

Norman Van Aken

Pamela Katz Zakheim, M.Ed.

Parker Thomson, Esq.

Paul George, Ph.D.

Randy and Laurie Shannon

Redmond Burke, M.D.

Rene Murai, Esq.

Robert and Tracey Moehling

Robert M. Heuer

Robert McCammon

Romero Britto

S. Anthony Wolfe, M.D.

Shannon Hori

Steven Raichlen

Steven Stylianos, M.D.

Terence Riley

Trudy Novicki

William M. Hoeveler, The Honorable

Fairchild Tropical Botanic Garden, Tropical Fruit Program

1 Bleu Restaurant, Gerdy Rodriguez

A Fish Called Avalon Seafood Grille, Brian Cantrell

Alta Cocina, Juan Mario Maza and Vani Maharaj

AltaMar Restaurant, Claudio Giordano

Anacapri On Ponce, Giuseppe Zuoco

Andú Restaurant & Lounge, Nate Martin

Atrio Restaurant, Michael Gilligan

Azul, Clay Conley

Balans Miami, Paula Pirichinsky

Barton G., Renaud Gonthier

Berries in the Grove, Jay Ruff

Blue Door Restaurant, Philippe Pinon

Cacao Restaurant, Edgar Leal

Café Pastis, Philippe Jacquet

Caffè Abbracci, Nino Pernetti

Casa Juancho, Alfonso Perez

Casa Tua, Sergio Sigala

Casablanca Seafood Bar & Grill, Maribel Sanchez

Chef Allen's, Allen Susser

Chispa Restaurant & Bar, Adam Votaw

Chocolate Fine Argentinean Cuisine, Rodolfo Fernandez

City Cellar Wine Bar & Grill, Jeff Haskell

Dolores But You Can Call Me Lolita Restaurant & Lounge, Christian Quarato

Emeril's Miami Beach, Tom Azar

Escopazzo Organic Italian Restaurant, Giancarla Bodoni

Evolution Restaurant, David Bouley

Francesco Restaurant, Segundo Matienzo

Garcia's Seafood Grille & Fish Market

Gourmet Creations, Jorge Montes and Andres Alarcon

Grass Restaurant & Lounge, Michael B. Jacobs

House of India

Hy Vong Vietnamese Cuisine, Tung Nguyen

Ishq, Kavita Kamlani

Jake's Bar & Grill, Lou Callahan

Joe's Stone Crab, JoAnn Bass and Stephen Sawitz

John Martin's Irish Pub & Restaurant

Jumbo's Restaurant, Ricardo Girdwood

Karu & Y, Alberto Cabrera

La Cofradia, Jean Paul Desmaison

La Marea at the Tides, Pietro Rota

La Palma Ristorante, Vittorio Amadi

Lan Pan Asian Café, Johnson Teh

Le Croisic, Adriana Fatat

Le Provençal Restaurant, France Ingraham and Christian Antoniotti

Lido, Mark Zeitouni

Lotus Garden

Mark's South Beach, Mark Militello

Maroosh Mediterranean Restaurant, Samir Al-Barq

Michael's Genuine Food & Drink, Michael Schwartz

Michy's, Michelle Bernstein

North One 10 Restaurant, Dewey LoSasso

Novecento Restaurant, Gabriel Medici

O Asian Grill, Todd Dae Kulper

Oriente at Cardozo, Rufino Rengifo

Ortanique on the Mile, Cindy Hutson

Osteria del Teatro, Martin Perez

Palme D'Or, Philippe Ruiz

Pascal's on Ponce, Pascal Oudin

Perricone's Marketplace & Cafe, Steven Perricone

Poblano Cocina Mexicana, Eddie and Leticia Berrones

Prime Blue Grille, Tindaro LoSurdo

Shula's Steakhouse, Patrick Lapaire

Soyka's Restaurant Café & Bar, Luis Lopez

Table 8, Govind Armstrong

Talula Restaurant & Bar, Andrea Curto-Randazzo and Frank Randazzo

The Cafe at Books & Books, Bernie Matz

The Captain's Tavern Restaurant, Dale Palomino

The Oceanaire Seafood Room, Sean Bernal

The RIVER Oyster Bar, David Bracha

The Rusty Pelican Restaurant, Peter Knezevic

Timō Restaurant & Bar, Tim Andriola

Touch Catering, David Tornek & Sean Brasel

Trattoria Sole, Maurizio Farinelli

Tutto Pasta Ristorante, Joao Carlos Olivera

Two Chefs, Jan Jorgensen

Two Sisters Restaurant, Sebastien Layen

Versailles Restaurant, Alfonso Perez

Yuga Restaurant, Johnson Teh

RECIPE FOR THE ACKNOWLEDGEMENT CAKE

INGREDIENTS FOR THE BATTER

10 cups of gratitude to Cargill, Inc. for underwriting and caring

12 kudos, or more, to Miami's outstanding chefs and city leaders for contributing their delicious recipes

10 hearty pats on the back for all participating members of the Community Council, especially for Tess Doheny, Marilyn Liedman, Linda McKenzie, Debbie Schottenstein, Joann Stylianos, and Sandi Chamyan

6 heaping tablespoons of devotion to Merlyn Marenco at Miami Children's Hospital Foundation for technical assistance mixed with cheerful encouragement

1 overflowing quart of warm appreciation to Mitchell Kaplan for professional advice and guidance

Place all of the above ingredients in a large bowl and mix well. Pour into book-shaped molds and bake in a preheated oven at 350° F. for 1 hour. Serve warm with a large dollop of appreciation for everyone who made this book possible and everyone who purchases it.

The Frosting on the Cake:
In addition, many good friends became recipe scouts and supporters during production. To Ann Lyons, Larry Carrino, Courtney Recht, Henry Burnett, Janet and Bryan Latham, Michael Cesarano, Olin McKenzie, and Louis Stinson...many glasses of sparkling thanks!

CHEERS!

BILTMORE Photo Credit: Biltmore Resort & Spa, Coral Gables, Miami

INTRODUCTION

Miami Flavors is like no other cookbook. It provides an unparalleled collection of favorite recipes from dozens of top chefs in Miami as well as a number of Miami civic leaders and local celebrities. All these incredible individuals, individually and collectively, help give Miami the unique flavors, diverse cuisines and singular style that has become famous the world over and whose efforts are enjoyed and savored daily by hundreds of thousands of tourists and residents alike.

Miami Flavors is also a "feel good" cookbook because 100% of the proceeds from the sales of Miami Flavors will be donated to Miami Children's Hospital, thanks to a grant from Cargill, Inc. The cookbook was a truly collaborative effort created by the Community Council, volunteers of the Miami Children's Hospital Foundation, who love and cherish children, the Miami experience, and making a difference.

Miami Flavors is a delightful cookbook that is chock full of terrific recipes and many longtime Miami favorites. We hope you purchase it for yourself and also buy a copy to give to others. We know that it will become a favorite on your kitchen shelf and will provide you, and your family and friends, with many memorable meals at the family table.

JUAN CARLOS MAS
Chairman, Miami Children's Hospital

As Chairman of Miami Children's Hospital I am extremely proud of the members of Miami Children's Hospital Foundation Community Council who have devoted many volunteer hours over the past year to compile and produce this beautiful Miami Flavors cookbook featuring recipes from our diverse Florida community. I know you will enjoy reading and tasting the eclectic variety of recipes.

As a parent I have witnessed first hand the benefit of having a world-class facility like Miami Children's Hospital dedicated only to children. Miami Children's is a place that is made up of a compassionate and loving group of individuals whose life calling is to serve children. I am very proud to be associated with an institution whose core mission is to provide not only excellent medical care but to provide the family and the patient an environment of compassion and caring that nurtures hope and healing from the caregivers to the janitorial staff.

As you embark on trying these great recipes: take the time to appreciate the beauty of the great fruits and vegetables that someone has spent months caring for, enjoy the great smells that emanate from your kitchen and serve as a dinner bell for your family, but most importantly appreciate those who break bread with you and have an important place in your life. We will continue to strive for excellence and provide the families that visit us with the same dedication and passion you bring to yours.

Thank you for supporting us with this purchase, we welcome you to continue your involvement in support of the kids. With your support Miami Children's Hospital will continue to pursue greatness and be at the cutting edge of technology, serving the noblest of endeavors, the future of our children.

FOREWORD

Speaking from my own experience as a parent of premature twin boys who spent more than a month in incubators as newborns and who, by the way, are now strapping, healthy teenagers, I can most certainly appreciate the incredible efforts, skill and care that a pediatric hospital like Miami Children's provides to the children and parents of both the Miami community and the international community as well. It is truly an invaluable resource that every parent dearly cherishes, whether they have ever had a seriously ill child or even if they have had the very good fortune of healthy children. Unquestionably, the loving care of our children is closest to every parent's heart and Miami Children's provides abundant hope and the absolute best care in some of our most anxious hours as parents. Certainly, our children are our future and that future is so unwaveringly shepherded and cared for by all the wonderful doctors, nurses and staff of Miami Children's Hospital. Leading the way in supporting those vital efforts is the Miami Children's Hospital Foundation. The Foundation is a group of dedicated professionals and an enthusiastic and tireless volunteer membership who devote countless hours to support and advance the mission of the hospital. Among those many tremendous efforts is the unique and beautiful cookbook you hold in your hands.

Miami Flavors brings together a wonderfully diverse collection of chefs, restaurateurs, civic leaders, artists, musicians and celebrities from the Miami community, all of them united in the singular endeavor to support the mission of the Miami Children's Hospital. The *Miami Flavors* cookbook is a consummate labor of love and is a direct result of the tremendous efforts by the volunteers of the Community Council, an affiliation of the Miami Children's Hospital Foundation. All of the recipes in *Miami Flavors* are either illustrative of an acclaimed chef's artistry, a celebrity's cherished recipe from childhood, a special dish for entertaining friends or, simply, a longtime family favorite. Notwithstanding their origins, however, every recipe lovingly represents a flavor, an approach, an ingredient or an individual that is somehow unique to Miami. *Miami Flavors* is undeniably a community-wide celebration of the diverse cultures, cuisines and individuals who comprise the unique place that is Miami. It is a cookbook that reflects the heart and soul of Miami through the outstanding recipes that you'll find from beginning to end in this marvelous collection. After all, *Miami Flavors* is all about cooking and caring.

Mitchell Kaplan
Books & Books

MIAMI CHILDREN'S HOSPITAL

In 1983, Miami Children's Hospital embarked on a mission to create the best hospital for children in the southeastern United States. Today, as the largest independent freestanding pediatric teaching hospital, in this part of the country, Miami Children's Hospital (MCH) is receiving accolades from around the world for its state-of-the-art specialized services to over 185,000 children annually.

Miami Children's Hospital Foundation (MCHF), founded by Ambassador David M. Walters, works tirelessly to generate funds and awareness for MCH, the only institute for which it raises funds. The generous financial support of individuals, corporations, and foundations has truly made this the "Diamond of the South" and a premier pediatric hospital recognized by national media such as *US News & World Report*. Volunteer organizations, such as Hugs & Kisses, the MCH Auxiliary, and the Community Council, work to help the Foundation reach their goals. The women of the Community Council donate their time and energy to generate funds by developing community projects that support patient services and patients' families. This special cookbook is one such project and is an example of the dedication of the Community Council members in supporting the vision of MCHF.

Miami Children's Hospital is more than just Miami. With Ambulatory Care Centers in Weston, Miami Lakes, South Dade, Doral and West Kendall, MCH is reaching out to provide state-of-the-art pediatric care to more and more children. More than a local hospital, MCH provides care for children from around the world and, with continued support, will always shine like the "diamond" that it is. For more information, go to www.MCHF.org or www.MCH.com.

STARTERS
APPETIZERS

KEY BISCAYNE LIGHTHOUSE Photo Credit: Islander News, Key Biscayne

Since opening his first restaurant, Mark's Place, in Miami in 1988, Mark Militello has continually been hailed as the chef responsible for putting South Florida on the national culinary map with his original contemporary American cuisine. A steady stream of the nation's top awards have been bestowed upon Militello, including a James Beard Award for "Best Regional Chef," Food & Wine Magazine's *"Ten Best Chefs in America," and a Distinguished Restaurant Award from* Conde Nast Traveler, *among many others. Today, Militello oversees four restaurants bearing his name, from South Beach to Palm Beach. Each restaurant prepares a daily menu based on ingredients available in the local marketplace.*

SERVES 6

1½ pounds fresh Bahamian conch or cleaned calamari

½ cup, plus 1 tablespoon lime juice, freshly squeezed

7 tablespoons extra virgin olive oil

2 tablespoons dry white wine

2 tablespoons red onion, minced

½ small red onion, sliced

1 teaspoon fresh thyme leaves, minced

Salt and freshly ground black pepper

2 jalapeño peppers

¼ cup red bell pepper, minced

¼ cup tomato, minced

16 good quality green olives (such as picholine),
 pitted and minced

2 tablespoons scallion, minced

2 tablespoons cilantro leaves, minced

1 ripe Haas avocado

6 leaves bib lettuce

Cut off hard narrow end of conch, and discard or grind it for conch cakes or chowder. Slice meat in thirds on the bias and pound each piece flat between sheets of waxed paper with a meat mallet. For calamari, remove tentacles and discard or reserve to deep-fry. Cut bodies in half lengthwise and lightly score surface in crisscross pattern with a sharp knife.

In a medium bowl combine 1/4 cup lime juice, 2 tablespoons olive oil, wine, 2 tablespoons minced red onion, thyme, salt, and pepper. Add the conch or calamari. Marinate for 30 minutes.

Heat a grill or stovetop grill pan. Grill sliced red onion and whole jalapeños until charred on all sides; set aside on a plate for 20 to 30 minutes. Grill conch or calamari about 20 seconds on each side, until lightly seared; set aside on a plate for 20 to 30 minutes. Seed and mince jalapeños. Also mince the grilled sliced red onions and the conch or calamari; place all in a bowl with any juices from the seafood. Add the bell pepper, tomato, jalapeños, olives, scallions, cilantro and minced grilled red onion. Mix well. Dish can be prepared up to this point, covered, and refrigerated.

Lightly beat ¼ cup lime juice and 2 tablespoons olive oil together and add to the seafood mix. Fold all the ingredients together and add to the seafood. Season to taste with salt and pepper. Set aside at room temperature until ready to serve, no more than 30 minutes.

Halve and pit the avocado. Remove flesh, chop, and place in food processor or blender with remaining tablespoon of lime juice. Process until smooth, scraping the sides of the container from time to time. With machine running, carefully drizzle in the remaining 3 tablespoons olive oil to emulsify. Periodically scrape the container, and process briefly until well blended. The mixture may look slightly separated. If so, transfer and beat vigorously with a small whisk, about 30 seconds, or until mixture is smooth. If you use a blender, you may have to scrape the container more often, but mixture will emulsify better. Season with salt. If not for immediate use, cover and refrigerate up to 1 hour. If the mixture starts to separate, whisk again before serving. Place a lettuce leaf in each of 6 martini glasses or wine goblets. Spoon in conch or calamari mixture. Top each with a dollop of avocado butter. Garnish with a small lime wedge and serve.

SERVES 6

6 medium sized Vidalia onions

5 tablespoons butter

1½ cups chicken stock

1 teaspoon lemon zest, minced

16 dried apricot halves, chopped

½ pound ground lamb

1 teaspoon ground cinnamon

Salt and freshly ground black pepper

3 tablespoons parsley, finely chopped

3 tablespoons fresh mint, finely chopped

2 tablespoons coarse fresh bread crumbs

Michael's Genuine Food & Drink is a neighborhood place that feels like the real deal. There's always something you want on the menu, and what goes into the dishes is simple, fresh and pure. Michael Schwartz, an accomplished and talented chef, has been hard at work in the kitchen since he was 14, evolving into the nationally renowned chef he is today. With his latest venture, he has created a showcase for the type of cuisine that he does best: homemade, unpretentious, delectable, with an emphasis on local and organic ingredients.

Without peeling the onions, cut about 1 inch off the top of each, and just enough off the bottom so that onions stand upright. Reserve the tops. Remove all but the outer two layers of each by scooping out the centers of the onions with a paring knife or pushing them up through the top. Set the shells and tops aside, then finely chop the remaining centers.

Melt 3 tablespoons of butter in a skillet over medium low heat. Add the chopped onions and cook until soft, about 15 minutes. Meanwhile, bring the chicken stock to a simmer in a saucepan over medium heat. Add the lemon zest and apricots and cook until soft, about 10 minutes. Preheat an oven to 400° F. Add the ground lamb and cinnamon to the onions. Increase the heat to medium and season with salt and pepper. Cook, continually stirring until the lamb is crumbly and just cooked through, about 5 minutes. Remove from the heat. Stir in the chicken stock and apricot mixture and 2 tablespoons each of chopped parsley and mint. Cool slightly. Spoon the filling into the onion shells and place in an ovenproof dish. Heap bread crumbs on top (lay onion tops alongside), and dot with remaining butter. Pour ¼ cup water into the dish. Bake, basting twice, for 20 minutes, then cover with aluminum foil and bake until the onions are tender, approximately an additional 20 minutes. Garnish with the remaining mint and parsley. Serve with the onion tops.

Bang Bang Shrimp
CHEF BRIAN CANTRELL, A FISH CALLED AVALON

Award-winning food, casual elegance, and indoor or streetside patio dining makes A Fish Called Avalon the perfect choice for South Beach dining. Try this South Beach tradition once and you'll be hooked. Zagat rates A Fish Called Avalon as "Excellent," CitySearch 2007 awarded it "Best Seafood," and Wine Spectator gave them an "Award of Excellence."

From Atlanta before working through Palm Beach, Nantucket, New Orleans, Birmingham and then back to South Florida at Nemo's on South Beach, Chef Brian Cantrell has been the master chef in some A-list kitchens. Now the culinary expert is bringing his best dishes to Ocean Drive at A Fish Called Avalon at the Avalon Hotel. His cooking philosophy is "What grows together, goes together" and "Non-confusion cuisine." Cantrell is passionate about delivering the highest quality product possible and exceeding guest expectations. He believes in keeping the cuisine simple and understated, yet providing a wide range of styles, ingredients, and cooking techniques.

Blend all of the marinade ingredients together. Add the shrimp and marinate shrimp overnight in the refrigerator. Arrange the julienned cucumbers on an appetizer plate. On top of the cucumber ribbons, spoon the avocado guacamole. Place the orange and grapefruit segments on top of the guacamole and drizzle orange syrup around the rim of the plate. On a hot grill or grill pan, grill the marinated shrimp 3-4 minutes on each side. Arrange the grilled shrimp around the plate–three per person. Sprinkle with pistachio dust and eat!

SERVES 6
MARINADE INGREDIENTS

½ cup Mojo de Ajo *(this literally means "gravy of garlic" & is available, bottled, in Spanish & specialty food markets.)*
1 teaspoon ancho *chili powder*
1 teaspoon *paprika*
1 teaspoon *fresh oregano, finely chopped*
1 teaspoon *fresh cilantro, finely chopped*
1 teaspoon *cumin*
1 teaspoon Syracha *hot sauce (or any other good hot sauce)*
1 teaspoon *honey*
1 teaspoon *extra virgin olive oil*

OTHER INGREDIENTS

1 cucumber, julienned or cut like ribbons
1 orange, in segments
1 grapefruit, in segments
½ cup avocado guacamole
Drizzle of orange syrup
1 teaspoon toasted and ground pistachio "dust"
18 colossal (or approximately 2¼ pounds) shrimp, peeled and deveined

Crabavocat
EXECUTIVE CHEF PHILIPPE PINON,
BLUE DOOR RESTAURANT

Located in the heart of South Beach and directly on the ocean, the Blue Door Restaurant & Brasserie is in the Delano. The Delano is the ultimate world-class urban resort and self-contained destination. It is a cool haven of relaxation in the middle of one of the world's most vibrant cities. The Brasserie, with its hand-etched mirrored bar, soaring mirrored screen, and comfortable living room style furniture, is the perfect spot for a more casual, relaxed meal. The Blue Door Terrace is the ideal place to dine alfresco, during the day while enjoying the warm ocean breeze, or at night under the brilliant stars.

SERVES 12
AVOCADO MOUSSE INGREDIENTS

5 ripe avocados, chopped

Juice of two limes, freshly squeezed

½ small Spanish onion, chopped

4 cloves garlic, chopped

1 tablespoon Tabasco sauce

Salt and pepper

1 tablespoon cilantro, chopped

1 tablespoon chives, chopped

5 tomatoes, diced

Olive oil

CRABMEAT INGREDIENTS

1 pound crabmeat, cooked

3 tablespoons mayonnaise

Salt and pepper

Avocado Mousse:

To make the avocado mousse, cut the avocados in halves, remove the pits and scoop out each half of the flesh and then cut into big cubes. Quickly place the cubes in a bowl and put into the freezer for 30 minutes. Meanwhile, mix all of the remaining ingredients and seasonings in a bowl. Add the avocado cubes from the freezer and mix very slowly. Take a round mold ring and fill 1/4 full with the avocado mixture. Then spoon in enough of the crabmeat mixture (see recipe) to cover the avocado mix and fill 3/4 of the mold. Add enough of the remaining avocado mixture to finish filling the mold to the top. Place the mold ring in the refrigerator for at least two hours. Repeat this procedure with additional mold rings until you have approximately a dozen servings (Note: You can buy round mold rings at most cookware shops or, for a homemade substitute, you can use empty tuna fish cans. Just cut the bottoms out of the cans, remove the paper labels and wash well.)

Crabmeat:

Mix the crabmeat in a bowl with the mayonnaise and then season to taste.

Tomtato Coulis:

Peel, seed and chop the tomatoes and purée them in a blender. Then add tomato paste, lemon juice, salt and pepper. Lastly, slowly whisk in the olive oil.

Shrimp or Crab Claw Garnish:

Season and bread the shrimps and deep fry until golden. Remove from the oil and set aside.

To assemble the finished dish, gently pour a ladle of the tomato *coulis* in the center of a medium shallow plate. Remove the molded avocado and crabmeat from the refrigerator and place a single mold in the center of the coulis and carefully remove it. Top each Crabavocat with some *hijiki* and a golden fried shrimp or crab claw, and garnish with a chive sprig.

TOMATO COULIS INGREDIENTS

12 tomatoes
3 tablespoons tomato paste
1 tablespoon lemon juice
3 tablespoons olive oil
Salt and pepper

SHRIMP OR CRAB CLAW GARNISH INGREDIENTS

12 jumbo shrimps or crab claws
Chive sprigs
Hijiki (dried seaweed)
¾ cup plain bread crumbs
Vegetable oil for deep frying

Edgar Leal is an accomplished and impassioned chef who has filtered a global experience to create one of South Florida's most critically acclaimed restaurants. Cacao was named "Best New Restaurant" by Food & Wine Magazine *and* The Miami Herald. *Chef Leal has been featured by* The New York Times, TIME Magazine *and has appeared on NBC's* Today Show. *Chef Leal was named StarChefs Rising Star in 2004. In 2006, Cacao was named one of America's top 20 restaurants in South Florida by the* Zagat Guide.

Dice the salmon into half inch pieces. Place the salmon in a bowl and add the lime juice, the fish sauce, 3 tablespoons of Tabasco sauce, 3 tablespoons cilantro, 3 tablespoons red onion, 3 tablespoons red peppers, and the finely diced leeks. Mix well and let it rest for five minutes.

Guacamole:
Cut and pit the avocado. Remove the flesh of the avocado and in a small bowl mash the avocado with a fork. Then add the onion, the rest of the cilantro, red peppers, red onion, and the remaining Tabasco sauce and salt. Mix well.

Mound the guacamole in the middle of a serving platter. Surround the guacamole with the salmon *ceviche* and complete the presentation with an outer ring of blue tortilla chips.

SERVES 4

1 pound fresh salmon, diced

4 tablespoons red pepper, cut in very small dice

4 tablespoons red onion, cut in very small dice

4 tablespoons Tabasco sauce

6 teaspoons cilantro, finely chopped

1 tablespoon Thai fish sauce

8 tablespoons lime juice, freshly squeezed

4 teaspoons leeks, finely diced

1 avocado

½ onion, finely diced

Blue tortilla chips

Salt

Mango Salsa
NORIS LEDESMA, CURATOR OF TROPICAL FRUIT
AT FAIRCHILD TROPICAL BOTANIC GARDEN

This mango salsa is redolent of the tropics with the zing of fresh ginger and fresh cilantro. Chile peppers pack an added punch while the essence of lime paired with the heady sweetness of mangoes provides great contrast and depth in this dish. It can be served as an appetizer or can accompany a savory main dish that features pork or beef.

Mix all ingredients in a large bowl, cover and chill for at least an hour.

Note: Mango varieties recommended: *Mallika, Nam Doc Mai, Alampur Baneshan*

SERVES 6

2 large mangoes, peeled, cut from the pit and diced
1 inch piece of fresh ginger, grated
½ cup fresh cilantro, chopped
½ large red onion, chopped
2 jalapeño peppers, seeded and diced
Dash salt
2 tablespoons lime juice

Tuna & Watermelon Tiradito *with Jalapeños, Mint & Lime*
EXECUTIVE CHEF & OWNER MICHELLE BERNSTEIN, MICHY'S

SERVES 4

1 pound fresh sushi quality tuna, diced (½ inch)

2½ cups watermelon, medium diced (same size as tuna)

1 tablespoon lime juice

2 tablespoons soy sauce

¼ cup scallions, thinly sliced (white part only)

2 tablespoons fresh ginger, peeled and finely chopped

3 tablespoons mint, roughly chopped

3 tablespoons basil, roughly chopped

½ jalapeño chile, sliced into very thin rounds

¼ cup corn nuts, plain flavor

Michy's is the homegrown, yet modern bistro created by the husband and wife team David Martinez and renowned chef and TV personality, Michelle Bernstein. Located in the up and coming neighborhood of Miami's "Upper East Side," this 50-seat restaurant is quintessential Miami: vibrant, full of tropical hues, just a shade sexy, with a decidedly Latin touch and totally cosmopolitan. Bernstein draws upon local farmers and fishermen to create whimsical bistro dishes, a style she coins as "luxurious comfort food." The menu is comprised of an eclectic range that includes Michelle's Jewish-Argentinean background, classical French training and a love for all things Spanish and Italian.

Have all the ingredients ready in the refrigerator. As your guests arrive, toss all ingredients together except for the corn nuts. Top with the corn nuts and serve immediately.

Grouper Ceviche
CHEF BERNIE MATZ, THE CAFÉ AT BOOKS & BOOKS

The Miami Herald *writes, "The new Café at Books & Books brings to mind South Beach in the old days. Maybe it's the chef, Bernie Matz, who is back in the neighborhood where he opened the quirky Wet Paint Café in the mid 1980s and gave chef Douglas Rodriguez his start. Matz has created a cutting-edge yet comforting menu for Mitchell Kaplan's beloved bookshop: burgers and fries, quesadillas, wraps, salads, hummus and pita as well as tropical-tinged dishes like guava-glazed pork tenderloin and shrimp in coconut milk…A meal here is like eating in the kitchen of a good home cook. Nothing is too fancy or exotic, but everything seems honest and full of flavor. That's the idea, according to Matz's cookbook,* Bernie's Kitchen: New South Florida Cuisine, *'Cooking South Florida style means being fresh, sophisticated, fruity, stylish and healthy,' he writes."*

With a very sharp knife clean and dice the fish fillets about ¼ inch thick, then marinate the diced fish in the juice of 2 limes for about 15 minutes while you make the dressing. In a bowl, combine the onion, scallions, celery, cilantro, vinegar, olive oil and remaining lime juice and orange juice and mix with a whisk or fork. Remove the excess lime juice from the reserved fish and gently incorporate the dressing into the fish. The *ceviche* is ready to serve immediately. It will, however, continue to cook in the marinade. So, it's also good in the refrigerator for 24-48 hours and can be served well chilled.

SERVES 6-8

2 pounds grouper fillet
¼ cup red onion, diced
¼ cup scallions, diced
¼ cup celery, diced
2 tablespoons white vinegar
2 tablespoons olive oil
4 limes, freshly squeezed
½ orange, freshly squeezed
2 tablespoons cilantro, chopped
Salt and fresh ground pepper

Casa Cristina's Ceviche
CRISTINA SARALEGUI, INTERNATIONALLY RENOWNED
TV PERSONALITY AND LATIN TALK SHOW HOST

Cristina Saralegui is a 30-year veteran journalist who is recognized as one of the most influential role models for today's Hispanic woman. In 2005, Cristina was named one of the "25 Most Influential Hispanics in America" by TIME *Magazine. She was also the first Latina to be inducted into the Broadcasting & Cable Hall of Fame.*

SERVES 8

1 cup lemon juice

1 cup of red onion, sliced julienne style, not rounds

½ cup tomato juice

1 teaspoon mustard

2 pounds small cooked, peeled shrimp without tails

2 pounds fresh tilapia fillets cut into strips or small pieces

Salt and pepper to taste

¼ teaspoon cilantro, chopped

Pour the ½ cup of lemon juice over the cut fish and the cooked shrimp in a large, shallow glass bowl. Cover with plastic wrap and let marinate in the refrigerator for 30 minutes. Add the onions and the rest of the ingredients and stir well, adding the other ½ cup lemon juice. Cover the container and leave in the refrigerator for 2 hours, minimum, until the lemon marinates and cooks the fish and shrimp. Optional: You can also add hot sauce, and corn at the end.

Black Bean Dip

FREDA COFFING TSCHUMY, Sculptor & Artist

Freda Coffing Tschumy is a sculptor and artist who has exhibited widely in the U.S.A. and Canada. She received the first Metrorail sculpture commission, for the University of Miami station, and her sculpture of Marjory Stoneman Douglas is on view at Fairchild Tropical Botanic Garden.

This recipe is tasty, quick, non-fat, and always popular. Except for the beans and salsa, the quantities can be adjusted to taste.

Put all of the ingredients in a food processor and process until chopped but not completely smooth. Place in a bowl, garnish with fresh cilantro sprigs, chill, and serve with tortilla chips.

Serves 4

1 can (15-ounce) black beans, drained
1 bottle (16-ounce) of tomato-based salsa;
mild, medium, or hot, to taste
4 to 6 cloves of garlic
⅓ bunch of fresh cilantro, washed and stems trimmed

31

SERVES 4

CEVICHE INGREDIENTS

3 ounces pasteurized lump crab meat

3 ounces shrimp, any size will do, raw, peeled & deveined

3 ounces salmon, cleaned

3 ounces snapper, cleaned

3 ounces swordfish, cleaned

3 ounces lobster meat, claws, tails, knuckles

1 cucumber, diced in brunoise

1 red bell pepper, diced in brunoise

½ bunch cilantro, chopped

15 lemons

10 limes

3 oranges

1 tablespoon garlic, minced

3 ounces ginger, grated, with juice

2 ounces soy sauce

2 tablespoons ají amarillo *(yellow Peruvian pepper paste), you can substitute any pepper purée depending on spice level*

Kosher salt to taste

Black pepper to taste

At Andú Restaurant & Lounge, we've created a new haven for sexy cuisine, style and sophistication. Andú will excite your senses and satisfy your cravings. Our talented executive chef, Nate Martin, in collaboration with consulting chef Jason McClain, has designed a tantalizing menu of Mediterranean cuisine with international influences. Using the freshest, highest quality ingredients, our menu entices even the most discerning of palates at price points that don't offend the wallet.

Chop all of the seafood, except for the crab, into small ¼ inch pieces and set aside. Into a bowl, squeeze the juice from the lemons, limes, and oranges, discarding the seeds. Squeeze the juice from the grated ginger as well. Then combine and whisk the garlic, soy sauce, *ají amarillo* and season with salt and black pepper. Reserve a small amount of sauce for plating. Next, add all of the chopped seafood, crab, diced cucumber and diced bell pepper into the sauce and marinate overnight or for at least 4-6 hours.

Yucca Chips:

Peel yucca root and thinly slice using a meat slicer, a food processor with a slicing blade or a mandoline. As you slice, place the pieces in ice water to remove some of the starch. After soaking for a couple of minutes, pat slices dry with paper towels. Fry the slices in hot oil at 350° F. degrees until they float and cease to sizzle in the oil. Quickly remove them from the oil and place them on a plate lined with a paper towel to drain the excess oil. Before they cool, lightly season them with the dried spices and salt.

Tuna:

Pre-mix the dried spices in a small bowl and set aside a container with an ice water bath big enough to hold the tuna. Generously season the tuna loin

with the salt and coat with the spice mix. In a medium sauté pan over high heat, sear the tuna loin on all sides for approximately five seconds each. Once tuna is completely seared, remove from the pan and directly submerge in ice bath. This will immediately stop the cooking process. Let stand for one minute, remove from water and pat dry. Using long and even strokes, slice the tuna loin into several thin pieces.

To serve the *ceviche*, arrange yucca chips on a plate or platter. Place a small one ounce portion of marinated *ceviche* on top of the yucca chips and gently wrap a slice of tuna over the top. Dress the *ceviche* pieces with the extra dressing and garnish with the chopped cilantro.

YUCCA CHIPS INGREDIENTS

1 Yucca root (cassava)
2 tablespoons chili powder
1 teaspoon ground cumin
Kosher salt to taste
Deep pan or deep fryer with enough vegetable oil to submerge chips

TUNA INGREDIENTS

8 ounces Ahi tuna loin, sushi grade, "Big Eyed"
2 tablespoons chili powder
2 tablespoons ground ginger
2 tablespoons paprika
1 teaspoon cayenne pepper
Kosher salt to taste
¼ cup canola or blended vegetable oil for searing

Fried Olives Stuffed with Spicy Lamb Sausage
CHEF GOVIND ARMSTRONG, TABLE 8

SERVES 8

SPICY LAMB SAUSAGE INGREDIENTS

1 tablespoon unsalted butter, chilled

½ onion, finely diced

¼ teaspoon garlic, chopped

⅛ cup sherry vinegar

Salt

1 pound ground lamb

¼ teaspoon cayenne pepper

¼ teaspoon hot paprika

¼ teaspoon ground cumin

Pinch of ground fennel seed

Pepper to taste

Canola oil, for frying

16 giant cocktail olives, pimentos removed

1 cup all-purpose flour

1 large egg, beaten with 1 tablespoon water

1 cup Panko Dustin' Mix (see recipe)

Table 8 in South Beach features the acclaimed French and California-influenced cuisine of celebrity chef Govind Armstrong, who began his career at 13 in the kitchen of Wolfgang Puck's legendary Spago LA. He then worked with Nancy Silverton and Mark Peel at Campanile, Susan Feniger and partner Mary Sue Milliken at City Restaurant, Joachim Splichal at Pinot Bistro, and Postrio in San Francisco. Armstrong serves his innovative cuisine – simple food created with the freshest, natural products and local ingredients – while drawing upon the region's diverse stock of fish and produce. Govind is also author of the cookbook, Small Bites, Big Nights: Seductive Little Plates for Intimate Occasions and Lavish Parties.

Panko Dustin' Mix:

Finely grind the *panko* in a food processor. Mix all ingredients together and store in an airight contianer.

In a saucepan over high heat, melt the butter. Add the onions and caramelize for about 6 minutes. Add the garlic and sauté until golden brown, making sure it doesn't burn. Deglaze with the sherry vinegar, stirring constantly and working very quickly. You want the vinegar to evaporate, but you don't want the pan to be bone dry. Remove the mixture from the heat and allow to cool.

Fill a large bowl with ice, and sprinkle salt on the ice to keep the temperature cool. Place another bowl on top and add the ground lamb, the cooled onion mixture, the cayenne, paprika, cumin, and fennel. Add a pinch of salt and pepper and mix well with a spoon.

Heat a small saucepan with 2 inches of canola oil to 350° F., using a candy thermometer to reach the correct temperature. Split the olives almost all the way lengthwise and stuff with the spicy lamb sausage. Place the olives quickly in the refrigerator to allow them to set.

Place the flour, egg wash, and *Panko* Dustin' Mix in three small bowls. Roll the olives in the flour, then dip in the egg wash, and finally give them a nice roll in the *Panko* Dustin' Mix. Place the breaded olives in the hot oil and fry for about 4 minutes, or until crisp and golden. Drain well on paper towels and serve immediately.

Chicken Enchilada Dip
DAN LE BATARD, SPORTS WRITER & RADIO PERSONALITY

Dan Le Batard, an ESPN Magazine *and former* Miami Herald *columnist and host of* 790 the Ticket *AM Radio's "Dan Le Batard Show" is proud to share his mother's recipe for this classic favorite of all sports fans.*

SERVES 6

½ pound skinless & boneless chicken breast strips or halves

½ cup Mojo Criollo *(look for it in the Spanish section of any supermarket)*

3 ounces cream cheese, softened

4 ounces mayonnaise

4 ounces cheddar cheese, shredded

2 ounces green chili peppers, diced

¼ jalapeño pepper, diced

Pinch of salt and pepper to taste

Marinate the chicken breasts in the *Mojo Criollo* sauce. Then preheat an oven to 350° F. Place the marinated chicken breast pieces on a medium baking sheet and bake chicken in the preheated oven for 20 minutes or until no longer pink. Remove from the oven, cool and shred. Place shredded chicken in a medium bowl, and mix well with cream cheese, mayonnaise, cheddar cheese, green chili peppers, jalapeño pepper and a pinch of salt and pepper. Be aware that the *Mojo Criollo* contains some salt. Transfer the mixture to a medium baking dish. Bake uncovered in the oven for 30 minutes, or until the edges are golden brown. Serve with crackers or tortilla chips.

Molded Salmon Mousse
HUMBERTO CALZADA, Artist

Humberto Calzada was born in 1944 in Havana, Cuba, and has resided in Miami since 1960. He became a professional artist in 1976 following his first exhibition at the Bacardi Gallery in 1975. He describes the subject of his paintings as being spaces "that might never exist physically, but which are as real to me as the soil on which my soul is now planted, and the soil on which my heart still walks."

Dissolve the gelatin in the boiling water. When dissolved, add the cold water. Combine and pour into a shallow mold and put mold in freezer until the sides start to set. While this first layer is setting, combine the salmon, mayonnaise, red onion and dill in a bowl. Mix well and set aside. Prepare a ring or fish-shaped mold by spraying with vegetable oil. Combine all of the ingredients; pour in the mold and chill well until time to serve. When serving, remove the mousse from the mold and decorate with slices of lemon and lime, an olive slice for the eye, if using a fish mold, and sprigs of dill. Serve cold with crackers of your liking.

SERVES 6

1 package gelatin, lemon flavor
1 cup boiling water
½ cup cold water
1 tablespoon lemon juice
¾ cup mayonnaise
1 7-ounce can of salmon, or a 6-ounce foil pack, drained and flaked
1 tablespoon red onion, very finely minced
½ teaspoon dried dill
Slices of lemon and lime
An olive slice for the eye, if using a fish mold
Sprigs of fresh dill
Vegetable oil spray
Water or other suitable crackers

Ceviche

CHEF GABRIEL MEDICI, Novecento Restaurant

Call it a bistro, parrillada, Argentinean social club, or local hang-out, Novecento is all these and more. The food and wine are affordable and always delicious. The atmosphere is lively and moves to a decidedly Argentine rhythm.

Contrary to what would be expected due to his great talents, Gabriel Medici never thought he would become a chef. His mother was a cook, and when he was a little boy, he ate everything he found in her kitchen, even if it was raw. At 18 years old, Medici began a culinary exploration of Europe on motorbike. He discovered exotic delights, as well as, horrible food. This is how he discovered the world's tastes and its people. Today he continues to discover the world through his cooking.

Serves 8

2¼ pounds of grouper, red snapper, or white fish

2 cups lime juice, freshly squeezed

2 garlic cloves, minced

2 fresh jalapeños, seeded and minced

2 tablespoons ginger, minced

Cilantro and watermelon for garnish

Pinch of salt

Cut and cube the fish in bite size pieces. Clean and cut the jalapeños and garlic and set aside. Mix the lime juice, jalapeños, ginger, garlic, and pinch of salt in a steel or glass bowl. Place the fish in the bowl with the other ingredients and mix gently. Place the bowl in the refrigerator for one to two hours. Serve by placing a fair amount of fish and marinade on a plate and garnish with fresh cilantro and cubed watermelon.

Hot Crab Dip

SENATOR BILL NELSON AND
HIS WIFE MRS. GRACE NELSON

Perhaps the two most defining events in Bill Nelson's life occurred in 1972: he married Grace Cavert and was elected for the first time to public office. Today, over three decades later, he has earned a reputation as a principled family man, a staunch advocate for all Floridians, and a moderate voice in the increasingly partisan world of national politics.

Florida's own Bill Nelson was elected to the U.S. Senate in November 2000, after serving six years as a member of the Florida Cabinet. He currently serves on the Senate Commerce, Armed Services, Budget, Foreign Relations, Intelligence, and Aging committees and is recognized as the leading congressional expert on NASA.

Mix all the ingredients in a medium bowl, then warm gently in a double boiler. Serve in a chafing dish with toast points on the side. Simple and delicious!

SERVES 6

1 pound fresh (or canned) Florida crab meat

1 cup mayonnaise

1 cup Parmesan cheese

Mrs. Wolfson's Pickled Shrimp

MICHELE OKA DONER & MITCHELL WOLFSON, JR., AUTHORS

It is rumored that Ada Brodus, a longtime Wolfson housekeeper, created most of the Wolfson dishes, but for the public record, Mrs. Wolfson appeared to be a hands-on cook. Mrs. Wolfson's Pickled Shrimp can be made two days ahead.

Michele Oka Doner and Mitchell Wolfson. Jr. are authors of the book, Miami Beach: Blueprint of an Eden. Lives Seen through the Prism of Family and Place, *2005.*

SERVES 6

⅔ cup corn or safflower oil

1 teaspoon dry mustard

⅔ cup vinegar

3 bay leaves

2 limes, juiced

½ teaspoon cayenne pepper

1½ tablespoons sugar

2 pounds shrimp, unpeeled

1 teaspoon dill seeds

½ large onion, sliced

1 teaspoon cracked black peppercorns

½ cup fresh cilantro, chopped

Combine all of the ingredients, except the shrimp, cilantro and onion, in a saucepan and bring to a boil. Simmer for ten minutes. While the sauce is simmering, peel the shrimp, and devein them by making a slit along the back or outside of the shrimp, lifting out the black vein, and discarding it. Rinse the shrimp and add them to the saucepan. Simmer very gently for three minutes (the shrimp will become rubbery if brought to a hard boil). Drain the shrimp, reserving the cooking marinade. In a large bowl, layer the onion slices and the shrimp, alternating until both are used up. Sprinkle the cilantro into the reserved hot marinade and pour over the mixture. Cover tightly with plastic wrap. Chill for about 48 hours.

Remove the shrimp from the marinade and serve on wooden skewers, or slice and place on pumpernickel rounds decorated with fresh cilantro leaves.

Beer Bread

MEG GREEN, Certified Financial Planner and Columnist

Here is one of my favorite "secret weapons." It's a fast and delicious homemade bread…no bread machine needed. Keep these ingredients in your pantry at all times and you can throw this together in a flash when needed. I keep at least one can of beer hidden in the house for "emergencies." Don't tell anyone how ridiculously easy it is to make! Fair warning, one loaf goes pretty fast! Going to someone's house for dinner? Bring it wrapped up and still warm.

In addition to being a certified financial planner, Green is a Miami Herald *columnist.*

Preheat an oven to 350° F. Mix together all the ingredients in a bowl, blending the beer into the flour and sugar mixture with a wooden spoon. When blended, it will be thick and a bit sticky. Pour or scrape the batter into an ungreased loaf pan. Bake for one hour. Remove from the oven, whether it looks done or not. Cool in the pan for about 10 minutes. Remove from the pan and spread a fair amount of butter on the top of the loaf while still warm. Let the butter melt and be absorbed by the bread. Slice and serve with butter.

Makes 1 Loaf

3 cups self-rising flour
⅓ cup white sugar
1 can good brand beer

SERVES 6

¼ cup lime juice, freshly squeezed

1 habanero pepper, seeded and diced

4-5 garlic cloves, finely chopped

1 tablespoon extra virgin olive oil

1 pound shrimp, firm sea bass, halibut or scallops,
   cleaned and cut into ½ inch dice

3 scallions, white & light green parts only,
   thinly sliced on the bias

1 cucumber, cut into matchstick or julienne (optional)

¼ cup fresh mint leaves

¼ cup fresh cilantro leaves

1 avocado, pitted and the flesh cut into ½ inch dice
   (optional)

Salt and freshly ground black pepper

The successor to the Center for the Fine Arts, the Miami Art Museum was founded in 1996 as a contemporary art museum with a permanent collection. It is dedicated to engaging a broad public with art from the twentieth century through the present. Miami Art Museum's collection, which Art in America *magazine called "the quintessential Miami collection" in 1999, looks at international art from the perspective of the Americas and reflects the cosmopolitan makeup of Miami, forging connections among diverse groups and ideas.*

Please note that the seafood ceviche *is not cooked in the traditional way, but will be "cooked" in the lime juice mixture. The acid of the citrus "cooks" the fish, and when the flesh becomes opaque and firm it is ready to eat. Enjoy!*

In a non-reactive bowl (either glass or ceramic), combine juice, habanero, garlic and olive oil. Add the seafood and combine well. Cover with plastic wrap and place in the refrigerator. Chill until the flesh of the seafood is opaque, most likely overnight, stirring occasionally. Remove from the refrigerator and add the remaining ingredients. Season with salt and pepper. Give one last toss and serve.

Savory Herb-Stuffed Mushrooms

DWIGHT LAUDERDALE, Retired WPLG-TV Local 10 Anchor

Dwight Lauderdale was born and raised in Columbus, Ohio. He began his career in broadcasting at the age of 17, at WSYX-TV in his hometown. Lauderdale did everything from processing black and white film to news writing, producing and substituting for on-air talent. He quickly adopted South Florida as home when he began reporting for WCKT-TV in 1974. Dwight Lauderdale joined Local 10 in 1976 and has been a fixture in South Florida ever since. The area was a perfect fit for him. Since his arrival, he has rejected several opportunities to work in larger cities, saying, "I love this community, and all that it has to offer." Among his many awards and honors are the National Academy of Television Arts and Sciences Silver Circle Award, the prestigious Ohio State Award and two Florida Emmy Awards. In 1998, readers of the Sun Sentinel *voted Lauderdale the number one anchor in the market and* South Florida Magazine *named him best news anchor in 1990. Dwight Lauderdale retired in 2008 after 32 years at WPLG and 40 years in broadcasting.*

SERVES 6

24 medium mushrooms, about 1 pound
6 tablespoons reduced-fat stick margarine
1 small onion, chopped
¼ teaspoon garlic powder, or 2 cloves garlic, minced
1 3-ounce package low fat cream cheese, softened
3 tablespoons Parmesan cheese, grated
2 tablespoons fresh parsley leaves, chopped or 2 teaspoons dried parsley flakes
1 cup packaged herb-seasoned stuffing croutons

Preheat an oven to 425° F. Remove stems from mushrooms. Chop enough of the stems to make 1 cup. Melt 2 tablespoons margarine in a saucepan. Brush mushroom cap tops with the melted margarine, place mushrooms top-side down in shallow baking pan and brush undersides of caps. Heat remaining margarine in the same saucepan. Add chopped mushroom stems, onion and garlic. Cook until tender. Stir in cream cheese, combining with a fork, if necessary. Add Parmesan cheese, parsley and herb seasoned stuffing. Mix thoroughly. Spoon about 1 tablespoon stuffing mixture into each mushroom cap. Bake until heated through.

Note: To make ahead, prepare as directed but do not bake. Cover and refrigerate up to 24 hours. Bake as directed.

SERVES 6

¼ cup onions, chopped

1 tablespoon drippings or other fat

½ cup water

2 tablespoons vinegar

1 tablespoon Worcestershire sauce

¼ cup lemon juice, freshly squeezed

2 tablespoons brown sugar

1 cup chili sauce

½ teaspoon salt

¼ teaspoon paprika

1 teaspoon pepper

1 teaspoon mustard

Don Noe was the Chief Meteorologist at Channel 10, a position that he held for 27 years. Don has also made special guest appearances on Good Morning America *and* The Hollywood Squares. *He has been featured in* People *and* Miami *magazines.*

This is his favorite chicken grilling sauce and it covers about 2 pounds of cut-up chicken.

In a medium sauté pan, sauté the onions in the fat or oil until they begin to caramelize and turn brown. Add these to a saucepan and add the remaining ingredients. Bring to a simmer and cook for 20 minutes.

Before you dip the chicken parts into the sauce, reserve some of the sauce in a dish for table-top dipping.

I find it works well to bring the pan of sauce out to the grill and dip the chicken parts directly in the pan and put them back on the grill. However, it is very important that you do this only within 10 or 15 minutes of the time before the chicken is done as the sauce will tend to become bitter if left on the chicken too long. Place the reserved dipping sauce on the table.

Sea Bass Ceviche *with Jicama and Avocado Slaw*
CHEF NORMAN VAN AKEN

This recipe forthrightly demonstrates the new thinking on ceviches in Peru. As we have seen in some other recipes, the idea nowadays is to greatly reduce the marinating period. In a sense, you are making a dressing rather than a marinade. So now you don't have to plan to make this the day before you want it; you can stop at your fishmonger on the way home and have ceviche on the table that very night. Here I serve it side by side with sea bass in a bowl over ice and the salad components chilled next to it. It is more or less a Japanese approach, and, in fact, I use chopsticks to eat this meal.

Note: You will need several chilled bowls of varying sizes to make this recipe.

First, thinly slice the fillets and then cut them into 3/4 inch bite-size squares. Keep them very cold while you prepare the rest of the recipe.

Marinade/Dressing:
Combine the ingredients in a bowl. Set that bowl inside a larger one, filled with ice. Now prepare the salad.

Jicama Avocado Salad:
In a small bowl, whisk together the olive oil, onion, cilantro, cumin, salt and pepper. Then, in a larger bowl, toss this vinaigrette with the avocado and *jicama*. Set aside. To finish the dish, gently mix the sea bass and the marinade/dressing and let stand for about 10 minutes. Into four chilled bowls, spoon the *ceviche* with its liquid, equally. Serve the salad, family-style, and encourage the guests to top their *ceviche* with salad. If you can get *cancha* (Latin American corn nuts) and toast them, they make a fantastic and authentic addition to this dish. I sometimes like to drizzle coconut milk onto the citrus juices. Or, I season the dish with tiny dots of soy sauce and sesame oil.

SERVES 4
CEVICHE INGREDIENTS
12 ounces skinless sea bass fillets

MARINADE/DRESSING INGREDIENTS
½ cup lime juice, freshly squeezed
1 cup grapefruit juice, freshly squeezed
½ small red onion, thinly sliced
2 tablespoons cilantro leaves, coarsely chopped
1 jalapeño pepper, minced
Kosher salt to taste

SALAD INGREDIENTS
ASSEMBLE IN CHILLED BOWLS
2 tablespoons extra virgin olive oil
2 tablespoons red onion, minced
2 tablespoons cilantro leaves, chopped
¼ teaspoon freshly toasted ground cumin
Kosher salt and freshly toasted, black pepper to taste
1 cup jicama, peeled and sliced into matchstick pieces
1 avocado, peeled, pitted and diced into ¼ inch pieces

Escopazzo is the first organic Italian restaurant in America and features not only organic produce and dairy products but also presents diners with grass-fed beef and pork that is free of hormones and chemicals. Escopazzo features both traditional Italian favorites and contemporary dishes that reflect a deep respect for sustainable agriculture and local farmers and providers. Chef Giancarla is an environmentalist who believes that by cooking and eating healthy, organic food we can "protect our children for generations to come."

SERVES 4

EGGPLANT ROLLS INGREDIENTS

1 medium eggplant

3 cups goat cheese, approximately 24 ounces

½ cup pistachio nuts, chopped

Black pepper

¼ cup extra virgin olive oil

RAGU OF CALAMARI INGREDIENTS

3 pounds fresh calamari tubes and tentacles, use 3-5 inch size, preferably

¼ cup extra virgin olive oil

1 large garlic clove, minced

¼ cup white wine

1 pint fresh grape tomatoes

1 sprig fresh mint

Pinch of red pepper flakes

Slice the eggplant paper thin with a slicer or mandoline and place on a hot grill. You may also use a hot grill pan or skillet and lightly sear the slices on both sides. For the filling, mix the chopped pistachios, goat cheese and black pepper in a bowl until the ingredients are well incorporated.

Place the eggplant slices on a flat working surface. Place a teaspoon of the goat cheese filling on the end of a slice of eggplant and roll it up and set aside. Repeat this with all of the eggplant slices until the goat cheese is exhausted.

For the ragu of calamari, first cut the calamari into rings, leaving the tentacles intact. Pour the olive oil into a pot over high heat and add the chopped garlic and red pepper flakes. Before the garlic turns color add the calamari, and then add the white wine. Lastly, add the tomatoes and mint. Cook the ragu at high heat for 5 minutes. Meanwhile, oil a large sauté pan and lightly sauté the goat cheese rolls in the hot oil until golden. To serve, place equal portions of the ragu of calamari on shallow, rimmed plates and place the goat cheese & eggplant rolls on top.

Grilled Chicken Thigh Skewers

CHEF MICHAEL BLOISE

As a former executive chef of Wish in Miami Beach, rated one of the top 20 restaurants in the country by Esquire magazine, Michael Bloise has worked at top Miami restaurants including The Gaucho Room and Tantra. Recently, Michael was invited to prepare a five-plus course dinner at The James Beard House in New York City, an honor bestowed on a select few culinary artists from around the world.

Mix the beers with the water, sugar, salt, and crushed garlic until well dissolved. This is the "brine" that will be used for the chicken. Slice the thighs in half, thread on the skewers, and let soak in the brine for 12 hours, or overnight, in a covered container in the refrigerator. Remove the skewers and let air dry for 15-30 minutes before grilling. Grill on a medium high part of the grill until the internal temperature of 180° F. on an instant-read meat thermometer has been reached and holds for 3 minutes.

For the sauce, place the butter in a mixing bowl and whisk in the cilantro, garlic, and lemon and lime juices. Add the remaining ingredients. Adjust to taste with the salt and hot sauce. Toss the grilled skewers in the sauce, arrange on a platter and serve!

SERVES 8

4 chicken thighs, boneless and skinless

8 bamboo skewers

½ cup sugar

½ cup kosher salt

1 quart water

6 cloves garlic, crushed with the side of a knife

3 bottles beer, lager

½ pound butter, unsalted and very soft

3 ounces or more hot sauce

½ bunch cilantro, chopped

Juice of 1 lemon, freshly squeezed

Juice of 2 limes, freshly squeezed

1 clove garlic, chopped fine

Salt to taste

STARTERS
SOUPS

SAILING IN MIAMI BEACH Photo Credit: Paul Picone

Sopa de Ajo (Garlic Soup)
CHEF & OWNER MICHELLE BERNSTEIN, MICHY'S

SERVES 6

8 garlic cloves, peeled

¾ cup extra virgin olive oil, plus extra to
   serve at the table

3 shallots, thinly sliced

½ teaspoon cayenne pepper

1 teaspoon fresh thyme, finely chopped

1 teaspoon fresh rosemary, finely chopped

2 bay leaves

12 cherry tomatoes, cut in halves

4 cups chicken stock

¼ cup Spanish sherry

3 tablespoons sherry vinegar

1 cup day old bread, diced

Salt and freshly ground black pepper

4 organic or free range chicken eggs

1 cup Manchego cheese, grated

Michy's is the homegrown, yet modern bistro created by the husband and wife team David Martinez and renowned chef and TV personality, Michelle Bernstein. Located in the up and coming neighborhood of Miami's "Upper East Side," this 50-seat restaurant is quintessential Miami: vibrant, full of tropical hues, just a shade sexy, with a decidedly Latin touch and totally cosmopolitan. Bernstein draws upon local farmers and fisherman to create whimsical bistro dishes, a style she coins as "luxurious comfort food." The menu is comprised of an eclectic range that includes Michelle's Jewish-Argentinean background, classical French training and a love for all things Spanish and Italian.

On a low flame, place the garlic cloves in a small sauté pan and cover with the extra virgin olive oil. Cook the garlic over low heat until very soft, about 20 minutes. Remove from the heat; strain the garlic, reserving the oil. In a large saucepan, heat 3 tablespoons of the garlic oil over medium heat; add the shallots and cook for 5 minutes. Add the diced bread, cook for 5 minutes, stirring the mixture all the while. Add the soft cooked garlic, cayenne pepper, herbs, bay leaves, tomatoes and cook for 5 minutes more. Then add the sherry, vinegar and chicken stock. Season with salt and pepper and cook for 20 minutes. Remove the bay leaves. Carefully purée the hot soup in a blender until very smooth.

Ladle the soup in bowls and top the soup with the grated cheese. The soup can also be topped with your favorite croutons.

For a special addition to the soup, crack an egg right in the center of the soup, if so desired. The heat from the soup will cook the egg very softly. If your guests prefer, you can either fry or poach the egg before placing it in the center of the soup.

Cream of Canistel Soup
NORIS LEDESMA, CURATOR OF TROPICAL FRUIT AT FAIRCHILD TROPICAL BOTANIC GARDEN

The canistel is a member of the mamey sapote family. Native to Central America, it is highly adaptable to Florida where it is grown in some home gardens. Canistel or "egg fruit" has similar characteristics to cooked pumpkin. It is delicious when mixed with milk products and won't sour the milk like many other fruit do. The yellow flesh is relatively firm and mealy with a few fibers. The fruit matures from November through March. Canistel can be eaten fresh, in milkshakes, or used in pies, puddings and bread. The fruit is picked when mature (yellow-color) and can be stored at room temperature for 3 to 10 days. If you wish to store the flesh you can freeze it for up to 6 months. Before freezing, mix the flesh with sugar.

Sauté butter, onion and garlic in a saucepan over medium heat for 2-3 minutes. Add chicken stock and remaining ingredients and stir constantly for 15 minutes. Serve with a dollop of whipped cream and sprinkling of chives.

SERVES 6

2 cups milk
1 cup canistel, peeled and mashed
4 cups chicken stock
1 teaspoon butter
½ teaspoon ground pepper
¼ cup onion, finely chopped
1 teaspoon garlic powder
1 envelope instant chicken soup
Salt to taste
Whipped cream for topping
Fresh chives, chopped fine for garnish

Asturian Broth a la Casa Juancho
CHEF ALFONSO PEREZ, Casa Juancho

SERVES 5

1 pound large dried white beans, such as cannellini or
  Great Northern beans

¼ pound salt pork

1½ pound ham hock

1 blood sausage (morcilla)

1 Spanish sausage (chorizo)

1 bay leaf

Minced garlic and onion to taste

Salt to taste

Pinch of saffron

(Note: Toast saffron on the stove in a small saucepan,
  moving it continually back and forth. Then pulverize
  the saffron using a flat-bottomed glass on a cutting
  board or, better yet, a mortar and pestle.)

Casa Juancho has been bestowed with numerous awards and proclaimed by various national magazines as a "must" when dining out in South Florida. The award winning Spanish cuisine is prepared with the freshest ingredients of Spain and South Florida. Also, the extensive wine cellar offers over 450 aged and vintage wines and has the rarest collections of Spanish wines in the United States. From the moment you enter Casa Juancho, you feel as though you are in Spain.

Place the ham hock and salt pork in a bowl of warm water. Soak the dried beans covered in cold water overnight or 10 to 12 hours. Then drain the beans. Place all of the ingredients in a large pan with enough water to cover. Bring this to a boil, and then simmer on low heat with the lid ajar, making sure that the beans are always covered so they will conserve their skin. Add water as needed in small amounts. The cooking process should be slow and the pan needs occasional shaking to prevent the beans from sticking to the bottom. Add the saffron that has been lightly toasted and very finely pulverized. Season the broth once it has cooked. Press several tablespoons of the cooked beans through a fine mesh colander, then add this to the broth to thicken it. Continue cooking for a few more minutes. Let rest for approximately 20 minutes before serving, if convenient.

Note: All the ingredients can be found at Spanish markets. In Miami, try Sedano's, Bravo's or Navarro, which are all located on *Calle Ocho* (SW 8th Street). Typical bodegas are also plentiful like *La Vasca* or *Brizas de Espana* also on *Calle Ocho*. *Delicias de Espana*, a Spanish specialty store, is on Red Road at Bird Road (SW 57th Avenue at SW 40th Street).

Gazpacho Bowl
MANAGER CHRISTIAN QUARATO,
DOLORES BUT YOU CAN CALL ME LOLITA
RESTAURANT & LOUNGE

The Mediterranean fusion restaurant, Dolores But You Can Call Me Lolita, features signature dishes from cuisines as far flung as Peru, Argentina, Spain and Brazil. Their Gazpacho recipe pays homage to tradition with a distinct flair.

In a blender or food processor, blend all ingredients together and chill in the refrigerator for at least 4 hours.

Place 2 tablespoons of diced peppers in bowl; pour blended ingredients over the peppers and serve. Be certain to always serve well chilled.

SERVES 4

3-4 pounds fresh tomatoes

1 cucumber

2 tablespoons red wine vinegar

2 green or red bell peppers

(plus 2 tablespoons diced peppers for garnish)

1 clove garlic

1 cup water

1 cup olive oil

3 slices bread

1 pinch ground cumin

Salt to taste

SERVES 6

From a roasting hen or large broiling chicken use the neck, wings, back and giblets

1½ quarts of cold water, brought to the boil

1 white onion, thinly sliced

3 stalks celery (with leaves), diced

1 carrot, diced

1 teaspoon salt

1 green bell pepper, diced

⅛ teaspoon paprika, preferably sweet roasted

⅛ teaspoon garlic powder

½ cup parsley, finely chopped

1 can (16-ounces) cream-style corn

Cleveland Bell, III is not only the Executive Director of Riverside House, a non-profit community based re-entry facility for men and women, but is also a world famous chef, at least in his own mind anyway! When Mr. Bell is not overseeing the operation of the halfway house, attending a community meeting, conducting a speaking engagement, or singing, he enjoys cooking for himself and his family.

This Chicken and Corn Chowder is a simple but favorite dish of everyone in the Bell family. It is a terrific way to use those leftover parts of a roasting chicken to their best advantage: by using them to make a fresh chicken stock with the vegetable "trinity" of onion, celery and green bell peppers. Add the sweetness of carrots and creamed corn and you can enjoy a heart-warming and healthy chowder.

Place the pieces of chicken in large pot or kettle with water, onion, celery, carrot, salt, bell pepper, paprika, garlic powder, and half the finely chopped parsley. Bring to a boil. Cover and simmer until all the ingredients are tender, about 30 minutes. When cooked through, remove the chicken pieces from the pot. Carefully slip the meat from bones, cut into bite-size pieces and return to the broth. Add the corn and simmer 10 minutes more until heated through. Serve piping-hot in soup platters or wide soup bowls, garnished with the additional parsley.

Mango Soup
NORIS LEDESMA, CURATOR OF TROPICAL FRUIT
AT FAIRCHILD TROPICAL BOTANIC GARDEN

One of the world's most popular fruits, the mango works well in both sweet and savory dishes. Fresh mangoes can be sliced and served as a simple but elegant dessert or combined with other fruit for fruit cocktails. Many people like the flavor of green or semi-ripe mangoes that can be used in pies, chutneys, salads and achar. Green mangoes are also delicious sprinkled with salt and pepper.

Different varieties of mango vary in flavor and pectin content and consequently the recipes may require some specific varieties. Varieties like Mallika, Sandersha, *and* Nam Doc Mai *are recommended for chutneys. Almost all of the mango varieties can be dehydrated but the best ones for this purpose are* Kent, Zill *and* Tommy Akins. *For cooking purposes and for jams, chutneys, sauces, dressings or ice creams,* Alphonse *and* Florigon *are good choices.*

Note: Mango varieties recommended for the soup: Carabao, Carrie, Florigon, Bombay

In a blender or food processor, blend the mango until smooth and combine with the ginger, lemongrass, and chicken stock in a large bowl; stir well. Add yogurt and chill. Before serving, garnish with cilantro and decorate edge of bowl with the shrimp.

SERVES 6

2 large ripe mangoes, peeled, cut from the pit & chopped
½ cup plain yogurt
½ cup chicken stock
½ tablespoon fresh lemon grass, minced
½ teaspoon fresh ginger, grated
2 tablespoons fresh cilantro, chopped fine for garnish
6 large shrimp, steamed and chilled

SERVES 6

SOUP INGREDIENTS

1½ to 1¾ pounds calabaza *(West Indian pumpkin)*

2 tablespoons unsalted butter

1 onion, diced

1 carrot, diced

2 ribs celery, diced

3 cloves garlic, diced

2 jalapeño chilies, seeded and diced (optional)

4 to 5 cups chicken stock

2 bay leaves

2 sprigs fresh thyme or 1 teaspoon dried thyme

¼ cup fresh Italian (flat-leaf) parsley, finely chopped

Salt and freshly ground black pepper, to taste

½ cup half and half, light cream, heavy cream or whipping cream

SPICE- SCENTED WHIPPED CREAM AND GARNISH INGREDIENTS

½ cup heavy or whipping cream

¼ teaspoon ground cumin

¼ teaspoon ground coriander

¼ teaspoon cayenne pepper

Salt and freshly ground black pepper, to taste

1 tablespoon fresh chives or scallions, finely chopped

Television personality and former fashion model Hunter Reno spent a year showcasing the city of Miami on WAMI-TV's Ocean Drive with Hunter Reno *prior to her current role as host of Florida's WPBT's television magazine program* Wild Florida. *She had also participated in a series that focused on the accomplishments of female athletes for Oxygen Sports, and, while hosting the Travel Channel's* Exotic Islands, *Reno visited some of the world's most breathtaking destinations. In addition, she has served as the master of ceremonies for the Sony Ericsson Open Tennis Event on Key Biscayne.*

Using a sharp knife cut the rind off the *calabaza*. Scrape out any seeds with a spoon and cut the flesh into 1 inch pieces. Melt the butter in a large saucepan over medium heat. Sauté the onion, carrot, and celery until soft but not brown, about 3 to 4 minutes. Stir in the *calabaza*, 4 cups of the stock, the herbs and seasonings, and bring to a boil. Reduce the heat and simmer the soup uncovered, until the vegetables are very soft, about 30 minutes. Remove the bay leaves and thyme branches, and purée the soup in a blender. Return the soup to the saucepan and stir in the cream. If the soup is too thick, add more stock. Correct the seasonings, adding salt or pepper. To prepare the spice-scented whipped cream, beat the cream to soft peaks in a chilled bowl. Whip in the spices and salt and pepper. To serve, ladle the soup into bowls and place a dollop of the spice-scented whipped cream in the center of each. Sprinkle the cream with the chives and serve at once.

Reprinted with permission from *Miami Spice: The New Florida Cuisine* by Steven Raichlen, Workman Publishing

Roasted Butternut Squash Soup
with Gorgonzola Beignets
CHEFS JORGE MONTES AND ANDRES ALARCON, GOURMET CREATIONS

After nearly a decade of working in various kitchens, hosting cooking classes, and special events in Miami, Chefs Jorge Montes and Andres Alarcon opened their very own culinary spot, Gourmet Creations. Located in South Miami, the quaint store offers customized service for catering events, private parties, corporate events and gourmet take-out lunches. This savory soup with cheesy beignets is a long-time favorite of their clients.

Preheat an oven to 400° F. Cut the squash in half lengthwise and remove the seeds. Place squash in a baking pan with a little olive oil and salt. Bake for 20 minutes or until tender. Remove skin and discard. In a large pot, melt butter and sauté onions until translucent. Add squash and spices; mix well and sauté for another three minutes. Add the cream and chicken stock. Bring to a boil and simmer for 15 minutes. Purée the mixture in a blender or food processor and then pass through a fine mesh strainer or *chinoise*.

Gorgonzola *Beignets*:
In a saucepan, heat the water and butter over moderate heat. Whisk in the flour and slowly bring to a boil. Once the mixture reaches a boil, pour into a bowl in a stand mixer and mix for 2 minutes on low. Add the salt, pepper and paprika. Then add eggs one at a time while continuing to beat the batter. Gently fold in the crumbled gorgonzola. Heat vegetable oil one-inch deep in a sauté pan to 325° F., using a candy thermometer or by placing a heaping tablespoon of the batter in the oil to be sure that the oil bubbles vigorously around the batter. Repeat this process and deep-fry all of the batter, tablespoon by tablespoon. *Beignets* will float and turn by themselves. Cook for two minutes until golden brown. Remove with a slotted spoon and place on paper towels to drain. To serve, ladle soup into individual shallow soup plates and top with the cheesy *beignets*.

SERVES 4-6
SOUP INGREDIENTS
2 large butternut squash (a small pumpkin can also be used in the same manner)
1 small onion, diced
4 ounces unsalted butter
2 teaspoons cumin
2 teaspoons cinnamon powder
½ cup sugar
1½ quarts chicken stock
1 cup heavy cream
Salt

GORGONZOLA *BEIGNETS* INGREDIENTS
1 pound unsalted butter
5 cups flour
1 cup water
12 eggs
1½ cups gorgonzola cheese, crumbled
1 teaspoon paprika
Salt & pepper to taste
Vegetable or canola oil for deep-frying

Lobster Bisque

CHEF & OWNER PASCAL OUDIN, PASCAL'S ON PONCE

Pascal Oudin's restaurant is the culmination of an illustrious and award-winning culinary career—working with such star chefs as Alain Ducasse, Roger Verge, and Jean Louis Palladin. Food & Wine Magazine named him as one of "America's Best New Chefs" and Esquire declared him to be the "Best New Chef in Florida." Pascal's on Ponce has garnered acclaim from Gourmet Magazine, the NY Times and the Zagat Guide. Featuring the finest in contemporary French cuisine, Oudin highlights the preparation of the freshest local ingredients to order using classic French techniques he has learned from the masters of French cooking.

SERVES 8

1½ pound Florida or rock lobster body

4 tablespoons olive oil

2 tablespoons butter

1 pinch cayenne pepper

1 small red onion, diced

1 small carrot, diced

1 rib of celery, diced

1 head garlic, cut in half

1 sprig of fresh thyme

1 sprig of fresh basil

1 sprig of fresh tarragon

1 tablespoon dry fennel seed, coarsely ground

¼ cup brandy

1 cup dry white wine

1 cup fresh tomatoes, chopped

1 tablespoon tomato paste

2 cups fish stock

2 cups heavy cream

Salt and pepper to taste

2 tablespoons uncooked white rice

Chop the body of the lobster into small pieces. Heat the olive oil in a large saucepan over medium heat. Add the lobster meat, cayenne pepper and fennel. Cook covered for 5 minutes, until the lobster shells are red. Stir in the onion, carrot, garlic, celery and herbs and let cook for 5 minutes longer. Add the brandy and wine. Turn the heat to high and cook uncovered for 2 minutes, until reduced slightly. Add the tomato paste, fresh tomatoes, fish stock, salt and pepper. Bring to a boil, then add uncooked rice, reduce heat and simmer for 30 minutes. Add the cream and cook uncovered for 10 minutes. Strain the soup through a medium strainer, pressing on the lobster shells so as to get all the meat from the shells. Purée the soup in a blender, then return the soup to the pan, and season to taste with salt and pepper. *Bon Appétit!*

Strawberry Gazpacho
CHEF MICHAEL BLOISE

Chef Bloise got an early education in food from his Italian father and Vietnamese mother — and an exposure to the deep, rich, complex flavors that are present in his cuisine today. A graduate of Johnson & Wales in Miami, he went on to work around the city, most notably at Miami Beach's Tantra restaurant and The Gaucho Room formerly at the Loews Hotel. This unique and colorful soup is a cool, tropical interpretation of the classic dish from the Andalusian region of southern Spain. Only in Miami!

Blend strawberries, cucumbers, garlic, tomatoes, and the jalapeño pepper in a blender. Add the sherry vinegar to taste. Season with salt and pepper and reserve the *gazpacho* in the refrigerator until well chilled. Dress the julienned *jicama* and chives with olive oil, thyme, and black pepper. Then place the *jicama* salad in the center of large, shallow bowl. Place the *chevré* balls in the center of *jicama* salad. Surround the *jicama* salad with the chilled soup and serve.

SERVES 4

3 pints strawberries, stems removed and coarsely chopped
2 English cucumbers, any seeds removed,
peeled and coarsely chopped
3 cloves garlic
4 plum tomatoes, coarsely chopped
1 jalapeño pepper
Salt and freshly ground pepper
½ cup sherry vinegar
½ bunch chives, sliced as batonette (¼ inch x 2-2½ inches)
1 pound jicama, *peeled and cut into julienne*
Extra virgin olive oil, Spanish, if possible
¼ bunch thyme, leaves stripped from the stems
8 ounces chevré *(or goat cheese) divided into four 2-ounce balls*

STARTERS
SALADS

AMERICAN AIRLINES ARENA Photo Credit: Denis Bancroft

Jackfruit Salad
NORIS LEDESMA, CURATOR OF TROPICAL FRUIT
AT FAIRCHILD TRPOICAL BOTANIC GARDEN

SERVES 4

6 cups fresh ripe jackfruit, coarsely chopped

Juice of one lime, freshly squeezed

1 cup sweetened, shredded coconut

¾ cup golden raisins or sultanas

16 ounces sour cream

¾ to 1 cup toasted walnuts (optional)

Jackfruit is believed to be native to India and is cultivated throughout the Far East including India, Myanmar, the Philippines, southern China and Indonesia. David Fairchild collected a variety in Sri Lanka, which was planted on his property in Coconut Grove. Large and ungainly, this green fruit is covered with spiny protrusions and may weigh upwards of 30 to 70 pounds. Inside the leathery exterior are starchy seeds surrounded by aromatic flesh which, when ripened, is extremely sweet, with a distinctive flavor reminiscent of bananas and Juicy Fruit gum.

This is one of the most versatile fruits I know and here in the subtropics we live in a veritable paradise of unique fruits. Immature, or green, it can be used as a vegetable, stuffed or sautéed with any kind of meat and/or cheese, boiled and mashed, or served in a casserole. Ripe fruit can be served plain, chilled or mixed in a fruit salad. Boiled and roasted, the seeds make tasty snacks. Use your palate as a guide when being creative with the largest tree-borne fruit in the world.

In a large mixing bowl, combine the jackfruit, lime juice, coconut, raisins and sour cream. If, after combining all the ingredients, you feel the mixture needs more of any of the above, slowly add according to taste. Mix in toasted walnuts, if desired, just before serving.

Note: To toast walnuts, spread them on a cookie sheet in a single layer, and toast for 8 to 10 minutes in a preheated 300°F. oven. Turn walnuts over after 4 or 5 minutes. After removing the walnuts from the oven, let them cool before adding to salad.

Cherry Tomato Salad
With Pine Nuts, Red Miso and Thai Basil
CHEF MICHAEL BLOISE

As a former executive chef of Wish in Miami Beach, rated one of the top 20 restaurants in the country by Esquire magazine, Michael Bloise has worked at top Miami restaurants including The Gaucho Room and Tantra. Recently, he was invited to prepare a five-plus course dinner at The James Beard House in New York City, an honor bestowed on a select few culinary artists from around the world.

In a mixing bowl, combine the *miso* paste, olive oil, and lemon juice. Season with fresh ground black pepper to taste, then fold in the remainder of the ingredients. Place a small portion in a porcelain spoon, preferably an Asian-style soup spoon. Place spoons in a decorative pattern on a serving platter.

MAKES 30 HOR D'OEUVRES

30 plump cherry tomatoes, quartered

1 cup pine nuts, lightly toasted

1 tablespoon red *miso* paste, available in specialty and Asian markets

½ cup extra virgin olive oil, Spanish if possible

1 bunch Thai basil, cut into thin strips or chiffonade

1 tablespoon lemon juice

Fried Calamari Salad
CHEF AUDREY BOWERS &
EXECUTIVE CHEF DALE PALOMINO, The Captain's Tavern

For more than thirty-six years, the family run Captain's Tavern has been one of the go-to places for fresh seafood in Miami. The lunch and dinner menus feature more than fifteen different varieties of fresh fish and seafood, as well as an award-winning wine list. The most "hopeless of landlubbers" will have a "trusty pair of sea legs" by meal's end. This Fried Calamari Salad is a classic example from Chef Dale Palomino's kitchen.

For the sauce, combine all of the ingredients in a non-metallic bowl and place in the refrigerator until needed.

For the calamari, take a large sauté pan, add the vegetable oil and heat until it is ready to fry the calamari. (You can test the oil by adding just a single piece of calamari and if the oil bubbles, it is ready.) Combine the Supreme Breader® and Lawry's Seasoned Salt® in a shallow bowl or platter. Lightly bread the calamari rings and carefully add them to the hot oil in the pan. Fry until they are lightly golden, about 20 seconds or so. Remove the calamari from the pan with a slotted spoon and place evenly on paper towels so that the excess oil can drain off. In a large bowl place the tomatoes, onions, and then gently toss together with enough of the sauce to coat the vegetables. Add the fried calamari and half of the cilantro and toss lightly. On a platter, serve the calamari and vegetable mixture over the shredded lettuce, drizzle with a little more of the sauce, garnish with the remaining cilantro and the lemon wedges and serve.

Serves 8
Salad Ingredients

2 pounds squid, cleaned and cut in ½ inch rings

4 cups Supreme Breader® (available at your local grocery store)

6 cups vegetable oil for frying

1 teaspoon Lawry's Seasoned Salt® (available at your local grocery store)

1 medium red onion, julienned

2 cups grape tomatoes, cut in halves

¼ cup cilantro, chopped

2 lemons for garnish

1 head Romaine or head lettuce, shredded

Sauce Ingredients

¼ cup olive oil

2 cups Thai-style sweet chile sauce

½ cup water

1 tablespoon fish sauce

1 tablespoon garlic, finely chopped

1 teaspoon Tabasco sauce

¼ cup lemon juice

1 tablespoon Worcestershire sauce

Freda's Salad Dressing
FREDA COFFING TSCHUMY, Artist & Sculptor

Freda Coffing Tschumy is a well-known artist and creator of the sculpture of Marjory Stoneman Douglas currently on view at Fairchild Tropical Botanic Garden.

For a pot-luck dinner, people often ask me to bring the salad because they like this dressing. It was inspired by a salad dressing that we had at Bandera Restaurant in Scottsdale, Arizona many years ago.

Place all of the ingredients in a cruet and shake vigorously until well mixed. This mixture can be kept at room temperature and used over a period of two to three weeks. To serve, pour the amount desired over a salad of mixed greens, tomatoes, scallions, avocado, craisins or raisins, toasted salted nuts or corn, or other combination. It's always interesting to include with the greens something red or yellow, something sweet, and something crunchy. This dressing is also nice on a simple green salad. Enjoy!

1 cup good extra virgin olive oil

⅙ cup rice wine vinegar

⅙ cup lemon juice

⅙ cup balsamic vinegar

2 tablespoons Dijon mustard

1 teaspoon salt

¼ teaspoon pepper (I often use ground cayenne here)

3 cloves garlic (or more to taste),
crushed through garlic press

1½ tablespoons dried herbs such as
basil, thyme, or oregano

SERVES 6

3 large bunches parsley

2 large tomatoes, diced small

¼ cup olive oil or vegetable oil

⅓ cup cracked wheat (or bulgar wheat)

2 cups water

⅓ cup lemon juice (or to taste)

4 green onions, with ends

¼ cup fresh mint, chopped or 2 tablespoons dry mint

1 ½ teaspoons salt

¼ teaspoon pepper

In 1986 the Hispanic world was introduced to Lili Estefan, and her signature smile, when she joined the cast of Sabado Gigante. *Sabado Gigante, broadcast in the United States on the Univision Television Network, is the number one rated and viewed international television program, transmitted to 25 other countries including Chile, Spain and México, reaching 80 million viewers weekly. Estefan, a Cuban native, has gained worldwide popularity during her career as an entertainer, film actor, music columnist and entertainment reporter.*

Wash the parsley well, drain and shake out the excess moisture. Soak the cracked wheat in water in a large mixing bowl for 2 minutes. Drain well. Set aside while preparing other ingredients. Remove the stems from the parsley and discard. Chop parsley very finely. The 3 bunches should equal 5 cups. Add to the wheat. Chop onions finely and add to the mixture along with the remaining ingredients. Do not add the tomatoes and onion until just before serving. Toss well. Serve with romaine lettuce leaves. Tear leaves into bite size pieces and use to scoop up salad for eating.

Avocado Carambola Salad
NORIS LEDESMA, CURATOR OF TROPICAL FRUITS
AT FAIRCHILD TROPICAL BOTANIC GARDEN

The avocado has been part of the human diet for thousands of years. Native to the tropics and sub-tropics, records of its usage occur from 7000 B.C. in Mexico. There are three major types of avocados: Mexican (grown in California) and Guatemalan types, which are relatively small fruited compared to Florida grown avocados (West Indian types), which have a large fruit. Florida avocados are large, smooth-skinned and lower in calories and fat compared with Mexican and Guatemalan avocados.

Arrange a bed of lettuce on each salad plate. Layer the remaining ingredients in the order listed. Repeat until all ingredients have been used. Add the dressing of your choice.

SERVES 2
Iceberg lettuce leaves, torn

2 tomatoes, sliced

½ red onion, chopped

1 avocado, sliced

2 carambolas (star fruits), sliced

Peanut Chicken Salad
CHEF JOHNSON TEH, LAN PAN ASIAN CAFÉ

Lan Pan Asian Café specializes in East and Southeast Asian cuisine including dishes from Japan, China, Korea, Thailand, and Vietnam. Chef Johnson Teh, has over twenty years of restaurant experience, both in Asia and in the United States. He often creates dishes that are traditional but are reinterpreted with a light contemporary touch bringing new tastes and textures to classical favorites. Lan Pan Asian Café has been highly rated by the New Times, The Miami Herald, The Sun Sentinel, *and* The Zagat Guide.

Mix well all of the ingredients for the peanut sauce and set aside.

In a large pot of salted boiling water, cook the noodles according to the directions on the package. When done, drain the pasta and toss it with the oil to keep the noodles from sticking together. Chill the noodles in a large bowl in the refrigerator until needed. Heat a grill pan over medium high heat. Season the chicken breasts with salt and pepper. When the grill is hot, brush the surface with oil and place the chicken breasts on the grill pan. Let them cook for 4 to 5 minutes undisturbed before turning the chicken breasts over. Cook the chicken for another 4 to 5 minutes or until the juices in the chicken breasts run clear. Remove the breasts and set aside to let the chicken cool and then cut the breasts into thin slices.

Cut the cucumber into thirds, then thinly slice the thirds, lengthwise. Stack the resulting cucumber slices, and again slice thinly to yield matchstick-like or julienned pieces. To the bowl of noodles add 1 cup of the peanut sauce and mix well. Place equal portions of the noodles into 4 shallow dishes and top each serving with the chicken, bean sprouts, cucumber, and scallions. Garnish each serving with sprigs of cilantro and serve with additional peanut sauce at the table.

SERVES 4
CHICKEN SALAD INGREDIENTS

1 pound thin Asian wheat noodles or thin spaghetti

1 tablespoon canola or vegetable oil

1 pound boneless, skinless chicken breasts

1 English or seedless cucumber

8 ounces bean sprouts

½ bunch scallions, thinly sliced

2 cups peanut sauce (the recipe below yields more than you need)

Cilantro for garnish

Salt and pepper

Canola oil for the grill

PEANUT SAUCE INGREDIENTS

1¾ cups rice wine vinegar

½ cup soy sauce

½ cup Worcestershire sauce

½ tablespoon chile paste

¼ cup sugar

¼ cup honey

2 cups smooth or chunky peanut butter

½ can (use 7-fluid ounces) coconut milk, well shaken

½ cup sake, optional

Octopus Salad *with Cherry Tomatoes and Wild Asparagus*
CHEF SERGIO SIGALA, CASA TUA

Casa Tua is a cozy but elegant restaurant, featuring simple, authentic Italian food. Sigala's every dish reflects a perfect harmony of flavors and textures, as well as the chef's unmistakable reverence for each ingredient. Fresh herbs and regional Italian olive oils figure prominently in his dishes. Restaurant guests may dine in the casual-chic dining room or at the "friends" table next to the open kitchen. The "friends" table seats 18-20 people and is intended for those who wish only a quick dish of pasta and a glass of vino *or for groups who wish to have a separate room for entertaining. From the menus that resemble family albums to the flower arrangements and the fragrant tropical plant garden, Casa Tua is an oasis to please all the senses of the most sophisticated clientele.*

SERVES 4
SALAD INGREDIENTS
8 green asparagus tips
8 green asparagus stems, cut in quarters lengthwise
12 grape tomatoes, cut in quarters
2 pounds fresh imported octopus

COURT BOUILLON INGREDIENTS
(Note: This broth is used to boil the octopus)
1 gallon water
1 carrot
1 celery stalk
1 yellow onion
1 glass of dry white wine
1 lemon
1 teaspoon whole black peppercorns

MUSTARD DRESSING INGREDIENTS
½ cup extra virgin olive oil
1 tablespoon of Dijon mustard
1 teaspoon of fresh tarragon, finely chopped
1 cup orange juice
Salt and pepper, to season

Salad:
Place the asparagus tips and stems in a small pot of salty water and boil over medium heat until they are blanched. Then remove and quickly chill in a bowl of ice water. Set aside.

Court Bouillon:
Boil the octopus in the court bouillon for about 40 minutes or until tender. Allow the octopus to cool down in the court bouillon, and then remove from the pot. Remove the skin and cut the cooked octopus into rounds.

Mustard Dressing:
Blend all the ingredients with a hand blender, set aside in a cool place.

In a large bowl dress the octopus rounds, asparagus and tomatoes with the mustard dressing, add salt and pepper, if needed. Assemble the dish on a large platter or serve in a big bowl, family style.

Palta (Avocado) Salad *with Salsa Golfito*

CHEF RODOLFO FERNANDEZ, Chocolate

Chocolate offers its own spin on traditional Argentine cuisine. The restaurant is colorful and cheery with great artwork on the walls. Chocolate is a sweet place to eat!

SERVES 6

PALTA SALAD INGREDIENTS

6 avocados, halved, flesh scooped out, diced and
  shells reserved
24 shrimp, cleaned and cooked
6 ounces pineapple, cubed
4 ounces hearts of palm, sliced into rounds
Salt and pepper to taste

SALSA GOLFITO INGREDIENTS

1½ ounces mayonnaise
1 ounce ketchup
1 ounce angostura bitters

Combine the diced avocado, pineapple and hearts of palm in a bowl. Add salt and pepper to taste. Mix the *Salsa Golfito* ingredients together until blended. Gently mix the salsa into the salad ingredients. Evenly divide the dressed salad between the reserved avocado shells, arranging the shrimp on top as garnish.

Ensalada de Pulpo (Octopus Salad)
EXECUTIVE CHEF SEAN BERNAL,
THE OCEANAIRE SEAFOOD ROOM

Sean Bernal has gained national acclaim for his creative Latin-Asian styled cuisine. His cooking blends perfectly with the hot Florida sun, using fresh local tropical fruits, Latin heirloom quality vegetables and, of course, "ultra-fresh" fish and shellfish from local waters, blending influences from traditional Caribbean, Latin, South American, and Asian cuisine that fit in perfectly with Oceanaire's daily changing menu. According to Bernal, "If it swims, floats, or crawls in the ocean, you'll find it on our table."

Slice octopus thinly and fan around a serving platter. Mix together the peppers, capers, onion, olives and herbs. Make a simple vinaigrette with the sherry vinegar, olive oil and salt and pepper to taste. Mix with the other ingredients and spoon this vinaigrette over the octopus and serve.

SERVES 6

8 ounces octopus, cooked
⅓ cup red bell pepper, diced
⅓ cup green bell pepper, diced
2 tablespoons capers
⅓ cup red onion, diced
4 tablespoons green olives, chopped
1 tablespoon fresh oregano, chopped
2 tablespoons cilantro, chopped
2 cups olive oil
1 cup sherry vinegar
Salt and pepper to taste

DONNA E. SHALALA, President, University of Miami

Serves 4-6

1 cup fine cracked wheat

Juice of 5 to 6 lemons (about 1 cup)

2 cups of Italian parsley leaves, chopped

1 cup fresh mint leaves, chopped

1 cup tomato, seeded and chopped

3 bunches scallions, trimmed and sliced

1 tablespoon extra-virgin olive oil

Salt and freshly ground pepper

Donna E. Shalala became Professor of Political Science and President of the University of Miami in 2001. President Shalala has more than 25 years of experience as an accomplished scholar, teacher, and administrator. She served as President of Hunter College of CUNY from 1980 to 1987 and as Chancellor of the University of Wisconsin-Madison from 1987 to 1993. In 1993 President Clinton appointed her U.S. Secretary of Health and Human Services (HHS) where she served for eight years, becoming the longest serving HHS Secretary in U.S. history. At the end of her tenure as HHS Secretary, The Washington Post *described her as "one of the most successful government managers of modern times." President Shalala has a host of other honors, including the 1992 National Public Service Award, the 1994* Glamour Magazine *Woman of the Year Award, and in 2005 was named one of "America's Best Leaders" by* U.S. News & World Report *and the Center for Public Leadership at Harvard University's Kennedy School of Government.*

It's important to dry the parsley and mint and drain the tomatoes well. You may replace some of the lemon juice with water. Soak the cracked wheat in the lemon juice and enough water to cover overnight. Using your hands, squeeze as much liquid as possible from the soaked wheat and place it in a serving bowl. Add the parsley, mint, tomato, and scallions. Drizzle on the oil and toss. Season to taste with salt and pepper.

MAIN DISHES
MEAT

FREEDOM TOWER Photo Credit: Nick Tzolov

Goat Cheese Crusted Lamb Loin
CHEF NATE MARTIN, ANDÚ RESTAURANT

At Andú Restaurant & Lounge, we've created a new haven for sexy cuisine, style and sophistication, all at a price you can afford. Andú will excite your senses and satisfy your cravings. Our talented Executive Chef, Nate Martin has designed a tantalizing menu of Mediterranean cuisine with international influences. Using the freshest, highest quality ingredients, our menu entices even the most discerning of palates.

SERVES 2

10 ounces lamb loin

4 ounces goat cheese

1 tablespoon Sun-Dried Tomato Tapenade (see recipe)

2 tablespoons pesto

1 tablespoon Herbs de Provence

2 tablespoons bread crumbs

1 cup orzo pasta, cooked

1 cup Ratatouille *(see recipe)*

3 ounces Parmesan cheese

1 sprig basil, cut in chiffonade *or little ribbons**

½ cup lamb stock

1 tablespoon unsalted butter

1 cup lamb sauce (see recipe)

Kosher salt to taste

Black pepper to taste

1 tablespoon canola oil

Preheat an oven to 350 ° F. In a mixing bowl, thoroughly incorporate the goat cheese with the *Herbs de Provence*, the tapenade and the pesto. Season this with salt and pepper to taste. Place a sauté pan on high heat with canola oil. While the pan heats, generously season the lamb loin with salt and pepper. Once the oil is at smoking temperature, sear the lamb on both sides. Once seared, remove from the pan and smear the goat cheese mixture over the top of the loin. Sprinkle with bread crumbs and finish in an oven until the desired temperature on an instant read thermometer is reached. While the loin is cooking, place the orzo pasta, *ratatouille*, and lamb stock in a sauté pan and begin to reheat. Once the stock reduces by about half, fold in the butter, Parmesan cheese, and basil. The butter and cheese should emulsify into the remaining liquid and form the "risotto". Season to taste.

Note: *Chiffonade* is accomplished by stacking the basil leaves, rolling them tightly, then cutting across the rolled leaves with a sharp knife, producing fine ribbons.

Sun-Dried Tomato Tapenade:
Place all of the ingredients in a blender and purée until smooth. The mixture should form a spreadable paste.

Ratatouille:

In a sauté pan over high heat, separately sauté the zucchini, squash, eggplant, onions and peppers. Since each vegetable requires different cooking times, keeping them separate will allow you to achieve nice caramelization on the vegetables without overcooking. Sauté the vegetables until they are cooked half way. In a larger sauté pan sweat the garlic, add the sautéed vegetables and deglaze with the slurry. Add the sprig of basil and cook until it is sec or dry. Cooking the slurry down until it is sec or dry will rid the tomato paste of its overwhelmingly raw taste. Sprinkle with Parmesan and season with salt and pepper to taste. Remove the basil sprig.

Lamb Sauce:

Place the lamb stock, sage, tomatoes, and roasted garlic in a small saucepan and begin to reduce over medium heat. Once reduced by half, emulsify the butter and season to taste. To serve, portion out the risotto and lay the sliced loin over the top. Spoon the lamb sauce over the edge of the lamb and the risotto.

SUN-DRIED TOMATO *TAPENADE* INGREDIENTS

4 ounces sun-dried tomatoes

1 clove garlic, roasted

1 tablespoon capers

2 anchovy fillets

2 tablespoons Sherry vinegar

2 ounces extra virgin olive oil

RATATOUILLE INGREDIENTS

2 ounces zucchini, diced

2 ounces yellow squash, diced

2 ounces red bell pepper, diced

2 ounces tomato, diced

2 ounces eggplant, diced

2 ounces red onion, diced

½ cup tomato paste "slurry"

(2 parts wine/1 part tomato paste)

1 teaspoon garlic, minced

1 sprig basil (whole)

2 ounces Parmesan cheese, grated

Kosher salt and black pepper to taste

LAMB SAUCE INGREDIENTS

3 cups lamb stock

1 teaspoon garlic, roasted

2 ounces sun-dried tomatoes, julienne

1 sprig sage, cut in chiffonade

1 tablespoon unsalted butter

Kosher salt and black pepper to taste

Grandma's Sweet Brisket

CHEF MICHAEL B. JACOBS, GRASS RESTAURANT & LOUNGE

Located in the Design District in Downtown Miami, Grass Restaurant & Lounge is an upscale venue and open-air eatery where diners feast under thatched huts. The foliage is lush and even the lighting has a floral bent, with a wall of illuminated apothecary jars housing colorful Polynesian flowers. The menu offers everything from a vegan-friendly tart stuffed with grilled peppers and zucchini squash to dishes like Ceviche *and* Kobe *beef.*

SERVES 6-8

2½ pounds beef brisket

2 Spanish yellow onions, thinly sliced

4 Idaho potatoes, cut into medium cubes

1 can (12-ounces) ginger ale

2 cans (6-ounces each) pineapple juice

1 cup of vegetable or beef broth

4 large carrots, cut into 1 inch pieces

3 stalks celery, cut into 1 inch pieces

2 parsnips, cut into 1 inch pieces

3 tablespoons brown sugar

12 cloves

2 bay leaves

4 fresh sprigs of thyme

2 tablespoons unsalted butter

3 tablespoons all purpose flour

Salt and white pepper to season

Preheat an oven to 400° F. Pat the brisket dry and season with salt and pepper. Stud the brisket on the top fatty part with cloves and the two bay leaves. Add the onions, carrots, celery, potatoes and parsnips to the bottom of a roasting pan. Place the brisket with the cloves and bay leaf on top of the vegetables. Rub the top of the brisket with a mixture of salt, brown sugar and white pepper. Pour in the ginger ale, pineapple juice and broth. The liquid should just about cover a quarter of the brisket. Braise in an oven for two-and-a-half hours, starting out at 400° F. for 30 minutes, uncovered. After 30 minutes, cover with aluminum foil and turn the oven down to 325° F. for two hours. When done, transfer the brisket and vegetables with a slotted spoon to a serving plate. Cover and keep warm. In the roasting pan, add the butter to the dripping juices and then add the flour. Cook over medium high heat for 3-8 minutes, stirring constantly. Pour the sauce over the finished brisket. Serve and enjoy!

Baby Rack of Lamb with Provençal Panis, Goat Cheese Mousse, Sautéed Zucchini & Black Olive Sauce
CHEF PHILIPPE RUIZ, Palme D'Or at The Biltmore

Seductive French cuisine and extraordinary wines take center stage at the award-winning Palme D'Or, recognized by Zagat as one of the best French restaurants in the country. Chef de Cuisine Philippe Ruiz along with Head Sommelier Sébastien Verrier, deliver delectable dishes paired with exceptional service, in a sophisticated, contemporary setting.

In a sauté pan, roast the garbanzo flour with 1 ounce of the olive oil over medium heat. Add chicken stock and the chopped rosemary. Cook for 2-3 minutes until you obtain a dry paste. Season with salt and pepper. Spread the hot paste across a plate until it reaches a ½ inch thickness. Reserve in the refrigerator. Once the paste is cold, cut the hardened paste in a preferred shape, such as rounds or triangles, and fry them in a sauté pan with 2 ounces of the olive oil, and reserve. Mix soft goat cheese gently with whipped cream and scallions. Check the seasoning and reserve.

Cut the zucchini in half and season with salt and pepper. Sear them cut side down in a sauté pan over high heat with 1 ounce of the olive oil. After a bit, turn them skin side down and add chopped garlic, scallions, fresh thyme leaves and cover them with aluminum foil. Cook slowly for approximately 5 minutes, then reserve. In another sauté pan over very high heat, sear the seasoned lamb with the remaining olive oil and cook until the lamb reaches the desired temperature. Place the lamb in the middle of the plate and reduce the lamb stock with the sliced black olives in a saucepan over medium heat. Reduce until it reaches a syrupy consistency. Place the zucchini in the center of the serving plate toward the upper right of the lamb. Arrange the *Provençal panis* on top of the zucchini, towards the left. Pour the glazed lamb stock around the rack of lamb and add the goat cheese *mousse* on top of the lamb. Garnish with one stick of rosemary and sprinkle with micro basil.

SERVES 8

2 pieces rack of lamb (8 bones each)
3 ounces soft fresh goat cheese
2 ounces heavy cream, whipped
½ bunch scallions, chopped
4 small zucchini
6 ounces olive oil
1 ounce garlic, chopped
2 branches fresh thyme
8 ounces lamb stock
2 ounces black olives
4 ounces garbanzo flour (chickpea flour)
5 ounces chicken stock
9 branches rosemary, chopped
1 ounce micro basil
2 ounces butter
Salt & pepper

Chickpeas with Spanish Chorizo
ARTURO SANDOVAL, MUSICIAN

Arturo Sandoval is fluent in at least four musical languages. He can burn through an Afro-Cuban groove, tear up a bebop tune, soar over a Mozart concerto and soothe you with a luscious ballad with equal power and grace.

Born in Artemisa, a small town in the outskirts of Havana, Cuba, Sandoval was granted political asylum in July 1990 and U.S. citizenship in 1999, Sandoval and his family now call Miami home.

A protégé of the legendary jazz master Dizzy Gillespie, Sandoval began studying classical trumpet at the age of twelve, but it didn't take him long to catch the excitement of the jazz world. He has since evolved into one of the world's most acknowledged guardians of jazz trumpet and flugel horn, as well as a renowned classical artist, pianist and composer.

SERVES 6

4 cans (14-ounces each) of chickpeas (garbanzo beans)

4 Spanish chorizo, *cubed*

3 smoked pork ribs

½ bacon strip

4 pig's feet

1 onion, finely chopped

1 bell pepper, chopped

5 garlic cloves, minced

½ cup pitted olives

2 cans (14-ounces each) tomato sauce

4 tablespoons of seasoning of your preference

1 tablespoon cumin

1 tablespoon oregano

Bring the pig's feet to a boil in a large pot without a lid. Let it slowly boil until the meat is tender. Dispose of the water and add to the large pot, the chickpeas, chorizo, smoked pork ribs, bacon, onion, garlic, oregano, seasoning, bell pepper, tomato sauce and olives. Add water until all ingredients are completely covered and boil for 90 minutes without a lid. Let it boil until the liquid thickens and is reduced. Add salt, if necessary.

Ali's Famous Chili Pie
BRETT AND ALI BIBEAU

Brett Bibeau is the Managing Director of the Miami River Commission and Ali Bibeau is the Group Sales Manager at The Adrienne Arsht Center for the Performing Arts of Miami-Dade County. Brett was featured in The Book of Leaders 2007, published by Miami Today. Brett and Ali are almost native Miamians both dedicated to making Miami a wonderful city to live in and, naturally, to visit.

The Miami River Commission was created in 1998 by the Florida Legislature as the official coordinating clearinghouse for all public policy and projects related to the Miami River. The river plays a vital role in the city's international trade, commerce, employment opportunities, and water front residences. Thanks to the Miami River Commission, the Miami River has taken on a new and vibrant life.

In a large sauté pan, brown the beef or turkey and then add the onions, garlic, and green pepper. Sauté on medium high heat until pepper and onion are soft. Add the red pepper flakes, fresh tomato, canned tomatoes, kidney beans, chili powder, salt and pepper. Simmer on medium low heat for 15-20 minutes.

Preheat an oven to 350° F. Prepare the corn muffin mix as directed on the box, but add a bit more water or milk as directed, so that batter is not too thick. Once the chili has simmered for 15-20 minutes, pour the chili into a 9 x 13 inch baking pan. Pour the batter evenly over the chili. Bake for 10-12 minutes or until the corn topping is golden and done. Remove from the oven and cut into square portions and enjoy. But be careful–it's hot!

Vegetarian Version: Sauté broccoli, zucchini and yellow squash together instead of the meat.

SERVES 6-8

1 pound ground beef or turkey
1 can (16-ounces) red kidney beans
1 can (16-ounces) diced tomatoes
1 medium tomato, diced
1 clove garlic, chopped
1 tablespoon dried red pepper flakes
4 tablespoons chili powder
Salt & pepper to taste

TOPPING INGREDIENTS

1 small box of cornbread or corn muffin mix
(8½-ounce Jiffy Corn Muffin Mix or 6-ounce Martha White Corn Muffin Mix, both work well.)

Veal Scaloppine *with Prosciutto and Arugula*
OWNER NINO PERNETTI, CAFFÈ ABBRACCI

Caffè Abbracci is a longtime Coral Gables favorite with locals and visitors alike. Featuring the Northern Italian cuisine of Nino Pernetti, it is an elegant and up-market eatery. The pasta is always fresh, the antipasto plentiful, the veal is a house specialty and the tiramisu memorable.

SERVES 4

8 3-ounce veal scaloppine (veal round), ¼ inch thick
  and pounded and thinned to ⅛ inch

All-purpose flour for dredging

6 tablespoons extra virgin olive oil

⅔ cup sliced Italian prosciutto, julienned, divided

2 large garlic cloves, minced

2 tablespoons Modena balsamic vinegar

3 tablespoons chicken stock

3 tablespoons butter

1 pound arugula, leaves only, chopped

1 pound plum tomatoes, chopped

Salt and pepper to taste

In a large skillet or sauté pan, heat 2 tablespoons of the olive oil. Add ⅓ cup prosciutto and garlic and cook over moderate heat, stirring, until the garlic is golden, about 4 minutes. Transfer to a plate. Dredge the veal scaloppine in the flour. Heat 1 tablespoon of the olive oil and ½ tablespoon of the butter in a large skillet or sauté pan over medium heat. When the butter is completely melted, add the freshly dredged *scaloppine*, fitting as many in the pan as you can, without touching each other. Sprinkle with salt and pepper. Briefly cook the *scaloppine* on both sides. Remove the *scaloppine* from the pan to a warm plate and cover with aluminum foil to keep warm.

Add the balsamic vinegar and chicken stock to the pan and continue to cook, scraping up any browned bits from the bottom of the skillet until the liquid has nearly evaporated. Add the arugula and toss until wilted, about 2 minutes. Add the chopped tomatoes and the reserved prosciutto and cook over high heat for 2 minutes, stirring occasionally. Season with salt and pepper. Place the reserved *scaloppine* into the pan and cook for 2 minutes more. When done, place the *scaloppine* on warmed dinner plates and spoon the arugula and tomato mixture over the veal and serve.

Wild Rice & Sausage Casserole
ARVA MOORE PARKS, Author and Editor

A lifelong Miami resident, Arva Moore Parks graduated from the University of Florida in 1960 and earned a master's degree from the University of Miami in 1971. She is the author of more than a half-dozen books on South Florida, including Miami, the Magic City. *She has produced films on Miami and Coconut Grove and has received several honors, including an Emmy from the Florida Academy of Television Arts and Sciences. In addition to her service on a number of civic boards and committees, Parks chaired the Florida Endowment for the Humanities.*

Put the package of wild rice into a saucepan of warm water, stir and drain. Repeat twice. Then wash the rice with flowing water. Put the rice in a saucepan of hot water over medium heat and boil for 5 minutes. Drain this and put the rice into a sauce pan of fresh hot water; 3 parts water to 1 part rice. Add salt and cook on low heat for 1 hour until fluffy. While the rice is cooking prepare the rest of the casserole.

In a skillet, fry the hot bulk sausage, breaking it into small pieces and drain. Sauté the shiitake mushrooms in 4 tablespoons butter until tender. Remove the mushrooms and set aside. Add 2 tablespoons butter and 2 tablespoons flour to mushroom juice. Mix well and add the cream. Add the mushroom soup thinned with the sherry. Add the 2 bay leaves and 1 teaspoon of the Kitchen Bouquet. Simmer while wild rice is cooking.

Preheat an oven to 350° F. Mix the cooked rice and sausage and mushrooms. Stir in the mushroom sauce. (Don't use too much, just enough to cover. I usually have some sauce left over.) Put into a long casserole dish and top with bread crumbs. Bake for about 45-50 minutes Can be made the day before. To re-heat, warm at 325° F. for about 40 minutes.

SERVES 6

1 package wild rice (1 cup of uncooked wild rice = 3-4 cups of cooked wild rice, adjust your recipe, as desired.)
1 pound of hot bulk sausage
1 pound shiitake mushrooms
6 tablespoons butter
2 tablespoons all-purpose flour
½ cup cream
1 can cream of mushroom soup
½ cup sherry
2 bay leaves
1 teaspoon Kitchen Bouquet
Bread crumbs

Cold Peppered Tenderloin of Beef
With Tarragon Sauce

FRANK RAVNDAL, CARGILL AMERICAS, INC.

SERVES 10

2 2-pound beef tenderloins,
  tied and at room temperature

2 tablespoons black pepper, coarsely ground

2 teaspoons kosher salt

4 tablespoons vegetable oil

TARRAGON SAUCE INGREDIENTS

1 large egg yolk (2 teaspoons egg yolk)

4 tablespoons heavy cream

4 tablespoons white wine vinegar

2 teaspoons Worcestershire sauce

3 teaspoons Dijon mustard

1 cup olive oil

3 teaspoons fresh tarragon

2 tablespoons capers, drained

4 tablespoons green onion, minced

Kosher salt to taste

"I moved from Minneapolis to Miami in mid-2005 with my wife, Donna and my two children, Stephen and Haley. I had the opportunity to come to Florida to lead several of Cargill's Grain & Oilseed businesses and to work from our Coral Gables office. Cargill is always eager to find worthy causes to support in the communities where we have a presence, and the chance to do something together with Miami Children's Hospital fit into this philosophy well. When I heard about the cookbook project through my wife's volunteerism with the Miami Children's Hospital Foundation Community Council and then subsequently had the chance to meet with Tess Doheny and hear about the project in detail, it was clear we had found a great cause to support. We are moving back to Minneapolis this Fall but hope that Cargill's involvement with Miami Children's Hospital will continue for many years to come." ~ Frank Ravndal

Preheat an oven to 500° F. Pat the beef tenderloins dry and coat them on all sides with salt and pepper. Heat oil in a skillet and brown both sides of the tenderloins. When browned, remove from the heat and roast in the skillet in the oven for 15 to 20 minutes or to 130° F. as shown on an instant-read meat thermometer for medium rare. The tenderloins may be roasted up to 2 days in advance. Wrap in plastic wrap and chill. When ready to serve, bring to room temperature. Slice and serve with sauce.

Tarragon Sauce:
In a blender, put the egg yolk, heavy cream, white wine vinegar, Worcestershire sauce, and Dijon mustard. Blend well. With the blender running add oil in a slow, steady steam. Blend the sauce until emulsified. Transfer to a bowl and add the tarragon, capers, green onion and salt to taste and then refrigerate. The sauce can be made one day in advance.

Note: The beef tenderloins must be at room temperature before cooking. Be prepared for your smoke alarm to go off!

Garlic Beef Tataki
CHEF JOHNSON TEH, YUGA RESTAURANT

Sister restaurant to Lan Pan Asian Café, Yuga specializes in East and Southeast Asian cuisine including dishes from Japan, China, Korea, Thailand, and Vietnam. Chef Johnson Teh has over twenty years of restaurant experience, both in Asia and in the United States. He often creates dishes that are traditional but are reinterpreted with a light contemporary touch, bringing new tastes and textures to classical favorites.

Mix the grated radish with the chile paste and set aside for garnish. Slice the skirt steak into thin 1 1/2 inch pieces against the grain of the meat. Heat a large skillet over high heat. When the pan just starts to smoke, add 1 1/2 tablespoons of the canola oil and add the spinach. It will make a loud sizzling noise when the spinach hits the pan. Quickly stir the spinach until it just starts to wilt, about 1 minute, season with salt and pepper to taste and place on a platter. Wipe out the same skillet with a paper towel and lower the heat to medium high. Add the remaining 1 1/2 tablespoons of canola oil and the skirt steak to the skillet and cook undisturbed for 2 minutes to let the meat brown. Stir the meat occasionally and cook to desired doneness, another 3-4 minutes for medium. Place the meat on top of the spinach and add all of the sauce ingredients to the pan except for the vinegar. Turn the heat to medium-high and simmer the sauce over the heat for about 1 minute, scraping any brown bits that are stuck to the bottom of the pan. Add the rice vinegar and take the sauce off of the heat. Pour the sauce on top of the meat. Garnish the dish with garlic, scallions, and chile paste, grated radish. Serve immediately.

SERVES 4

1½ pounds skirt steak
1 10-ounce bag baby spinach
2 tablespoons canola oil
Salt and pepper
¾ cup soy sauce
¼ cup mirin *(seasoned rice wine,*
you may substitute regular sake*)*
1 tablespoon sugar (only if using sake*)*
1 teaspoon powdered dashi *fish broth, optional*
(available at Asian markets)
2 tablespoons rice wine vinegar

GARNISHES

3 medium cloves garlic, minced
1 bunch scallions, finely sliced
1 2-inch round of daikon radish,
peeled and grated (optional)
1 teaspoon chile paste (optional)

Enrique's Almond Glazed Picadillo

JORGE ESTEVEZ, WFOR-TV/CBS4, WPFS/MY33 REPORTER

SERVES 6

2 pounds fresh ground sirloin

2 medium sized onions

1 teaspoon whole oregano

¼ cup butter toffee-glazed sliced almonds

¼ cup dried cranberries

1 tablespoon complete seasoning (Badia or Goya Sazón
  Natural and Complete)

2 medium red tomatoes, cubed

15-20 pitted olives, each olive sliced in 3 equal parts

1 teaspoon sugar

¼ cup of white cooking wine (Vino Seco)

Jorge Estevez came to South Florida after five years working in Central Florida as a Weekend Anchor for WFTV, the number one rated news station in Orlando. His first taste of television news was with the entertainment news magazine show **Access Hollywood,** *a job that found him spending many hours on red carpets interviewing celebrities. The son of Cuban immigrants, Estevez is looking forward to spending time in South Florida where most of his family currently resides.*

Picadillo is a traditional Cuban Dish that "mi mama" used to make. However, this dish has a special twist.

Heat a large pot over medium high heat and cook the ground sirloin. Stir it at first and then break it up as it cooks. Once the meat has cooked for 5 minutes (avoid over cooking), add the chopped onions. Then mix in and swirl around the oregano and the complete seasoning. Now you add the not so secret ingredient "sliced glazed almonds" and throw in the dried cranberries. (The berries add the zest many will be asking you about.) Keep in mind you need to constantly stir your ingredients to create an even texture and distribute the flavors properly. (Really, you just don't want to burn it.)

As the picadillo turns brown, lower the heat to medium and then add the cubed tomatoes and olives. Cook for 10 minutes, then add the cooking wine and the sugar, which adds to that glazed taste. Let it simmer for another 10 minutes. Serve hot over white or brown rice and don't forget to accompany this tasteful dish with some Cuban plantains! (Those I buy frozen, I microwave them and serve right from the box. It's so much easier!) Good luck and invite your friends over. This is a meal that could be made ahead of time in order to keep you away from the kitchen once the company arrives. (Don't show them the pre-made plantains box). *Bon Appétit!* No, wait that's French...so then in Cuba we say *Disfruten!*

Arroz al Horno (Hearty Baked Rice)

PAUL GEORGE, PH. D., HISTORIAN, RECIPE BY MRS. LAURA GEORGE

For almost two decades, Dr. George, who is a historian for the Historical Museum of Southern Florida, has toured his way to local, national and international acclaim with his continuing series of historical tours. As a South Florida native, author and Miami Dade College professor, Dr. George has gained fame for his uncanny ability to recall the most impressive details about the people and places that make South Florida so unique.

Preheat an oven to 400° F. Heat the oil in a shallow sauté pan and fry the garlic along with the potato slices. When the potatoes are browned, put the grated tomatoes in, and then add the sweet and smoked paprika. Combine well. Then pour this mixture into a large ovenproof earthenware casserole.

In the same pan in which you fried the potatoes, fry the individual baby back ribs until they are browned. Then add them to the ovenproof casserole as well. Next, add the green pepper and chickpeas and rice. Then add to the stock, the pinch of saffron threads, stir well and add this to the casserole. Check the seasoning and season to taste. Transfer the casserole to a hot oven and bake for 30 to 35 minutes. Taste a few grains of rice to check that it's done. Remove from the oven and serve.

SERVES 4

2 ¾ cups chicken stock

¼ cup olive oil

6 cloves garlic

2 or 3 medium size potatoes, sliced in ½ inch slices

3 small tomatoes, peeled and grated

1 teaspoon sweet paprika

½ teaspoon smoked paprika

2 cups long grain rice

4 ounces chickpeas, cooked

½ green bell pepper cut in big pieces

1 rack baby back ribs, separated

Pinch saffron threads

Salt

Sunday Sauce

OWNER STEVE PERRICONE, Perricone's Marketplace & Cafe

Serves 10-12

½ cup virgin olive oil

1 pound Italian sausage

1 pound baby back ribs

1 pound meatballs

1 cup white onions, chopped

1 cup dry white wine

8 cups ripe tomatoes, chopped

10 ounces tomato paste

2 tablespoons fresh garlic, minced

4 tablespoons fresh basil chiffonade

Salt to taste

The last thing you expect to discover on the outskirts of downtown Miami is a cozy New England barn sitting in a quiet park surrounded by lush vegetation. But that's exactly what you find at Perricone's Marketplace and Cafe. Its resistance to rampant modernity is a welcome surprise in the shadows of sky-scraping banks that line the famous Brickell Avenue along Biscayne Bay.

This is a cherished family recipe, only recently agreed to be released. Once you taste this masterpiece, you'll know just what to serve it with: everything, especially your favorite pasta.

In a large pot, using a few tablespoons of oil at a time, sear the meats, one kind at a time, over medium-high heat, then remove to a large plate. Add the remaining oil to the pot and cook the onions in it until they become translucent, about 5 minutes. Add the white wine to deglaze the pot. Add the chopped tomatoes, tomato paste, garlic and basil. Return the meats to the pot, cover and simmer on low heat for at least an hour. Salt to taste. To serve, pour the hearty sauce over perfectly cooked pasta and serve hot.

Laurie's Meatloaf with Purple Hull Peas

RANDY SHANNON, HEAD FOOTBALL COACH,
UNIVERSITY OF MIAMI HURRICANES, AND HIS WIFE, MRS. LAURIE SHANNON

Randy Shannon is the current head football coach of the University of Miami Hurricanes. He played college football for the University of Miami, starting as outside linebacker for the 1987 national championship team. After graduating in 1991, Shannon played briefly as a linebacker for the Dallas Cowboys.

Preheat an oven to 350° F. In a large bowl, combine all of the ingredients, being sure to mix them well so that you get a uniform consistency. Spray an 8 x 8 x 2 inch baking dish or pan with the vegetable oil. For the topping, mix together the brown sugar, ketchup and mustard in a small bowl. Place the loaf mixture evenly into the dish and spread the topping evenly over the meatloaf. Bake for an hour to an hour-and-a-half.

Serve with purple hull peas and mashed potatoes and gravy.

Purple Hull Peas:
In a sauté pan over medium heat, sauté the 1 cup chopped onion in 2 tablespoons bacon grease or butter until translucent. Place the purple hull peas in the pan and cover with water. Add salt and pepper and simmer for 1 hour. Add 1 tablespoon butter and cook 5 more minutes or until tender. Serve with the other ½ cup chopped raw onions on the side.

SERVES 6

1 cup dried breadcrumbs (Progresso Italian style is best)
1 pound ground beef
1 pound ground pork
2 eggs, slightly beaten
1 can (12-ounces) evaporated milk
1 teaspoon salt
⅛ teaspoon pepper
1 medium onion, chopped
Vegetable oil spray

TOPPING INGREDIENTS

3 tablespoons brown sugar
1 teaspoon dried mustard
1 cup ketchup

PURPLE HULL PEAS INGREDIENTS

1 bag frozen purple hull peas
1½ cups onion, chopped (reserve ½ cup for garnish)
3 tablespoons bacon grease or butter (separated)
Water
Salt and pepper

Stuffed Piquillo Peppers

CHEF JEAN PAUL DESMAISON, La Cofradia Restaurante

The cuisine at La Cofradia is a fusion of Mediterranean and Peruvian flavors created by Chef Jean Paul Desmaison. The flavors, aromas, textures and the palate of Peruvian cuisine arise from the variety of chiles, corns, fresh lime, cherimoya and cilantro. Chef Jean Paul also stirs in a dash of Mediterranean cuisine to highlight the fresh ingredients he chooses for his dishes.

In a large pot, add olive oil and sauté the onions, tomato and garlic. When the onions are brown, stir in the ground beef and pork. When meat is half way cooked, add the raisins and the chopped peanuts. Season to taste with salt. Let cool and set aside. Under a broiler in the oven, roast the piquillo peppers until they begin to blister.

In a small saucepan, mix the heavy cream and rosemary over low heat. When the cream starts to bubble, add the cheese and cook over low heat until it becomes thick.

Stuff the piquillo peppers with the pork and beef mixture and reheat them in the oven or microwave. To serve, spoon Parmesan sauce onto the center of each plate and place the stuffed peppers on top. Garnish with a sprig of rosemary.

Serves 4-6

8 roasted piquillo peppers

10 ounces ground beef

10 ounces ground pork

3 ounces onions, chopped

4 cloves garlic

3 ounces tomato, diced

2 ounces olive oil

2 ounces raisins

1½ ounces unsalted peanuts, chopped

Salt to taste

Sauce Ingredients

3 ounces Parmesan cheese

8 ounces heavy cream

1 sprig fresh rosemary

Mexican Enchilada Casserole

MAX MAYFIELD, WPLG-TV LOCAL 10 HURRICANE EXPERT AND FORMER DIRECTOR OF THE NATIONAL WEATHER SERVICE HURRICANE CENTER

Max Mayfield serves as WPLG's hurricane specialist, offering viewers an insider's view of severe weather. Mayfield became the director of the National Hurricane Center in January 2000 and led the coastal regions of the United States through the devastating hurricane seasons of 2004 and 2005 that spawned a record number of storms, including the catastrophic Hurricane Katrina. Mayfield is recognized as one of the world's most knowledgeable scientists with an expertise in forecasting the path and intensity of tropical storms. He has been honored by local, state and federal officials for his tireless efforts. Mayfield and his wife, Linda, have lived in South Miami-Dade County since 1972. They have three children.

Preheat an over to 350° F. In a large skillet, brown the ground beef and drain off any drippings. Add the 1/2 package of taco seasoning mix, add water and cook according to package directions. In a separate bowl, mix 1 cup cheese, the sour cream, 1/2 cup of the green onions, cumin and chili powder. Pour the enchilada sauce into a shallow bowl. Heat 6 tortillas on a plate in a microwave oven for about 1 minute. Repeat twice more. Dip the warmed tortillas in the enchilada sauce and add 2 tablespoons of meat and cheese mixture onto each tortilla, roll up and place in a 9 x 13 inch baking dish. Finally, add 3 cups of the cheese, the remaining green onions and sauce over the top of the rolled tortillas. Bake for 20-30 minutes.

SERVES 6

4 cups cheddar cheese, grated
1 cup green onions, chopped
1 teaspoon cumin
2 cans (10-ounces each) enchilada sauce
1 pint sour cream
18 corn tortillas
1 pound ground beef
1/2 package taco seasoning mix
1 tablespoon chili powder

Tenderloins Filet Tournedos

EXECUTIVE CHEF PATRICK LAPAIRE, SHULA'S STEAK HOUSE AT
THE ALEXANDER HOTEL

SERVES 4

4 - 5 ounce cuts of Angus beef tenderloin

Olive oil

1 Red Bliss potato

5 Yukon Gold potatoes, peeled

1 tablespoon garlic, chopped

2 tablespoon shallots, chopped

1 tablespoon heavy cream

1 tablespoon butter

1 tablespoon sour cream

¼ teaspoon nutmeg

Salt & white pepper to taste

6 ounces sliced wild mushrooms
   (shiitake, portobello, cremini)

8 fluid ounces demi-glace

1 yellow squash

2 asparagus, blanched in salted water

1 baby carrot

1 red bell pepper

Cognac for flambé

Red wine for deglazing

Rosemary for garnish

Don Shula, like most Americans, has always loved a great steak. When he came to Miami, he couldn't find a great steak anywhere. Therefore, when the Graham Family asked him to partner up to open the first Shula's steak house, he knew it was an opportunity he could not pass up. Their goal was to build the best steak house in Miami, which became one of the top ten steak houses in America. In order to be the best, he followed the same principles that made him the winning-est coach in football history: select the best talent available and give them the resources they need to succeed. That meant serving Premium Black Angus Beef® steaks, the best beef money can buy. You won't find a better steak anywhere.

A native of Switzerland, award-winning executive chef Patrick Lapaire graces the kitchen of Shula's Steakhouse with skills honed from many years of cooking on cruise ships.

Season both sides of the filets with salt and pepper and grill or pan-sear, 10 to 15 minutes for medium, or to taste. In a sauté pan over medium heat, add enough olive oil to cover the bottom of the pan, then add the shallots with the garlic and sauté in the pan. Add the wild mushrooms, *flambé* with cognac and deglaze with red wine. Add the *demi-glace* sauce. Cook peeled Yukon Gold potatoes in salt water and then mash with heavy cream, butter, sour cream, nutmeg, salt and white pepper. Cook the Red Bliss potato in salted water until *al dente*. Cut the potato in half and scoop out the middle with a spoon. Slice yellow squash on the bias and grill the squash, the asparagus and carrots. Cut the top and bottom of the red bell pepper and remove the seeds. Grill on the skin side and peel the skin. Finish with garlic drawn butter and seasoning. Place the shallot and mushroom mixture over each tenderloin. Arrange the tenderloins, the potatoes and the vegetables on a serving platter, drizzle the sauce over the beef and garnish with rosemary.

Picadillo
CONGRESSWOMAN ILEANA ROS-LEHTINEN

Since her election in 1989 to the United States Congress, Ileana Ros-Lehtinen has proudly represented Florida's 18th Congressional District in the United States House of Representatives. Forced to flee with her family from the regime of Fidel Castro, Congresswoman Ros-Lehtinen became the first Hispanic woman and first Cuban-American elected to Congress and a powerful voice for the South Florida community.

In a large skillet, melt the margarine and sauté the garlic until golden brown and then discard the garlic. Sauté the onion, green pepper and parsley until the vegetables are soft. Add the ground beef and brown, stirring with a fork to prevent lumps. Mix in the remaining ingredients. Cover and simmer, stirring occasionally, for about 15 minutes. Serve over white rice.

SERVES 6

1½ pounds lean ground beef

2 tablespoons margarine

1 clove garlic, chopped

1 large onion, chopped

1 green pepper, chopped

4 sprigs parsley, chopped

¼ cup seedless raisins

¼ cup blanched almonds, sliced

2 tablespoons pimiento, sliced

12 stuffed olives, sliced

1 tablespoon capers

1 bay leaf

1 teaspoon salt

¼ teaspoon pepper

1 cup tomato paste

¼ cup dry red wine

Marinated Pork Kabobs with Mango

S. ANTHONY WOLFE, M.D., CHIEF, DIVISION OF PLASTIC & RECONSTRUCTIVE SURGERY MIAMI CHILDREN'S HOSPITAL

SERVES 6-8

2 1-pound pork tenderloins

4-5 garlic cloves, finely minced or put through a garlic press

1 tablespoon fresh ginger, finely chopped

2 small red chiles, finely chopped

1 tablespoon fresh rosemary, finely chopped

⅓ cup olive oil

Sea salt and freshly ground black pepper

3-4 large mangoes, just between soft and firm, peeled, and sliced

4-6 limes (Key limes, if available)

Long bamboo skewers

Dr. S. Anthony Wolfe is a graduate of Harvard University Medical School. He completed his residency in general surgery at Peter Bent Brigham Hospital in Boston and in plastic surgery at the University of Miami. Dr. Wolfe holds two specialty board certifications, one from the American Board of Surgery and the other from the American Board of Plastic Surgery. He has been the recipient of numerous honors, including the Boylston Prize (Harvard Medical School), a Fullbright scholarship, and has been named one of the Best Doctors in America. Dr. Wolfe is a member of the American Association of Plastic Surgeons, the American Society of Plastic Surgeons, and many other professional organizations. In addition, Dr. Wolfe was a member of the Florida Governor's Advisory Council of Cleft Lip and Palate and Craniofacial Anomalies Program and has served as a consultant to the National Institutes of Health Special Studies Section Meetings. Dr. Wolfe has published numerous articles, books, chapters in selected books, and is an internationally renowned speaker, lecturer and panel discussant.

Here are two variations on the same theme, one easy, the other even easier.

Easy Version:

Combine all of the ingredients in a bowl to make a marinade for the pork. Cut the pork into 1 inch cubes, toss well in the marinade and refrigerate 4-6 hours. Soak the bamboo skewers in water for an hour. Thread the skewers with the pork and then grill the kebabs over a charcoal or gas grill. Serve the pork with mango slices on top

Easier Version:

Buy *lechon asado* at any Cuban take-out place that sells roasted pork (*La Lechoneria*, etc.) It usually comes in a heavy aluminum foil container. Use this to marinate the pork. Grill and serve as above.

Ossobucco Alla Veneta
CHEF VITTORIO AMADI, LA PALMA RISTORANTE

La Palma Ristorante is known to serve some of the best Northern Italian Cuisine in Miami. Owner Paolo Montecchi of Bologna and Chef Vittorio Amadi of Venecia always use only fresh ingredients combined with a personal touch that has garnered La Palma rave reviews. Zagat *2004 named La Palma "Most Romantic Dining in Town" and the* Miami Herald *says, "La Palma Ristorante puts a song in your heart."*

Preheat an oven to 450° F. Roll the veal shanks in the flour. In a large skillet or sauté pan, sear the veal shanks in olive oil on high heat to brown the exterior and seal in the juices and flavors. Meanwhile, in a large roasting pan sauté the vegetables and herbs in olive oil over medium heat. When the onions become translucent, put the seared veal shanks on top of vegetables, herbs, zests and pour chicken broth and red wine over all. Cover the pan with aluminum foil and braise in the oven for one hour. Serve over a bed of *Risotto Milanese* and top with vegetable sauce from pan.

Note: This dish is best cooked one day prior to serving. Prepare by reheating in a preheated oven at 450° F. for 45 minutes. Serve as directed above.

SERVES 5

5-10 center cut veal shanks
(One large shank portion per person or 2 medium)
1 cup all-purpose flour
¾ cup olive oil
2 onions, chopped
4 carrots, diced
1 bunch celery, diced
1 bunch Italian parsley, finely chopped
1 bunch thyme, finely chopped
Lemon zest
Orange zest
Dash of salt and pepper
Touch of bay leaf
1 cup red wine
4–5 cups chicken broth or stock

The Dish of Chesterfield Smith
PARKER THOMSON, Esq., COMMUNITY ACTIVIST AND LAWYER

Mr. Thomson was the Performing Arts Center Trust Chairman. He is committed to public service and has earned numerous awards for his contributions to the city, including his local assistance to the poor. He is the Managing Partner of Hogan & Hartson, LLP.

This dish is hefty and ample, if accompanied by a wet and sour green salad, garlic bread and a bottle of beer! It is neither a jambalaya, *or a* paella *or a* pilau; *it is simply "Chesterfield's Dish." While variations and innovations are acceptable, and usually the case, in general I do it something like I describe below. However, there are many other ways it can be done with great results, so do it your way. First, assemble all the ingredients into three groups.*

First, bring the chicken broth to a boil in a pot over medium high heat, then add the paprika, saffron, Worcestershire sauce, Sazon Goya and the olive oil. After lightly salting, stir and add the rice and again bring it to a boil. Do not stir after the rice is added. Reduce the heat to very low and cook for 30 minutes. The cooked rice is then set aside to cool. Quite frankly, great rice is the heart and soul of "Chesterfield's Dish."

Next, place the sun-dried tomatoes in a pot of boiling water until soft, then cut them into pieces. In another large pot, pour the canned mushrooms, pimientos and olives. Then add the tomatoes, bell peppers, onions, and the thawed, chopped okra. Bring this to a boil (if needed add water), and then let it simmer until the vegetables are limp. After draining off all of the liquid, add the garlic cloves, which are put through a garlic press. Next, fry the sausage in a skillet over medium heat for 10 minutes, then cut them into 1/2 inch long pieces. The shrimp are boiled, shelled and combined with the sausage.

SERVES 8-12
GROUP 1

2 cups of short grain rice

3 cups of chicken broth

1 teaspoon of paprika

1 teaspoon of saffron

1 teaspoon of Worcestershire sauce

2 packets of Sazon Goya with coriander and annatto

1 tablespoon of olive oil

GROUP 2

2 tomatoes, peeled and chopped

1 red bell pepper, seeded, cored and diced

1 green bell pepper, seeded, cored and diced

6–8 large cloves of garlic

2 large sweet onions, coarsely chopped

3 ounce package of sun-dried tomatoes

8 ounce can of mushrooms, pieces and stems

8 ounce can of diced pimientos

2 cups of frozen chopped okra, thawed

8 ounce can of chopped ripe olives

GROUP 3

2 pounds country style hot pork sausage

2½ pounds medium shrimp

Salt, pepper, olive oil, Tabasco sauce and other discretionary condiments

Preheat an oven to 300° F. Lastly, place the sun dried tomatoes and vegetable mixture in a large mixing bowl. Mix this carefully with the cooked mixture. Be very careful about stirring thereafter and do not mash or scrape the rice in any way. To season, add the salt, pepper and other seasonings. Other condiments may be added according to taste or personal preference. Add a tablespoon or two of olive oil. Seasoning is obviously a matter of taste and judgment, which can be best developed by repeated experiences. I like it spicy, so most often I add a good portion of Tabasco, but the amount is discretionary. The mixture should then be placed in a very large cast iron pot. Insert the pot into the oven for 20 minutes, or until all liquid has been absorbed. Then without stirring the rice and keeping the rice as stable and undisturbed as feasible, carefully mix the shrimp and sausage into the mixture as promptly as possible. Return the pot to the oven to cook for an additional 15 minutes. Serve this most pleasant concoction by starting with a large helping for everyone, together with garlic bread, a wet and sour salad with bleu cheese, lime juice, olive oil and vinegar. Add a cold glass of beer, or two.

SERVES 4

⅛ pound bacon, diced

1½ pound seasoned boneless beef chuck, cubed

2½ cups red Burgundy wine

2 tablespoons butter

1 carrot, diced

1 onion, diced

1 clove garlic, minced

1 tablespoon tomato paste

1 bay leaf

2 sprigs fresh thyme

1 tablespoon flour

½ pound mushrooms

Salt and pepper

Dr. Stylianos is a graduate of Rutgers University and the New York University School of Medicine. He completed his General Surgical training at Columbia-Presbyterian Medical Center, and subsequently spent two years as the Trauma Fellow at the Kiwanis Pediatric Trauma Institute in Boston. Dr. Stylianos completed the Pediatric Surgical fellowship at Boston Children's Hospital in 1992. He is Board-Certified in Pediatric Surgery, General Surgery and Surgical Critical Care.

Dr. Stylianos joined the medical staff at Miami Children's Hospital in 2005 and was elected Chief of the Department of Pediatric Surgery. Previously, he was at the Children's Hospital of New York/Columbia University College of Physicians & Surgeons where he was Director of the Operating Room and Director of the Regional Pediatric Trauma Program. Dr. Stylianos was named one of the "Best Doctors in New York" by New York Magazine *for six years. He organized and directed the 50-member team of physicians and nurses who separated conjoined twins at Children's Hospital of New York in 1993, 1995 and 2000.*

In a sauté pan, brown the diced bacon over medium heat and then remove from the pan and reserve. In the same pan, brown the beef chuck in the bacon fat and then remove from pan and discard excess oil. Add ½ cup of the Burgundy wine, scraping the brown bits from bottom of pan and pour resulting mixture over reserved beef. Melt 1 tablespoon of the butter, then add the carrot and onion, and sauté over medium low heat. When golden, add the garlic, tomato paste, the beef and pan juices, the additional 2 cups of Burgundy, plus the bay leaf and thyme. Allow mixture to simmer gently about 3 hours. Remove the herbs. Knead together 1 tablespoon of the butter and flour and stir into stew. Add mushrooms and reserved bacon and simmer an additional 20 minutes. Season with salt and pepper. Serve with a fresh baguette and more red Burgundy wine.

Photo Credit: Craig B. Smith

Pork Chops & Rice

ROMERO BRITTO, Artist

A modern day pop culture icon, Romero Britto is one of the premiere artists of our time. As the youngest and most successful Pop Artist of this generation, Britto has managed to create contemporary masterpieces that evoke a spirit of hope and convey a sense of warmth. His original artwork, dubbed the art of healing, brings together bright colors and playful themes with compositional elements of cubism. Britto's work provides art lovers around the world an open-minded and optimistic view of life, from the mental canvas of an artist who gains daily inspiration from the world around him. Embraced by the international community, Britto's paintings and sculptures are currently featured on five continents in more than one hundred galleries worldwide, including the Saatchi Gallery in London. In addition, Britto's artwork is included in some of the world's most impressive private collections. His artwork is also proudly on display at Miami Children's Hospital.

SERVES 4

4 pork chops

2 cups white rice

2 cups water

2 cans chicken noodle soup (I prefer Campbell's)

Mustard

Preheat an oven to 350 ° F. Coat pork chops in mustard and brown in a skillet over medium high heat. Place the browned chops on the bottom of an oven safe casserole dish. Cover with one cup of rice. Add one can of chicken noodle soup. Repeat by adding one more cup of rice and one more can of soup. Cover and bake for 45 minutes.

Cabernet Braised Short Ribs of Beef
With Basil Mashed Potatoes

GENE SINGLETARY, MIAMI CATERER

This recipe is the result of combining several versions of the dish from some of my favorite Parisian bistros and adding a few twists of my own over the years. The ultimate success of the dish depends on three things, a hearty cabernet, a good browning and slow cooking. To create a great sauce you must brown the ribs to a dark golden color in the beginning and then to bring out all the flavors in the meat, braise in a 275° F. oven for 4 hours in a good wine reduction. I prefer to use the cut of short ribs that are sliced in between the bones, not across the bones like those that are used for beef flanken. The best part about this dish is that you can make it 2-3 days before, just reheat and serve.

SERVES 8

¼ cup extra virgin olive oil

8 short ribs of beef (5-6 inches in length with excess fat trimmed off, about 6 pounds total)

Kosher salt and fresh ground pepper

Flour for dredging

3 bottles hearty cabernet sauvignon (reduced to half)

2 large onions, coarsely chopped

3 celery ribs, coarsely chopped

2 carrots, coarsely chopped

10-12 cloves garlic, finely chopped

1 leek, chopped and well rinsed (use both white and green parts)

12 sprigs Italian parsley

3 sprigs thyme

3 bay leaves

¼ cup tomato paste

3 quarts beef stock (unsalted)

Preheat an oven to 275° F. Reduce the wine by half by boiling it in a pot over medium heat. Dry and then season the ribs with salt and pepper and dust with flour. Heat the oil to medium high in a large 6-quart Dutch oven and sear the ribs until dark golden brown on all sides. Don't crowd the pan when searing. Transfer ribs to a platter and set aside. Lower the heat to medium and lightly brown the onions, celery, carrots, garlic, leek, and herbs. Stir in the tomato paste and cook for another few minutes. Add ribs, the wine reduction and beef stock and bring up to a boil. Cover and place in the oven. Braise for approximately 4 hours or until ribs are tender. You may skim off the surface fat and carefully rearrange the position of the ribs several times while cooking. Using tongs, gently transfer the ribs to a platter, removing any excess fat or connective tissue in the process. Cover to keep warm. It's okay if some of the bones fall away from the meat, just serve the meat portion and discard the bones.

Strain the remaining liquid through a fine sieve and discard solids. Do not press too hard on the solids while straining. Let the remaining liquid stand for a few minutes and then skim away any remaining fat. Reduce the remaining liquid by one half, stirring while the sauce continues to thicken. You should have approximately 1 quart. Season if necessary.

Note:

I also like to serve small sized young carrots (6-8 inches) with this dish. Just add the whole carrots into the Dutch oven the last hour of cooking and remove them before straining liquid.

Basil Mashed Potatoes:

To prepare the basil mashed potatoes, place the potatoes in a pot, cover with water, add salt and bring to a boil. When tender, drain into a colander, and then return potatoes to the pot. Place pot back on the burner and turn heat to lowest setting. Add warmed milk, melted butter and sour cream and mash with a potato masher. Fold in the chopped basil and season with salt and pepper. Serve immediately after mashing.

To serve, spoon a generous portion of mashed potatoes into the center of 8 plates (or large wide rimmed soup plates) and gently lay a rib half way on top of each mound. If you have added the carrots, place one or two around the meat and potatoes. Spoon the sauce around the remaining portion of the plate.

BASIL MASHED POTATOES INGREDIENTS

5 pounds Idaho potatoes, peeled and cut

3½ tablespoons kosher salt

1 cup warmed milk

1½ cup sour cream or Greek yogurt

1 stick melted butter, unsalted

Fresh ground pepper

1 cup basil, finely chopped

Cindy Hutson is a self-taught chef who developed a passion for cooking at the age of nine. Hutson focuses her culinary talents on the lighter side of fusion cooking. While traveling to and from Jamaica, Hutson developed a unique style of culinary skills which she refers to as "edible art," a "Cuisine of the Sun," by concentrating on the wonderful flavor combinations of fish, fruits, vegetables and traditional tropical seasonings, she avoids conventional island cooking techniques which rely on excess oil and heavy sauces for flavor. The award-winning and widely acclaimed Ortanique offers diners authentic Caribbean cuisine with a fresh, light attitude, a concept reflected in a menu replete with island delicacies such as ceviches, salads, bouillabaisse, *meats and fishes and delectable desserts.*

SERVES 8

4 pounds pork tenderloin

6 ounces kosher salt

12 garlic cloves, smashed

1 large yellow onion, diced

2 tablespoon ground cumin

4 tablespoons coriander seeds

1 bunch cilantro, chopped

2 tablespoons fresh oregano

2 quarts water

½ cup honey

Zest from 4 oranges

2 cups orange juice, freshly squeezed

MOJO DEMI SAUCE INGEDIENTS

½ pound salted butter

2 large yellow onions

1½ cups dark rum

1 cup orange juice, freshly squeezed

½ cup lime juice, freshly squeezed

½ cup lemon juice, freshly squeezed

5 garlic cloves, thinly sliced

1 bunch cilantro, tied with string

¼ cup sugar

2 tablespoons kosher salt

4 cups veal stock

Cuban Citrus Brine:

Combine all of the ingredients, except the orange juice and pork, in a pot and bring to a boil. Remove from heat, cover and chill in the refrigerator. When well cooled, remove from pot and place into airtight container. Add the orange juice and the pork, cover and allow to brine for 24 hours.

Mojo Demi Sauce:

Sauté the onions and garlic in the salted butter over medium heat in a 6 quart pot. When the onions and garlic are caramelized, add the orange juice and rum. Cook off the alcohol and reduce by half. Add the lime juice, lemon juice, cilantro and salt. Stir well to combine. Add the veal stock and reduce on a low simmer until the mixture reaches the consistency of light syrup. Remove the cilantro. With a slotted spoon, remove the onions and place in blender along with 1 cup of the reduced sauce. Blend well, then strain through a fine mesh strainer and return to pot.

Remove the pork from the brine and grill the tenderloins until medium-rare or 165° F. on an instant-read meat thermometer. When done, remove from the grill, then slice and drizzle the pork with the *mojo demi* sauce. Serve with Black Bean Corn Salsa and Cumin *Aioli*. (see recipes below)

Black Bean Corn Salsa:
Scorch the corn, onions, peppers, chipotle, and scallions in a very hot sauté pan with olive oil. Cool on a sheet pan. When cool, combine with the lime juice, cilantro, tomatoes and black beans. Season with salt and pepper.

Cumin *Aioli*:
Pulverize garlic in a food processor and add the eggs. Add salt and pepper to taste, the sugar and then cumin. Slowly drizzle in oil.

BLACK BEAN CORN SALSA INGREDIENTS

5 ears of corn, kernels removed from cob
½ cup red onion, diced small
½ cup red bell pepper, diced small
½ cup yellow bell pepper, diced small
1 cup scallions, green parts only, chopped
¼ cup olive oil
1 cup tomatoes, diced
½ cup lime juice, freshly squeezed
1 dried chipotle pepper, soaked in tequila for 24 hours
2 cups cooked black beans
½ cup cilantro, chopped

CUMIN *AIOLI* INGREDIENTS

10 cloves garlic, roasted
5 egg yolks
1 cup salad oil
Salt and pepper to taste
1 teaspoon sugar
2 tablespoons cumin

Poivrons Farcis de Veau La Provençale

OWNER FRANCE INGRAHAM AND CHEF CHRISTIAN ANTONIOTTI,
LE PROVENÇAL RESTAURANT

Le Provençal provides all the extravagance and flavor that has made French cooking so famous, without a heavy reliance on copious amounts of butter and cream. Instead, you will find an artistic use of herbs and savory vegetables to flavor many traditional French favorites. For example, it is hard to resist the Bouillabaisse, a seafood soup made with various fish and shellfish, served with toasted rounds of French bread. Simple, aromatic, and delicious!

SERVES 6

3 red bell peppers

2 pounds ground veal

1 onion, chopped

6 garlic cloves, chopped

A touch of fresh parsley, chopped

1 tablespoon olive oil

1 cup bread crumbs

3 whole eggs

1 cup milk

6 ounces Swiss cheese, shredded

¼ cup water

Salt and black pepper

Cut the red bell peppers in half from top to bottom. Clean out all the seeds and set aside. Heat a saucepan over medium heat and add olive oil. When the oil is hot, toss in the chopped onion. Cook on high heat until it starts to brown, then add the ground veal, chopped garlic, parsley and salt and pepper to taste. Let this cook for 25 minutes over moderate heat. Turn off the heat and mix in 3 whole eggs, a cup of milk and the bread crumbs.

Preheat an oven to 350° F. Stuff the bell pepper halves with the veal mixture and top with Swiss cheese. Put the stuffed peppers in a baking dish with ¼ cup of water and cover with aluminum foil. Bake for 25 minutes or until the tops of the peppers are brown. Serve with rice or mashed potatoes.

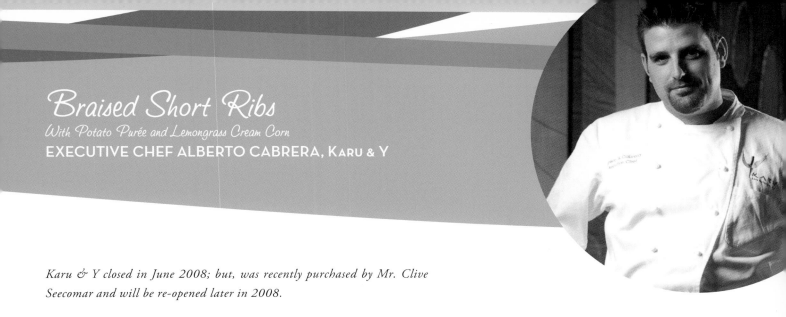

Braised Short Ribs
With Potato Purée and Lemongrass Cream Corn
EXECUTIVE CHEF ALBERTO CABRERA, KARU & Y

Karu & Y closed in June 2008; but, was recently purchased by Mr. Clive Seecomar and will be re-opened later in 2008.

Preheat an oven to 300° F. Season the short ribs with salt and the Five Spice powder and then sear on all sides in a large sauté pan over medium high heat. Remove the ribs and add the vegetables and roast in the pan until caramelized. Add the tomato paste and roast until caramelized. Deglaze with the soy sauce and reduce by half. Add the red wine and reduce by half. Place the short ribs and the sachet in the pan. Add enough water to cover. Braise in the oven for 3 hours.

Potato Purée:
Place the potatoes, skin on, in a pot of heavily salted water and simmer until cooked through. Remove the potatoes and skin them while still hot. Heat the cream in a saucepan over low heat. Mash the potatoes through a ricer into a bowl. Stir in the butter and heavy cream. Season with salt and white pepper. Keep warm.

Lemongrass Cream Corn:
In a saucepan over medium heat, reduce the heavy cream with the butter and the chopped lemongrass by half. Roast the corn on a grill and remove the husk. With a serrated knife, strip the kernels from the ears of corn and add the nibs into the cream and heat through. Serve alongside the Potato Purée and Braised Short Ribs.

SERVES 5
SHORT RIBS INGREDIENTS
5 16-ounce short ribs
1 carrot
1 celery stalk
1 onion
2 cloves garlic
1 head of fennel
1 knob of ginger
½ cup soy sauce
1 bottle dry red wine
2 tablespoons tomato paste
¼ cup Five Spice powder
1 sachet of Thai long pepper corns, bay leaf, thyme, star anise, and cinnamon

POTATO PURÉE INGREDIENTS
4 pounds Yukon Gold potatoes
1 pound butter
3 cups heavy cream
Salt and white pepper

LEMONGRASS CREAM CORN INGREDIENTS
2 cups heavy cream
¼ cup butter
2 stalks lemongrass, chopped
2 ears of corn

Rack of Lamb *With Red Wine & Dijon Mustard*
OWNER MAURIZIO FARINELLI, Trattoria Sole

At this beloved Italian eatery, you'll be treated to fantastic Northern Italian cuisine whipped up with style. The kitchen wows regular customers with skilled preparations of Veal Marsala, seafood fettuccine and tender cannelloni. Even better, the pastas hold center stage. They're made from scratch everyday and cooked to perfection.

SERVES 2

Whole rack of lamb, either New Zealand or domestic

1 teaspoon Dijon mustard

½ teaspoon fines herbes

1 tablespoon butter

½ cup Barolo wine or strong red wine

1 clove garlic, finely chopped

2 tablespoons extra virgin olive oil

½ cup demi-glace *of lamb or good beef broth*

Salt and pepper to taste

Preheat an oven to 425° F. Heat a medium size skillet over medium high heat and add the olive oil. Season the rack of lamb with salt and pepper and place in the skillet to sear. Cook until the rack is golden all around. Drain the oil from the skillet and place the skillet in the oven (be sure skillet is oven proof) for 15-18 minutes. Once the rack of lamb is ready, remove the skillet from the oven. Remove the rack of lamb and set aside. In the skillet, mix the beef broth with the red wine and the mustard and cook over medium heat. Allow the sauce to reduce. To add texture, add the butter and garlic and cook until golden. Add the *fines herbes*. Cut the lamb into individual chops, then serve and top with roasted potatoes and sauce.

MAIN DISHES
POULTRY

VIZCAYA Photo Credit: Bill Sumner

Chicken Fricassee

GLORIA ESTEFAN, SINGER & SONGWRITER
AND RECIPE BY HER MOTHER, MRS. GLORIA FAJARDO

SERVES 8

3 whole chickens, each cut into 4 equal parts

5 medium sized potatoes, peeled and cut into equal parts

2 large onions, sliced

1 green bell pepper, sliced

1 red bell pepper, sliced

1 onion, sliced

5 garlic cloves, minced

1 cup Spanish dry wine
  (Artañan is recommended, without salt)

2 small cans tomato sauce

2 teaspoons salt

½ cup olive oil

1½ sour or Seville orange

½ cup capers

¼ teaspoon pepper

1 chicken bouillon cube

1 can early or spring peas

Gloria Estefan is a Cuban American singer and songwriter. Named the "Queen of Latin Pop," she is in or near the top 100 of best selling music artists with over 90 million albums sold worldwide. With five Grammy Awards and several number one hits she is the most successful crossover performer in Latin music to date. She received the Ellis Island Congressional Medal of Honor, which is the highest award that can be given to a naturalized U.S. citizen. The singer is the recipient of the American Music Award for Lifetime Achievement. She is also the owner of a number of restaurants in South Florida and the Cardozo Hotel in South Beach.

Wash the chicken pieces and pat dry with a paper towel. In a large bowl, marinate the pieces of chicken with garlic, onions, sour orange, and sliced green and red peppers. Pour 2 cups of water in a saucepan with the cube of chicken bouillon and bring to a boil over medium heat to dissolve. When the bouillon is fully dissolved, remove from the heat and set aside.

Preheat an oven to 350° F. Remove the chicken pieces from the marinade and brown them in olive oil in a very large sauté pan or pot over medium high heat until golden, so as to seal the juices in the meat. It is best to use tongs to turn the chicken so as not to pierce the flesh and let the juices escape. When all the chicken is browned on both sides, add all the marinated ingredients. Then add the tomato sauce, capers, Spanish dry wine, and season with the salt and pepper. Then add the 2 cups of reserved bouillon. Cover the pan or pot and let cook for 20-25 minutes on medium heat until the chicken is tender. Add the potatoes, cover and cook for another 15 minutes. Lastly, place the covered pan or pot in the oven for 10 minutes. When done, remove from the oven and when serving you may add a can of early peas for a beautiful presentation.

Curried Chicken

CHEFS & OWNERS JUAN MARIO MAZA AND VANI MAHARAJ, Alta Cocina

Alta Cocina was established by the husband and wife team of Chef Juan Mario Maza and Chef Vani Maharaj. Vani, born in Trinidad and Tobago, grew up surrounded by the best and freshest organic ingredients. Her cooking is inspired with the love of the Caribbean. Together with her husband, Juan Mario, a Guatemalan native, their cooking is a beautiful fusion of Latin, Caribbean, and South Floridian flavors.

Season chicken with salt, pepper, chopped garlic, and onion. Allow to marinate for at least 24 hours. Heat the oil in a pot to the smoking point. Add water to curry to form a runny paste and then add curry paste to the hot oil. Allow the curry to cook for 3 minutes, being careful not to burn curry. Add the seasoned chicken to pot. Coat the chicken with curry in the pot and then add the chicken stock. Cook for 20 minutes. Lastly, fold in the ground cumin. Garnish with chopped cilantro and serve.

SERVES 6

3 pounds chicken breasts, cut in cubes

2 cloves garlic, chopped

½ onion, chopped

2 tablespoons curry powder

1 teaspoon ground cumin

¼ cup water

2 cups chicken stock

2 tablespoons oil

Chopped cilantro

Salt and pepper to season

Chicken in Spiced Tamarind Salsa

NORIS LEDESMA, CURATOR OF TROPICAL FRUIT at FAIRCHILD TROPICAL BOTANIC GARDEN

SERVES 4

4 chicken breasts

½ teaspoon white onion, chopped

2 tablespoons fresh oregano, chopped fine for garnish

1 pinch salt

1 pinch pepper

1 cup tamarind juice (approximately 10 tamarinds)

3 tablespoons flour

1 pinch fresh ginger, grated

⅛ cup red onion, diced

2 green chiles, seeded and diced

1 teaspoon cumin seed

½ teaspoon salt

1 tablespoon butter

1 tablespoon sugar

*Each person born in the tropics has a story to tell about the tamarind. As tamarind season approaches on the Eastern plains (*llanos orientales*) of Colombia, women make* tamarindada *or tamarind juice, to offer to the thirsty farmers following an intense day of work. In Trinidad and Jamaica, tamarind is a popular refreshing snack. Asians, particularly in Thailand and India, have a long tradition of eating and cooking with tamarind; creating delicious salsas, chutneys and sauces. The tamarind fruit "pod" is smooth and brittle to the touch. Inside, the pasty flesh clings tightly to the hardened dark-brown seeds. The tamarind tree grows easily in South Florida and requires little care. The fruiting season in Florida is February to May and tamarind paste is available year-round in Asian specialty stores.*

Mash 10 tamarinds and soak in water overnight. In the morning, strain through a colander, collecting the juice. Discard the seeds and the skin. Heat the butter, salt, onions, and chiles in a sauté pan over medium heat until soft. Add the flour and stir to make a *roux*. Add the chicken breasts, tamarind juice, and the remaining ingredients. Stir constantly until slightly reddish- brown in color. Cook until the chicken is tender and cooked through. To serve, plate the marinated chicken and spoon the tamarind sauce over the chicken. Garnish with the fresh chopped oregano.

Coq Au Vin
CHEF & OWNER ADRIANA FATAT, Le Croisic Restaurant

"This is a traditional French recipe that has been in my family for at least three generations. I am very lucky today to be able to use it in my restaurant as part of the specialties. I hope you can come to Le Croisic and try it!" – Chef Fatat

SERVES 10-12

3 whole free range chickens
½ bottle of full bodied Burgundy or other red wine
5 bacon slices, diced
½ pound button mushrooms
½ pound pearl onions
4 cloves garlic
2 celery stalks, chopped
2 carrots, peeled and quartered
¼ pound unsalted butter
Bouquet of fresh herbs (1 bay leaf & 3 sprigs of thyme)
Olive oil
Salt and pepper

In a large skillet heat the olive oil and butter together over medium heat and sear the chicken on both sides with salt and pepper until brown. Remove the chicken and set aside. Using the same skillet, add the garlic, herbs, and vegetables and cook for about 3 minutes. Then place the chicken back in the sauce pan with all of the vegetables and add the wine until the chicken and vegetables are covered. Add salt and pepper. Bring to a boil at a moderate heat. Cover and cook at low heat for 1 to 2 hours. While the chicken is cooking with the wine, in another skillet pour some olive oil and cook bacon, onion, and mushrooms until brown, or about 10 minutes. When the chicken is ready add bacon, onion, and mushrooms to the pan. Cook and stir for 3 to 4 minutes. Taste and correct the seasoning. Add parsley to the chicken when finished and serve with rice or boiled potatoes. *Bon Appétit!*

Turkey & White Bean Chili
ARTHUR AGATSTON, M.D., THE SOUTH BEACH DIET
QUICK & EASY COOKBOOK

SERVES 4

1 tablespoon extra virgin olive oil

1 medium onion, roughly chopped

2 garlic cloves, minced

1 pound turkey cutlets, cut into ½ inch pieces

1 tablespoon chili powder

1 teaspoon ground cumin

1 can (15-ounces) cannelloni beans, rinsed, and drained

1 can (14½ -ounces) Mexican diced tomatoes

1 cup low sodium chicken broth

Salt and freshly ground black pepper

Arthur Agatston, M.D., is a cardiologist and an associate professor of medicine at the University of Miami Miller School of Medicine. Dr. Agatston has authored over 100 articles and abstracts for scientific journals and he has participated as a speaker, faculty member, and organizer of numerous academic cardiology meetings and symposia. Along with his renown as a researcher, he is a lecturer, and pioneer in clinical and preventive cardiology. As a practicing cardiologist, Dr. Agatston did not set out to develop a weight-loss plan. But he did create what became known as the South Beach Diet in the mid-1990s to help his patients whose weight and blood chemistries were not improving on the standard, low-fat American Heart Association diet. His balanced approach became the basis for The South Beach Diet, *his first nonacademic book, which became an international best seller.*

This yummy chili can be made different ways, if you want to experiment. Try using chicken instead of turkey or navy, black, or pinto beans in place of white ones. Top it with a tablespoon or two of shredded low-fat cheddar or jack cheese, sliced scallions, or chopped cilantro. You can even use chipotle chili powder for a smoky taste in place of regular.

Heat the olive oil in a large saucepan over medium high heat. Add the onion and cook, stirring occasionally, until softened, about 5 minutes. Add the garlic and cook 1 minute more. Add the turkey, chili powder, and cumin. Cook, stirring often, until the turkey is no longer pink inside, for about 5 minutes. Add the beans, the tomatoes with their juice and broth. Bring to a boil, the reduce the heat to medium low. Cover and simmer until the flavors blend, about 15 minutes. Season with salt and pepper to taste and serve.

The South Beach Diet Quick & Easy Cookbook by Arthur Agatston, M.D., reprinted by permission of Rodale, Inc.

Stuffed Chicken Breasts in Mushroom Sauce
KRISTI KRUEGER, WPLG-TV LOCAL 10 ANCHOR & HEALTH REPORTER

Kristi Krueger has built a solid reputation as an award-winning medical reporter and effervescent anchor. She joined Local 10 as a co-anchor of the 5:30 p.m. newscast and Eye on Health *reporter in 1993. In addition to her anchoring duties, Kristi specializes in medical reporting in* Kristi's Good Health *segments. She is married to Todd Templin, Vice President of Boardroom Communications, a South Florida Public Relations firm. Todd and Kristi have two children, Troy and Kelsie. This is her favorite recipe when company is coming over. If you need to, just double everything for 8. It looks and tastes great and it's not difficult to make.*

Preheat an oven to 325° F. Combine the bread, spices, seasoning, onion, butter, and water in mixing bowl and mix well. Take the stuffing mixture, divide into four portions, and put on the chicken breasts. Fold chicken breasts around stuffing and secure with toothpicks using the skin of chicken. Roll the chicken breasts in 1/2 cup of the flour, 1/2 teaspoon salt, some paprika, and garlic salt. Melt one cube of butter in a baking dish, roll the breasts in butter, and bake for 1 1/2 to 2 hours, basting frequently.

Sauce:

Brown mushrooms and onions in butter and then add the soup and sour cream. Heat through, add wine when ready to serve and ladle over chicken breasts.

SERVES 4

4 chicken breasts, boned but skin left on

1/4 cup soft bread

1/4 teaspoon pepper

1/4 teaspoon paprika

1/4 teaspoon poultry seasoning

1/2 teaspoon salt

1 tablespoon onion, finely chopped

1/4 cup hot water

3 tablespoons butter, melted

1/2 cup flour

1/2 teaspoon salt

Dash paprika

Dash garlic salt

SAUCE INGREDIENTS

1/4 pound fresh mushrooms

1/4 cup onion, diced

2 tablespoons butter

1 can mushroom soup

1 small carton sour cream

2 tablespoons of Sauterne or Sherry

Duck Ropa Vieja
With Coconut Basmati Rice & Soy Chimichurri
EXECUTIVE CHEF RUFINO RENGIFO,
ORIENTE AT CARDOZO

Oriente at Cardozo is a new South Beach bistro presenting a taste of Cuba and the savory and exotic flavors of the far east. Award-winning Chef Rufino Rengifo has masterfully created a tantalizing fusion that is sure to stimulate everyone's culinary senses. Oriente, Cuba's most Eastern province is where the earliest European settlements began and is home to some of the best musical rhythms in all of Cuba.

SERVES 6

1 whole duck

3 oranges, cut in half and juiced

1 bunch cilantro, chopped

2 fresh knobs of ginger, peeled and very finely chopped

Salt to taste

1 tablespoon cumin

1 tablespoon paprika

1 tablespoon onion powder

1 tablespoon garlic powder

SOFRITO CRIOLLO INGREDIENTS

3 tomatoes

2 red bell peppers

2 green bell peppers

6 garlic cloves

2 sweet chiles

1 Spanish onion

1 bay leaf

1 pinch of cumin

1 pinch of Sazón Natural & Complete (Goya Brand)

Make a rub by combining all of the dry ingredients; the seasoned salt, cumin, paprika, onion powder, and garlic powder. Rub the mixture over both sides of the meat. Squeeze the orange halves over the duck.

Set aside, cover, and let marinate for three hours. Preheat an oven to 350° F. Roast the whole duck for an hour-and-a-half. Remove from the oven and allow to cool. When cool, cut the duck and shred into pieces. While the duck is roasting prepare the *Sofrito Criollo*.

Sofrito Criollo:

Pulse all of ingredients in a food processor. Place the mixture in a saucepan over low heat and gently simmer for 30 minutes.

Add the *sofrito* mixture to the shredded duck, return to the saucepan and simmer for another 10 minutes.

Rice:

In a large saucepan, boil the water, then add the rice with the 1 knob of ginger and butter. Prepare the rice until cooked *al dente*. Let cool. Once *al dente* and cool, add the coconut milk and the shredded coconut. Bring to the boil and remove from stove. This is then served with the Soy *Chimichurri*.

Soy *Chimichurri*:

Combine all of the ingredients in a bowl to create an emulsion. Then garnish the plate for an exquisite presentation.

COCONUT BASMATI RICE INGREDIENTS

2 cups basmati rice

1 knob of ginger

4 cups water

2 tablespoons butter

6 ounces coconut milk

4 ounces shredded coconut

SOY CHIMICHURRI INGREDIENTS

2 bunches of parsley, finely chopped

4 ounces garlic, chopped

3 ounces rice vinegar

1 ounce lemon juice

8 ounces extra virgin olive oil

1 ounce soy sauce

1 pinch crushed red pepper

Salt and pepper to taste.

SERVES 4

4 boneless, skinless chicken breasts

1 jar of your favorite spaghetti sauce

1 8-ounce package of shredded mozzarella cheese
  (part skim or fat-free)

Vegetable oil spray

Fresh parsley, chopped

Salt & pepper

Glenna Milberg joined Local 10 in 1999 to report on South Florida's top stories and community issues. She is a regular contributor to Local 10's public affairs broadcast, This Week in South Florida. *She's covered an eclectic collection of South Florida stories - among them: campaigns, crime, and category fives, from the Everglades to the ocean. She and her husband Michael have two bright and beautiful daughters.*

Heat a skillet over medium high heat. Spray the skillet with the vegetable oil and place the chicken breasts in the skillet. Brown the chicken breasts on one side for 3 minutes. Turn the chicken breasts over and season with salt and pepper. Liberally spoon the tomato sauce over the chicken breasts. It's okay if some of the sauce runs over into the skillet. Cover the skillet and cook over medium heat for 5 minutes. Uncover and sprinkle desired amount of cheese over each chicken breast and cover skillet. Continue cooking for another 2 to 3 minutes until cheese is melted. Sprinkle with parsley and serve.

Kadai Chicken

**M. NARENDRA KINI, M.D., PRESIDENT AND CEO,
MIAMI CHILDREN'S HOSPITAL AND HIS WIFE REKHA KINI, M.D.**

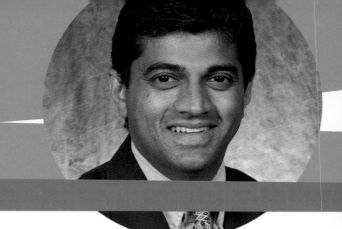

M. Narendra Kini, M.D., joined Miami Children's Hospital in January of 2008 as President and CEO. He is responsible for overseeing management of the 275-bed pediatric specialty hospital and its growing ambulatory services network. Dr. Kini brings to the post particular expertise in clinical care, informatics, quality care models and advocacy that will support Miami Children's in building on its reputation for clinical excellence and pediatric care leadership. Prior to joining Miami Children's, Dr. Kini served as Executive Vice President for Clinical and Physician Services at Trinity Health, the fourth largest Catholic health system in the U.S. Prior to his work with Trinity Health, Dr. Kini served at GE Medical Systems in various roles related to information technology. He was named Director of the GE Healthcare Leadership Institute. Dr. Kini obtained his medical degree in 1985 and completed a master's degree in hospital and health administration in 1988. He is board certified in general pediatric and pediatric emergency medicine through training at the Medical College of Wisconsin.

A kadai is a kind of dish cooked in a karahi, which is a type of thick, circular, and deep pot (similar in shape to a wok) used in Indian cooking. It is useful for shallow or deep-frying of meat, potatoes, sweets, fish, and for simmering of stews.

Grind the coriander seeds and whole red chile peppers into a coarse powder in a mortar and pestle or a small food processor. Set aside. Heat the oil in a large cast iron or heavy metal pot over medium heat. Add the bay leaves and sauté for about 30 seconds and then add the onions. Sauté until they turn a light golden brown. Add the ginger and garlic pastes. Let this sauté for about 3 minutes or so over medium to high heat. Now add the coriander seed and the reserved red chile and coriander powder along with the *garam masala* powder. Stir this well until it reaches a uniform consistency. Add the tomatoes and make sure they are fully cooked through. Finally, add the chicken pieces, the salt, and the red chili powder and simmer until the chicken is tender. Serve garnished with the chopped fresh cilantro. Enjoy!

SERVES 4

*1 whole chicken, cut in pieces, but keep pieces
moderately large
4 to 5 tablespoons of vegetable oil
(feel free to use heart healthy oil)
½ cup of onions sliced
1½ cups tomatoes, sliced and peeled
2 tablespoons fresh cilantro chopped, for garnish
1 tablespoon garlic paste
1 tablespoon ginger paste
4 teaspoons garam masala powder
(available at Whole Foods or any
ethnic grocery or online stores)
2 bay leaves
4 whole red chile peppers
2 teaspoons coriander seeds
1 teaspoon red chili powder
Salt as needed*

Duck Satisfaction
With Banana Mashed Potatoes - Two Ways
OWNERS DAVID TORNEK & CHEF SEAN BRASEL, TOUCH CATERING

Touch Catering is the vision of owners David Tornek and renowned chef, Sean Brasel, of Touch Restaurant, located on Lincoln Road on South Beach. They have taken the restaurant's innovative cuisine and signature style "on the road" to bring you a truly unique culinary experience.

This is a highly involved recipe so please take note that several days of preparation make this dish what it is.

SERVES 6

DUCK LEGS INGREDIENTS

6 large duck legs

⅓ cup kosher salt

⅛ cup herbs de provence

3 tablespoons paprika

1 tablespoon chili powder

1 tablespoon cumin powder

1 tablespoon garlic powder

1 tablespoon cayenne pepper

2 tablespoons black pepper

4 cups rendered duck fat

Vegetable oil, as needed

DUCK BREAST INGREDIENTS

6 pieces fresh 6-ounce duck breast, preferably Muscovy

¼ cup kosher salt

¼ cup brown sugar

1 tablespoon chile pepper flakes

1 tablespoon cinnamon

1 tablespoon Chinese Five Spice

1 tablespoon chili powder

½ tablespoon of star anise

Duck Legs:

Mix all of the seasonings together and set aside in an airtight container until needed. Clean off any excess fat from the duck legs. Place a generous amount of seasoning on the duck legs and place in the refrigerator uncovered for 48 hours. After the duck legs have set for two days, heat the vegetable oil in a sauté pan over medium high heat and place the duck legs in the pan to sear. Set all of the seared duck legs in a pot and cover with the rendered duck fat. Preheat an oven to 275° F. Bake for three hours.

Duck Breast:

Prepare the seasoning for the duck breast by mixing in a bowl and then set aside. Clean all excess fat from the duck breast and save for the leg confit oil. With a very sharp knife, score shallow cross hatch marks across the duck breast skin. Rub seasoning on all sides of the duck breast, place on a tray, cover and set in the refrigerator for four hours. After the duck breast has cured, place in a hot smoker for 10-15 minutes. Alternately, smoke in a cold smoker for at least 30 minutes. Cover and return the duck to the refrigerator until time to cook.

Banana Mashed Potatoes:

In a pot, boil the potatoes in water until soft. Strain off all of the water and place potatoes in an electric mixer with sour cream, butter, kosher salt, and white pepper. Whip the potatoes until smooth. Place the bananas on a grill with cut side facing down and grill until medium-dark grill marks appear. Remove bananas from the peel and chop. Fold in to the mashed potatoes.

Preheat an oven to 450° F. Place the duck breasts in a cold non-stick sauté pan with the skin side down. Place in the oven and cook for 10 minutes with the skin side down. In a separate pan, place the duck legs skin side up, and heat for 10 minutes over medium low heat. To serve, place the desired amount of the banana mashed potatoes in the center of a dinner plate with the duck leg pressed firmly up against it. Slice the breast length-wise, fanning the breast slices against the leg. Garnish with fresh berries.

BANANA MASHED POTATOES INGREDIENTS

1 pound Idaho potatoes, peeled and chopped

3 tablespoons sour cream

¼ pound butter

1 tablespoon kosher salt

½ tablespoon white pepper

2 unpeeled bananas, cut in half

Fresh berries to garnish

Breast of Duck *with Pomegranate Molasses*
MIKE MAUNDER, PH. D., EXECUTIVE DIRECTOR, FAIRCHILD TROPICAL BOTANIC GARDEN

SERVES 4

4 duck breasts with skin

2 tablespoons olive oil

2 tablespoons pomegranate molasses

2 pinches of ground cinnamon (optional)

Sea salt and black pepper

Pomegranate molasses is made from boiling down the juice of sour pomegranates to make an aromatic, auburn brown, very sticky treacle. The best quality molasses come from my wife's family's groves in the north of Lebanon; otherwise it can be bought in most Middle Eastern food stores in Miami.

Preheat an oven to 425° F. Score the skin of the duck breasts in a crisscross fashion, salt well and set aside for 15 minutes. Heat the olive oil in a large frying pan and place the duck breasts skin side down and sear them for a minute or so until browned. Turn them over and sear the other side. Then place the breasts in a roasting dish in the oven for about 15 minutes until pink. Remove them from the oven and let them rest under foil for about 10-15 minutes.

Heat the frying pan after removing the excess fat and add the pomegranate molasses and cinnamon. Reduce the liquid for a minute and season with salt and pepper. Slice each breast into three or four slices and pour the sauce over them. This is best served with roast vegetables and a large glass of good red *Rioja*.

Thai Chicken Wraps

CHEF JAY RUFF, BERRIES IN THE GROVE

Berries in the Grove features a wide variety of health conscious dishes and decadent favorites. For lunch, choose from an assortment of salads, wraps, smoothies and sandwiches. The dinner menu includes seafood, steaks and homemade pasta.

Salt and pepper chicken breasts to taste, grill, and cut into strips. Mix scallions, cucumber, minced garlic, minced ginger, basil, and mint together and set aside. Combine in a sauce pan the peanut butter, ginger powder, garlic powder, soy sauce, and heavy cream. Let simmer for 10 minutes. Lay the tortilla down, placing mixed greens down first, add scallion cucumber mix, chicken and then ladle about 2 ounces of peanut sauce over top. To assemble, fold the sides of the wrap in and roll up. Cut across the middle at an angle. Enjoy!

SERVES 8

8 whole-wheat tortillas
8 chicken breasts, skinless and boneless
16 ounces mixed greens
2 bunches scallions, cut on a bias
2 cucumbers, sliced thin
2 garlic cloves, minced
4 tablespoons fresh ginger, minced
6 tablespoons fresh basil, chopped
6 tablespoons fresh mint leaf, chopped
⅔ cup rice wine vinegar
⅔ cup peanut butter, chunky
2 teaspoons ginger powder
2 teaspoons garlic powder
½ cup soy sauce
1 cup heavy cream

Chicken Makhani (Indian Butter Chicken)

CLIFF DRYSDALE, Tennis Legend and ESPN Sports Commentator

Serves 6

2 tablespoons peanut oil

1½ shallots, finely chopped

⅜ cup white onions, chopped

3 tablespoons butter

1 tablespoon lemon juice

4½ teaspoons ginger garlic paste (made by combining equal parts of ginger paste & garlic paste)

3 teaspoons garam masala

1½ teaspoons chili powder

1½ teaspoons ground cumin

1½ bay leaves

⅜ cup plain yogurt

1½ cups half-and-half

1½ cup of tomato purée

½ teaspoon cayenne pepper, to taste

⅛ teaspoon salt

⅛ teaspoon black pepper

24 ounces boneless skinless chicken thighs, bite size pieces

4½ teaspoons cornstarch

⅜ cup of water

Both on and off the court, Cliff Drysdale is one of the most popular personalities in the international tennis community. This South African played forty-five Davis Cup matches for his former homeland over a six-year period. In 1972, Drysdale teamed with Roger Taylor to win the U.S. Open doubles crown. Drysdale was ranked several times in the world's top ten in singles, and he earned his way to being number one in the world on the senior tour in 1989. The highlight of Drysdale's singles career was a finals showing in the 1965 U.S. Championships. Cliff Drysdale went from making the shots to calling them. He is the game's preeminent tennis announcer and his insightful tennis commentary makes him a popular personality on ABC Sports and ESPN. When not traveling, Drysdale resides in Miami.

Heat 1 tablespoon oil in a large saucepan over medium high heat. Sauté shallots and onion until soft and translucent. Stir in the butter, lemon juice, ginger garlic paste, 1½ teaspoons garam masala, chili powder, cumin, and bay leaf. Cook, stirring for 1 minute. Then add the tomato purée and cook for 2 minutes more, stirring frequently. Stir in half-and-half and yogurt. Season with salt, pepper, and cayenne. Remove from the heat and set aside

Heat 1 tablespoon oil in a large heavy skillet over medium heat. Add the chicken thighs and cook for about 10 minutes or until lightly browned. Reduce heat and season with 1½ teaspoon garam masala and cayenne. Into the pan with the chicken stir about ⅓ of the sauce and simmer about 5 minutes until the liquid has reduced and chicken is no longer pink. Pour the rest of the sauce into the skillet with the chicken. Mix together the cornstarch and water, then stir into the sauce. Cook for 5 to 10 minutes or until thickened. Enjoy!

Quick & Easy Arroz con Pollo
DIANA GONZALEZ, WTVJ-TV/NBC6, HEALTH CONNECTIONS REPORTER

Diana Gonzalez is a veteran WTVJ reporter, originally coming on board in 1978 as a news reporter and producer for Montage, *a weekly magazine show. Today Gonzalez is NBC6's Health Connection Reporter, bringing South Florida the latest news in medicine and health care.*

From 1983 - 1993, Gonzalez worked as a medical reporter and midday anchor for ABC-WPLG. She then accepted the position of National Correspondent with CBS News. After three years of working for network news, Gonzalez returned to WTVJ in 1996 desiring to "report local news for a station that focused on quality." Throughout her broadcasting career Gonzalez has received numerous awards. Most recently, she was honored with the 2000 Food Science Journalism Award, by the Institute of Food Technologists, for her story on "Cancer Fighting Foods."

Soak the rice in water while removing the skin and bones from the chicken. In a 6 quart covered pot, sauté the onions, green peppers and garlic in olive oil over medium heat until soft. Add the jar of pimentos and the chicken pieces. Then add the drained rice along with the broth, wine, and water drained from the can of peas. Sprinkle *Bijol* seasoning over this and stir everything up until it's a deep yellow. Add the bay leaf, cover and cook on low heat until rice is soft. This should take about an hour from start to finish. When done, garnish with the green peas and enjoy!

SERVES 4

1 Mojo style pre-cooked whole roasting chicken (found at your local grocery store)
14 ounces "pearl style" short-grain rice
1 8-ounce container pre-diced onion
1 8-ounce container pre-diced green pepper
1 small jar diced pimentos (do not drain)
1 teaspoon garlic, minced
1 teaspoon salt
¼ teaspoon pepper
1 bay leaf
1 small can tomato sauce
2 cups chicken broth
1 ¾ cup dry cooking wine or beer
3 tablespoons olive oil
1 can green peas
Bijol seasoning or turmeric for color

Fettuccine with Chicken
CHEF & OWNER JOAO CARLOS OLIVERA,
Tutto Pasta Ristorante

SERVES 4

16 ounces fresh fettuccine pasta

8 ounces chicken breast, grilled

½ cup sun dried tomatoes

1 cup mushrooms

1 teaspoon garlic

2 teaspoons olive oil

3 cups tomato sauce

¼ cup fresh basil, chopped

Salt, pepper and oregano

Tutto Pasta is a family run restaurant that is centrally located in the heart of Miami. Chef and Owner Joao Carlos Olivera combines Italian cuisine with his Brazilian touch that creates flavors that will transport your palate to the Italian countryside. The Miami Herald *named Tutto Pasta one of the best in Miami-Dade County.* Zagat *raves that Tutto Pasta, "is the real thing." The pasta is made daily in an open kitchen.*

Add the garlic to a sauté pan with olive oil over medium heat and cook until lightly colored. Then sauté the chicken breasts, sun dried tomatoes, and mushrooms. Add the butter and tomato sauce, salt and pepper and oregano to taste. When the sauce thickens add basil. In a large pot of boiling water, cook the fettuccine just a few minutes until it is to your liking, preferably *al dente*, and serve with the sauce.

Ajiaco Santafereño
AMBASSADOR CARMENZA JARAMILLO,
Consul General de Columbia, Dean of The Consular Corps

Ajiaco *is a version of chicken soup from Colombia. Although several regions of Colombia have their distinct recipe the most famous is* Ajiaco Santafereño, *named after* Santa Fé de Bogotá, *the capital of Colombia, where it is a cultural mainstay. It typically contains pieces of chicken on the bone, large chunks of corn on the cob, two or three kinds of native potatoes (the tiny* papas criollas *that fall apart and thicken the soup, usually accompanied by chunks of the waxy* sabanera *and/or the soft* pastusa), *and* guasca, *a weedy, aromatic herb that lends the dish part of its distinctive flavor. In recent years, guascas have become easier to find in Latin American markets. Though purists may insist on using genuine* guascas, *others might substitute oregano in a pinch. The soup is typically served with heavy cream, capers and avocado, all mixed in just before serving.* Ajiaco *is so robust that, served with a side of white rice, it is usually considered a full meal.*

In a large pot, cook the chicken breasts combined with the green onions, bay leaves, cilantro, salt and pepper and the water for 30 minutes over medium heat. Remove the chicken and set aside. Strain the broth and skim off the fat. Place a bunch of *guascas* in the strained broth and bring to a boil. Add the *pastusa* potatoes, then 15 minutes later add the *sabanera* potatoes and, lastly, add the peeled *criolla* potatoes and the corn segments. Simmer for 20 minutes.

Add the second bunch of *guascas* and continue simmering on low heat for 10 minutes more, or until achieving the desired consistency. Remove the *guascas*. Bone and shred the chicken. Add a little warm broth to the chicken and serve separately. The capers, the cream, and the avocados should also be served separately so that diners can add them to the soup as they so desire.

SERVES 8

6 chicken breasts, bone in

3 stalks scallions or green onion

2 bay leaves

1 sprig cilantro

Salt and pepper to taste

12 cups water

2 bunches guascas

2 pounds pastusa potatoes, cut into chunks

1½ pounds sabanera potatoes

1 pound criolla potatoes, peeled

4 tender ears of corn, cut into segments

1 cup capers

1 cup cream

4 medium avocados, cubed

Arroz con Pollo a la Cubana
CHEF ALFONSO PEREZ, VERSAILLES RESTAURANT

SERVES 4

One 3 to 3½ pound chicken, cut into 8 pieces

2 teaspoons salt

½ teaspoon black pepper, freshly ground

½ cup extra virgin olive oil

1 large onion, finely chopped

4 large garlic cloves, finely chopped

1 medium green bell pepper, diced

2 ounces Spanish chorizo, diced

½ cup tomato sauce

½ cup dry white wine

5-6 cups concentrated chicken stock, warm

2 cups Valencia rice or pearl rice

½ teaspoon ground cumin

½ teaspoon Bijol con azafran or several threads of saffron

2 bay leaves

1 can or bottle (12-ounces) domestic beer, room temperature

½ cup pimientos cut in thin strips, for garnish

½ cup petite peas, fresh or frozen, briefly blanched
  and cooled, for garnish

Legend has it that Versailles started out as a French restaurant—on Calle Ocho? The French format didn't work so well, but the building and the location proved ideal for Cuban Felipe Valls, Sr. who created this now legendary restaurant back in 1971. Always popular with the locals, Versailles is a great place to take those out-of-town visitors for a complete immersion in Cuban culture. The restaurant is a lot like the Cuba of old—loud, boisterous, and full of excitement, just dripping in Cuban patriotism. Versailles has always had one of the largest Cuban food menus imaginable. If they don't have it on the menu, it's probably not Cuban food!

Preheat an oven to 375° F. Generously season the chicken pieces with some salt and pepper. Put the oil in a stovetop, ovenproof casserole or Dutch oven over medium high heat. Add the chicken and brown on both sides until golden brown, about 5 to 6 minutes. Add the onion, garlic, chorizo and green pepper and sauté for 5 minutes over medium heat. Add the tomato sauce, white wine, and hot chicken stock. Bring the liquid to a boil and add the rice, salt, pepper, cumin, azafran and bay leaves. Reduce the heat and simmer for 10 minutes, stirring gently. Cover and finish in the oven for about 10 more minutes. The rice should be tender and the chicken should be cooked through, so juice runs clear when pricked with a knife. Remove from the oven and pour the beer over the casserole. Garnish with pimientos and peas and serve.

Tasty Chicken Bolognese Pasta

EDWARD VILLELLA, FOUNDING ARTISTIC DIRECTOR AND CEO OF THE MIAMI CITY BALLET AND HIS WIFE MRS. LINDA VILLELLA

Edward Villella, certainly America's most celebrated male dancer, did much to popularize the role of the male in dance through the supreme artistry and virility he exhibited during his performance career. Offstage he has been as influential, accepting the role of Founding Artistic Director of Miami City Ballet in 1985 and achieving worldwide acclaim for the Company in a mere decade. He has been recognized by and performed for many Presidents and foreign Heads of State and has been awarded numerous honors, including the National Medal of Art and The Kennedy Center Honor. He and his wife, Linda, a former Olympic figure skater and Founder and Director of Miami City Ballet School, reside in Miami Beach.

Place the olive oil in a big pot over medium heat. Add the garlic and sauté until slightly brown. Add the onion and sauté until soft and translucent. Add the ground beef and continue sautéing until the meat is browned. Mix the can of tomato paste in with the meat. Add the diced tomatoes. Season with the salt, pepper, oregano, basil and thyme to taste. Last but not least, add the chicken legs into the sauce and simmer at low heat for one hour. Cook the pasta in boiling, salted water and serve in a large bowl or platter with the *Bolognese* sauce and enjoy!

SERVES 6

1 pound ground beef

12 chicken legs

1 pound pasta, cooked

2 cloves garlic, thinly sliced

2 small onions or 1 large onion, thinly sliced

8 ounces tomato paste

3 cans (16-ounces) diced tomatoes

3 tablespoons olive oil

Salt and pepper

Oregano

Basil

Thyme

Pad Thai
LOTUS GARDEN

For over twenty years, the Lotus Garden has been a treasured family-owned and operated restaurant. All of the authentic Thai dishes are made fresh with each order. Their Pad Thai is a Coral Gables favorite!

SERVES 4

1 (12-ounces) package of rice noodles

4 ounces of boneless, skinless chicken breast, cut into bite-sized pieces

3 tablespoons vegetable oil

1 egg

3 tablespoons white vinegar

3 tablespoons thin soy sauce

3 tablespoons white sugar

½ teaspoon paprika

⅛ teaspoon crushed red pepper (optional)

8 ounces bean sprouts

¼ cup crushed peanuts (optional)

2 green onions, chopped

Soak the rice noodles in cold water for 30-50 minutes, or until soft. Drain and set aside. Heat the vegetable oil in a wok over medium-high heat. Crack the egg into the hot oil and cook until firm. Stir in the chicken and cook for 5 minutes. Add the softened noodles, vinegar, thin soy sauce, and sugar. Add the paprika and crushed red pepper. Adjust seasoning to taste. Toss while cooking, until noodles are tender. Add bean sprouts, mix and continue to cook for 3 more minutes. Add the peanuts, if desired, and the green onions.

Lemon Chicken
OWNER SAMIR AL BARQ, MAROOSH MEDITERRANEAN RESTAURANT

Fine Mediterranean fare, with an emphasis on the Middle East, is all the rage in Coral Gables now that Maroosh has come to town. Enjoying great success in its new digs, a two-story historic Moorish building just off Ponce de Leon Boulevard, Maroosh has proven that only succulent lamb, beef or chicken kabobs upstage decadent platters of hummus, tabbouleh *and* baba ghanoush. *The beauty of quality ingredients, simply and carefully prepared, is showcased on every plate.*

In a food processor or blender add the garlic, lemon juice and olive oil. Liquefy and set the marinade aside. Wash and rinse the chicken and cut in 1 inch cubes. Marinate the chicken using half of the marinade and add the salt, pepper, oregano and nutmeg. Allow the chicken to marinate for 3 hours in the refrigerator. Reserve the reminder of the marinade.

Broil the chicken under an oven broiler or grill in a grill pan on the stove until chicken is done. Transfer the cooked chicken to a large sauté pan over low heat and toss together with the olive oil. Add the artichoke hearts along with the chopped cilantro. Cook thoroughly, then add the rest of the reserved marinade. Bring it to a boil, then remove and serve it on a platter along with your favorite side dishes, such as steamed vegetables, potatoes or a Mediterranean rice pilaf. Enjoy! *Sahatin!*

SERVES 6-8

2 pounds boneless, skinless chicken breast
or boneless, skinless chicken thighs
1 can (12-ounces) artichoke hearts
¼ cup of fresh garlic, chopped
¼ cup olive oil
½ cup lemon juice, freshly squeezed
½ cup fresh cilantro, chopped
2 tablespoons salt, or less depending on taste
1 tablespoon black pepper
1 tablespoon fresh oregano, chopped
½ tablespoon nutmeg

Chicken Adobo

STEVEN RAICHLEN, MULTI-AWARD WINNING AUTHOR, JOURNALIST, TEACHER AND TV PERSONALITY

SERVES 4

2 large boneless, skinless chicken breasts (about 1½ pounds), split in half (4 halves), washed and blotted dry

3 cloves garlic, coarsely chopped

1 shallot, minced

½ teaspoon ground cumin

½ teaspoon dried oregano

½ teaspoon dried thyme

1 tablespoon fresh cilantro, chopped

1 tablespoon fresh parsley leaves, chopped

3 tablespoon sour orange or lime juice, freshly squeezed

2 tablespoon extra-virgin olive oil

Plenty of salt and freshly ground black pepper

Steven Raichlen is the man who reinvented barbecue. His bestselling Barbecue Bible *cookbook series and* The Primal Grill *and* Barbecue University™ *TV shows on PBS have helped people all over the world ascend the ladder of grilling enlightenment. Raichlen's 28 books include* Barbecue Bible Sauces, Rubs, and Marinades; Beer Can Chicken; *the perennially popular* Miami Spice *(Workman Publishing), and the James Beard Award-winning* Healthy Latin Cooking *(Rodale). In all, he has won 5 James Beard Awards and 3 International Association of Culinary Professional awards, and his books have been translated into 12 languages. He lives with his wife, Barbara, in Miami.*

Mash the garlic, shallot, and herbs to a paste in a mortar with a pestle. Work in the remaining ingredients for the marinade. Alternatively, the ingredients for the marinade can be puréed in a blender or mini food processor. Transfer the marinade to a non-reactive baking dish and add the chicken breasts. Turn to coat the breasts with the marinade. Cover the dish and marinate the chicken in the refrigerator for 30 minutes to 1 hour. Turn the chicken breasts once or twice during that time.

Preheat a barbecue grill to medium heat or preheat the broiler with the broiler tray 3 inches from the heat. Grill the chicken breasts over medium heat until just cooked, about 2 to 4 minutes per side, or until the internal temperature on an instant-read meat thermometer (inserted into the thickest part of the breast) registers 160° F. Broiling time is about the same. Transfer to a plate or platter and serve immediately.

Reprinted with permission from *Miami Spice* by Steven Raichlen, Workman Publishing.

Turkey Roulade *with Jalapeño Cornbread Stuffing*
CHEF & OWNER JAN JORGENSEN, TWO CHEFS RESTAURANT

Located in the heart of South Miami, Two Chefs is the acclaimed restaurant owned by Jan Jorgensen, the classically trained chef whose European-inspired cuisine has made Two Chefs one of the region's landmark restaurants. A native of Denmark, Jorgensen fell in love with cooking at the age of 16, when he enjoyed a classic European apprenticeship at a local restaurant. He trained in some of the leading European cooking schools before moving to South Florida. Beyond his culinary endeavors, Jorgensen began to feed his passion for collecting rare and unique spirits and now boasts the largest back bar in the Southeast.

Jalapeño Cornbread:
Preheat an oven to 425° F. Render the bacon, then sauté the jalapeños and onions in the same pan. Let cool and purée. Combine the flour, baking powder, salt and sugar in a mixing bowl. Sift the mixture twice before adding the cornmeal. Mix in eggs, buttermilk and the purée. Grease a loaf pan or 6-cup muffin tin with the butter. Pour the batter in and bake for 20 minutes or until golden brown.

Preheat an oven to 350° F. In a sauté pan, sauté the onions, carrots and celery for two minutes over medium heat and set aside. Crumble the cornbread in a large bowl, add the vegetable mixture and mix well. Add salt and pepper to taste. Spread cornbread mixture on top of the flattened turkey breast and roll up. Wrap the roll with bacon strips and place on a baking sheet seam down. Tie with butcher string and bake for 30 minutes.

SERVES 8

1 large raw turkey breast, boned, fanned and pounded

10 strips bacon

½ cup celery, diced small

½ cup carrots, diced small

1 cup onions, diced small

3 cloves garlic

6 4-ounce jalapeño cornbreads (see recipe below)

Salt and pepper to taste

Butcher string

JALAPEÑO CORNBREAD INGREDIENTS

3 strips bacon, diced

5 jalapeños, diced (remove seeds)

1 onion, diced

2 cups flour

2 teaspoons baking powder

2 ounces butter

1 teaspoon salt

½ cup sugar

2 cups yellow cornmeal

2 large eggs

2 cups buttermilk

SERVES 6

1 pound ground turkey

10 ounces shiitake mushrooms, diced

4 tablespoons shallots, minced

1 tablespoon thyme, minced

1 egg

½ cup bread crumbs

2 tablespoons butter

Salt and pepper to taste

Emmy award winning journalist Belkys Nerey has been a TV junkie her whole life. It's no wonder she grew up to be a main anchor at one of the country's most dynamic television stations. Born in Havana and raised in Long Island and Miami, Belkys is a natural on-air personality who is completely bilingual. Nerey started her television career as a reporter for a South Florida cable station. She was a "one-man band" for more than two years (shooting her own video and editing her own stories), before heading for Connecticut to take a job as general assignment reporter for the ABC affiliate in New Haven. It wasn't long before she was covering some of the market's biggest stories, often beating the competition convincingly because she could speak Spanish. During her nine-year tenure at Miami's WSVN, Belkys has covered major news stories and you can catch her co-anchoring the evening newscasts.

Preheat an oven to 350 ° F. In a medium sauté pan, sauté the shallots and mushrooms in the butter. When cooked, allow to cool and combine with the egg, bread crumbs, thyme, and turkey in a large mixing bowl. Season the mixture with a pinch of salt and pepper and mix everything well. Place the mixture in a greased loaf pan and bake for 1 hour. Insert a knife in the middle of the loaf and when it comes out dry, it's done. Remove from the oven and let rest for 15 minutes. Remove the meatloaf from the pan and slice into individual servings.

MAIN DISHES
SEAFOOD

ARSHT CENTER Photo Credit: Robin Hill

Moules Marinieres, Frites

(Steamed Mussels in White Wine, Shallots and Roquefort with French Fries)
CHEF & CO-OWNER PHILIPPE JACQUET, CAFÉ PASTIS

SERVES 4

6 pounds mussels, cleaned and de-bearded

1 onion, chopped

4 shallots, chopped

2 tablespoons butter

½ cup olive oil

1 leek, chopped in medium pieces

½ pound Roquefort or bleu cheese

2 cups sauvignon blanc white wine

Café Pastis is a funky little bistro in the middle of South Miami that calls to mind the charming neighborhood eateries of Paris. Born in Marseille, trained in Paris, Chef Philippe Jacquet has partnered with Miami native Scott Price to bring you the most authentic country French dining experience this side of the Atlantic. From their cozy kitchen, Jacquet and team passionately prepare the homey palate pleasing cuisine of Provence. Here is a simple yet tantalizing recipe for the ever so versatile mussel, one of the favorite dishes at Café Pastis. Bon Appetit!

In a large sauté pan, cook the chopped onion and shallots with the butter and olive oil on low heat until translucent. Add the mussels, leek and white wine. Cover and cook on high heat for two minutes, shake the pan and add the *Roquefort* cheese, shake again and cook until all of the mussels have opened. Serve hot and steamy with a side dish of crispy French fries and a salad of simple mixed greens and don't forget the warm French bread.

Seafood Stuffed Lobster
CHEF MARIBEL SANCHEZ, CASABLANCA SEAFOOD BAR & GRILL

Casablanca Seafood Bar and Grill was established by the Lazaro and Jorge Sanchez families when their fish market was evicted from Watson Island in 2005. They relocated, changed the name and established a combination fish market and restaurant overlooking the Miami River. Their motto is, "From our boats to your table.", and the freshness of their fish and seafood is only exceeded by the caring preparation and presentation in the restaurant.

In a medium sauce pan lightly sauté the onions, garlic and butter over low to medium heat. Add the Lobster Base and saffron. Stir well and then add the flour, cook for one minute more and then pour in the wine, followed by the heavy cream. Stir and bring to a simmer. Add all of the seafood, except the lobster, and cook for about three minutes. Add the bread crumbs and adjust seasonings. Set aside.

Preheat an oven to 350° F. Cut the lobster in half and clean under running water, making certain to leave the cavity of the head empty. Season lobster and stuff it with the prepared seafood stuffing. Sprinkle with some Parmesan cheese and chopped parsley, if desired. Bake for about 30 minutes and serve.

SERVES 6

2 pounds whole lobster

6 ounces bay scallops, coarsely chopped

5 ounces small shrimp, peeled, deveined and coarsely chopped

7 ounces lump crabmeat

1 tablespoon garlic, chopped

2 ounces white onion, finely chopped

3 ounces unsalted butter

1 tablespoon Superior Touch Lobster Base (available at specialty food stores or online)

2 ounces all-purpose flour

3 ounces white wine

3 ounces heavy cream

3 ounces Japanese bread crumbs (Panko)

2 ounces Parmesan cheese

Complete seasoning, to taste

Pinch of saffron

1 tablespoon parsley, chopped

Red Snapper Fillet *With Fresh Baby Artichokes*
CHEF & OWNER CLAUDIO GIORDANO, AltaMar

SERVES 4

2 2-pound whole red snappers (take the fillets out
   and reserve the head and bones)

1 pound fresh baby artichokes

4 tablespoons extra virgin olive oil

2 tablespoons fresh Italian parsley, chopped

1 pint fish stock (see recipe)

2 lemons

1 pint white wine vinegar

2 celery stalks

1 large carrot

1 leek

1 white Spanish onion

4-5 bay leaves

Salt and pepper to taste

Chef and proprietor Claudio Giordano lovingly prepares the best local, fresh seafood in a predominantly Italian vein. But he also pairs each individual fish with whatever international influences best enhance its natural flavor. What makes AltaMar truly special is that Giordano, a fisherman at heart, respects the regional varieties and offers specialties that swim South Florida's waters but rarely appear on local Miami menus.

Fish Stock:

To prepare the fish stock, take 2 pints of water, combine in a pot with the bones and head of the fish, onion, celery stalks, carrot, leek and 4 or 5 bay leaves and boil for 30 minutes or until the stock is reduced by half. Strain the stock through a strainer and set aside.

To prepare the artichokes, trim the outer leaves of the artichokes and discard. Place the artichoke hearts into a bowl with just enough water to cover them and add the lemon juice to preserve their color. Boil the artichoke hearts in 3 pints of salt water with 1 pint of white wine vinegar for 20 minutes. Drain and cut into quarters lengthwise and set aside.

Salt and pepper the snapper fillets. In a large non-stick sauté pan, heat only enough olive oil to cover bottom of the pan until hot and place the previously salt and peppered fillets in the pan for 3 to 4 minutes. Turn the fillets, then add the artichokes and fish stock to the pan and continue cooking for 3 to 4 minutes. Remove the snapper and place individual servings on dinner plates. Add the parsley and remaining olive oil to the pan and simmer for 1 minute more. Pour the sauce over the snapper fillets and serve immediately.

Diver Scallops Anisado
With Potato Purée and Vanilla Oil
EXECUTIVE CHEF GERDY RODRIGUEZ, 1 BLEU RESTAURANT

1 Bleu offers a cornucopia of tantalizing fresh local and imported seafood, prime beef and organic poultry dishes, paired with superb regional and international ingredients. Guests can pamper their palates daily with lunch and dinner cuisine that is innovative and an atmosphere that is contemporary and comfortable. Led by acclaimed Executive Chef Gerdy Rodriguez the restaurant thrives on the philosophy of Art de Vivre (the art of living), which strives for excellence in every aspect of the culinary experience.

Season the scallops with sea salt and pan sear in a sauté pan over medium heat to medium rare, approximately 2-3 minutes on each side. Steep the potatoes in the heavy cream in a saucepan for 5 minutes, then add the butter and season with the salt. Then purée till smooth. Split vanilla beans lengthwise and scrape into canola oil and mix well. Finely dice the vegetables for the *brunoise* and mix with the chives.

Preheat an oven to 350° F. Place the water and sugar in a small pot, then cook over medium heat for 3 minutes, set aside and allow to cool. Dip the fennel slices in the water and sugar syrup and then place on a *Silpat* or silicone lined sheet pan, and heat for approximately 10 minutes or until crispy.

To serve, sauce the plate with 2 tablespoons of potato purée, then slice the seared scallops in half and arrange in the center of the plate. Top the scallops with the vegetable *brunoise* and drizzle the vanilla oil over the potato purée. Finally top the scallops with the fennel crisps and garnish with the fennel and *chervil* leaves.

SERVES 1
2 Diver scallops, (U-10 sized)
1½ pounds cooked potatoes
2 ounces butter
3 cups heavy cream
Salt to taste

VANILLA OIL INGREDIENTS
½ cup canola oil
2 vanilla beans

VEGETABLE *BRUNOISE* INGREDIENTS
1 teaspoon carrot, diced
1 teaspoon fennel, diced
1 teaspoon celery, diced
½ teaspoon chives, minced

FENNEL CRISPS INGREDIENTS
4 thinly sliced pieces of fennel (2-3 inches long)
½ cup sugar
½ cup water

Fennel leaves for garnish
Chervil leaves for garnish

141

Grilled Yellowtail Snapper
With Key Lime Chipotle Aioli

EXECUTIVE CHEF NATE MARTIN, ANDÚ RESTAURANT

SERVES 4

4 whole yellow-tail snapper fillets, butterflied

2 ounces gray salt or course sea salt

2 teaspoons ground coriander

1 teaspoon ground cumin

1 teaspoono white pepper

6 sprigs thyme

2 lemons

Olive oil, enough to marinate the fish

CHIPOTLE *AIOLI* INGREDIENTS

1 egg yolk

½ cup Key lime juice

2 cups blended oil or canola oil

2 ounces chipotle peppers in **adobo** *sauce*

1 ounce clover honey

2 tablespoons blackening spice (Cajun spice)

Kosher salt to taste

Andú Restaurant & Lounge has created a new haven for sexy cuisine, style and sophistication, all at a price you can afford. Andú will excite your senses and satisfy your cravings. Talented Executive Chef Nate Martin in collaboration with consulting Chef Jason McClain, has designed a tantalizing menu of Mediterranean cuisine with international influences. Using the freshest, highest quality ingredients, the menu entices even the most discerning of palates.

Preheat an oven to 400° F. Truss the snapper by cutting two small slits through the fish. Skewer the sprigs of thyme through the fish cavity and marinate the fish in the olive oil. Next mix the salt and spices together and season the snapper on both sides evenly. Grill mark the fish on a grill or a very hot grill pan in the oven for approximately 5 minutes. When cooked through, remove from the oven and dress generously with lemon juice.

Aioli:

Place the Key lime juice, egg yolk, chipotle peppers, honey and blackening spice in a blender. Start to blend the mixture and slowly add the oil to emulsify. Once the mixture thickens, and forms an *aioli*, season to taste with salt.

Florida Seafood Casserole
SENATOR BOB GRAHAM AND HIS WIFE, MRS. ADELE GRAHAM

Bob Graham was a United States Senator from Florida from 1987 to 2005 and the Governor of Florida from 1979 to 1987. Following a bid for the Democratic Party nomination in the 2004 presidential race, Graham was considered a possible running mate for John Kerry. Graham is now concentrating his efforts on the newly established Bob Graham Center for Public Service at his undergraduate alma mater, the University of Florida.

Preheat an oven to 400° F. Mix all ingredients together in a large mixing bowl, except the potato chips and paprika. Fill a large baking pan with the mixture and cover completely with the chips. Sprinkle with paprika. Bake for 20-25 minutes.

SERVES 12

½ pound crab

½ pound Florida lobster

1 pound shrimp

1 cup mayonnaise

½ cup green bell pepper, minced

¼ cup onion, minced

1 ½ cups celery, finely chopped

½ teaspoon salt

1 tablespoon Worcestershire sauce

1 cup crushed potato chips

Paprika

Chef Clay Conley is at the helm of Azul, located at the Mandarin Oriental Hotel. His diverse cuisine is a blend of Mediterranean flavors with Asian influences. The rising star chef honed his culinary reputation at Todd English's acclaimed Olives restaurant, where he served as executive chef and culinary director.

Take one cup of all-purpose flour, season with salt and pepper, and mix with one cup of semolina flour. Take the other cup of all-purpose flour and season it with salt and pepper. Dredge the oysters in flour, then dip in buttermilk, and then in the semolina mixture. Deep fry oysters until very crispy at 375° F. Spread out the slices of beef and fish, and place a fingernail-sized dollop of mayonnaise in the middle of each slice. Place a fried oyster on each dollop and wrap.

Respectively, the tuna sits on a small dollop of avocado, the crab sits on a small pool of mustard sauce, the beef sits on a small dollop of truffle mash and the salmon sits on a dollop of horseradish cream (see recipe).

Avocado Salad:
Mix all of the ingredients and let sit for a few hours.

Mustard Sauce:
Mix all of the ingredients and let sit a few hours.

SERVES 4

4 large oysters, shucked

4 - 1 x 4 inch slices of smoked salmon

4 - 1 x 4 inch slices raw beef

4 - 1 x 4 inch slices raw tuna

4 - 1 x 4 inch slices king crab leg meat, slightly pressed

1 cup buttermilk

1 cup semolina flour

2 cups all-purpose flour

3 tablespoons mayonnaise

Salt and pepper

AVOCADO SALAD INGREDIENTS

1 avocado

2 tablespoons red onion, minced

1 tablespoon cilantro, chopped

½ jalapeno pepper, minced, with seeds removed

Juice of 1 lime

Salt and pepper

Truffle Mash:

Cook the potato in boiling water. Remove and rice potato. Mix with all of the other ingredients and keep warm until serving.

Horseradish Cream:

Whip the cream until stiff peaks occur. Add horseradish, salt and pepper. Serve immediately.

MUSTARD SAUCE INGREDIENTS

1 cup mayonnaise

2 tablespoons yellow mustard

2 tablespoons Dijon mustard

1 teaspoon Coleman's mustard powder

1 ounce Worcestershire sauce

1 ounce A-1 sauce

2 ounces half and half

1 tablespoon honey

Juice of ½ lemon, freshly squeezed

Salt, pepper and cayenne pepper to taste

TRUFFLE MASH INGREDIENTS

1 potato

4 tablespoons cream

1 tablespoon white truffle oil

2 tablespoons black truffle peelings

1 tablespoon butter

HORSERADISH CREAM INGREDIENTS

8 ounces heavy cream

2 tablespoons horseradish

Salt and pepper

Crab Crusted Sea Bass
EXECUTIVE CHEF ADAM VOTAW, Chispa Restaurant and Bar

Since it opened in 2003 in the heart of Coral Gables, Chispa has remained an acclaimed and innovative fixture on Miami's restaurant scene. Under Executive Chef Adam Votaw, formerly of the acclaimed restaurant at Little Palm Island Resort in the Florida Keys, Chispa, Spanish for "spark," consistently draws accolades for its signature brand of contemporary Latin cuisine, served in an environment as sexy and chic as the city itself.

Preheat an oven to 350° F. First, make the crab cake mix as directed below. Season the sea bass with salt and pepper. On a roasting pan or large sauté pan, top the fish with the crab cake mix and bake for 15-18 minutes. Meanwhile, prepare the saffron, leek and tomato sauce. After about 20 minutes in the oven, the fish should be firm to the touch and the crab mix should be golden. Put a spoonful of the warm sauce onto a plate and place the fish on top. Garnish with chopped basil.

Crab Cake:

Drain both containers of crab meat. In a medium size bowl mix together the mayonnaise, egg, lemon juice, adobo, salt & pepper. Flake the back fin crab meat to make sure there are no shells, and gently do the same to the jumbo lump crab. Add the crab meat to the dressing and lightly fold until half incorporated. Dust the Panko bread crumbs over the mix and continue to fold until evenly mixed.

SERVES 4

4 sea bass fillets

6 ounces crab cake mix (see recipe)

12 ounces saffron, leek and tomato sauce (see recipe)

4 teaspoons basil, chopped

Salt and pepper

CRAB CAKE MIX INGREDIENTS

1 pound jumbo lump crab meat

1 pound back fin crab meat

½ cup mayonnaise

1 egg

1 tablespoon lemon juice

1 tablespoon adobo seasoning (Chispa makes this in house, but a store bought version is fine. Chef Adam suggests "Old Bay" seasoning)

1 teaspoon salt

½ teaspoon pepper

¼ cup parsley, chopped

½ cup Panko bread crumbs

Saffron, Leek and Tomato Sauce:

Lightly sauté leeks and garlic in olive oil. Add the saffron and white wine and continue to cook over medium heat until wine has reduced by three-quarters. Finish with tomatoes, parsley, salt and pepper.

Note: Leeks need to be throughly cleaned before using in any recipe. After chopping, place leeks in a bowl filled with water and separate the leek pieces allowing the bits of dirt to fall to the bottom of the bowl. Scoop out the leeks and dry with a paper towel. Now they are ready to be used.

SAFFRON, LEEK AND TOMATO SAUCE INGREDIENTS

4 cup leeks, julienned, cleaned well

4 teaspoons garlic, minced

1 cup white wine

1 cup tomatoes, chopped

4 tablespoons parsley, chopped

4 pinches saffron

Salt and pepper to taste

Quick & Easy Tilapia Fillet Dinner
CALVIN HUGHES, WPLG-TV LOCAL 10 ANCHOR

SERVES 3-4

1 pound fresh tilapia fillets

½ cup onions, diced

½ cup green peppers, diced

½ cup red peppers, diced

3 tablespoons olive oil

12 stalks of asparagus

1 tomato

Emmy Award-winning newscaster Calvin Hughes arrived in South Florida in November 2006 and serves as the weekday morning and noon news anchor with Kristi Krueger. Hughes comes to Local 10 from the CBS station in Philadelphia. He has also worked in Atlanta, Dallas, Lexington, Kentucky, and Evansville, Indiana, as an anchor and reporter. Hughes has interviewed a wide-ranging number of newsmakers, including President George W. Bush, Dr. Maya Angelou and the late Coretta Scott King.

"My wife and I have a one year old son. Each night, we try to prepare quick but healthy meals. Tilapia fish is one of our favorite dishes. Plus, if prepared at night, after my son goes to sleep, this meal could lead to a very romantic evening. Bon Appétit!"

Preheat an oven to 350° F. Make sure to clean your tilapia fillets before seasoning with your favorite spices. Add the olive oil, onions, red and green peppers and asparagus to a baking dish. With the tilapia on top, place dish in the oven and bake for 15-20 minutes. Make sure you turn the fish at least once to cook both sides to your desired taste.

Finally, cut the tomato into six slices and season with your favorite spices. When fish is cooked to your desired taste, serve on a plate with your sliced seasoned tomatoes.

Salmon & Sea Scallop Rolls
Topped with Basil Sauce and Vegetables
CHEF SEGUNDO MATIENZO, FRANCESCO RESTAURANT

Francesco Restaurant features Peruvian cuisine in the heart of Coral Gables. A taste of Francesco is but the beginning of a love affair with the culture and cuisine of Peru. Francesco specializes in seafood and was awarded the Miami Dade Top Food award and recognized by the Zagat Survey in 2004-2007.

Sprinkle salmon and scallops with salt, pepper and parsley. Roll up each butterflied scallop while enclosing the salmon. Cover the rolls with plastic wrap. Bring a medium saucepan of water to boil over medium heat and add the scallop and salmon rolls. Boil uncovered about 5 minutes. Remove the rolls and unwrap the film from the rolls. Meanwhile, heat the olive oil in a medium sauté pan over medium high heat. Sauté asparagus, carrot and bell pepper. Sprinkle with salt and pepper.

Combine the cream cheese, white wine, heavy cream and the fish fumet in a small saucepan until reduced, cooking for approximately 5 minutes. Finally, add the chopped basil. Cut the rolls in half and remove to a serving plate. Spoon basil sauce over rolls. Garnish with sautéed vegetables and serve.

SERVES 2-3

3 large sea scallops, butterflied
6 ounces fresh salmon, cut in thirds
6 basil leaves
2 jumbo Peruvian asparagus, trimmed
2 thin slices of bell pepper
1 medium carrot, trimmed and sliced
1 tablespoon parsley, finely chopped
1 tablespoon extra virgin olive oil
Salt and pepper

BASIL SAUCE INGREDIENTS

½ cup heavy whipping cream
1 tablespoon cream cheese
½ cup white wine
1 teaspoon basil, finely chopped
1 teaspoon fish fumet
Salt and pepper

Prawns in Cognac Sauce
GARCIA'S SEAFOOD GRILLE & FISH MARKET

Garcia's Seafood Grille & Fish Market, where South Florida's freshest seafood has been served since 1966, is a Miami River lunch-only joint, run by a family of second-generation "fisher-folk."

SERVES 1

8 ounces large prawns with head, cleaned & deveined

2 tablespoons shallots, chopped

1 tablespoon garlic, chopped

1 tablespoon parsley, chopped

1½ tablespoons butter

1 tablespoon olive oil

1 cup of cognac

Juice of ½ lime, freshly squeezed

In a large skillet or sauté pan, sauté the cleaned prawns in hot olive oil over medium high heat. When they are cooked, turn down the heat and add the shallots, garlic, and butter. Once they are browned add the cognac and *flambé* and then add the lime juice and parsley.

Serve with mashed potatoes and sautéed vegetables.

Seared Scallops *with Pineapple and Mango Salsa*
CHEF TUNG NGUYEN, HY VONG VIETNAMESE CUISINE

In 1975, Tung Nguyen fled war torn Vietnam and her journey led her to Kathy Manning whose church was helping to resettle refugees in the United States. The women shared a passion for food and dreamed of one day opening a restaurant to share their culinary gifts. Hy Vong, which means "hope" in Vietnamese, is the culmination of that dream.

Hy Vong pride themselves on using only the freshest ingredients and preparing each dish with the highest level of care and attention. Their fish is brought in by local fisherman daily, their fruits and vegetables are hand-selected and their rice paper is home-made. It is no wonder that Hy Vong has been a Miami favorite for nearly 30 years!

Rinse the scallops and season with salt and pepper. Set aside. Julienne mango and pineapple into 2 inch strips. After cutting, the mango and pineapple will look similar to matchsticks. Mix the pineapple and mango in a bowl and set aside.

Melt the butter in a sauté pan over medium heat. Add the scallops to the butter and brown on one side, approximately 5 minutes. Flip each scallop over and finish browning on the second side for approximately another 5 minutes. When they are finished browning, place the scallops on a plate for serving. Reserve the sauce from the scallops and butter in the pan. Add the garlic to the pan and sauté lightly over low heat. Add the lime or lemon juice to the sauce in the pan. Place the pineapple-mango salsa on top of the scallops and spoon the garlic-lemon butter over the salsa. Cut the cilantro into 2 inch strips and finish garnishing the plate.

SERVES 8

16-24 scallops (scallops should be large, dry-packed & all natural)
2 tablespoons salt
½ tablespoon pepper
4 tablespoons butter
2 tablespoons garlic
2 tablespoons lime or lemon juice
1 cup cilantro, julienned
1 cup pineapple, julienned
1 cup mango, julienned
Dash or two of hot peppers (optional)

151

Sea Bass in Spicy Sauce
OWNER JIMMY CEFALO, Cefalo's Wine Cellar in The Grove

Jimmy Cefalo's family has been making and selling wine for the past fifty years. His great grandfather was a wine maker in Central Italy. His grandfather carried a wine press to the United States at the turn of the century. Cefalo's was created for those who love wine. From the novice to the expert, Cefalo's has developed a unique concept at the historic Taurus site in Coconut Grove, Florida.

SERVES 4

4 sea bass fillets (or other firm white fish
  such as monkfish or grouper)
2 cans (28-ounces) of San Marzano tomatos
  with juice, crushed by hand
10-15 basil leaves, torn
5 tablespoons olive oil
5 garlic cloves, coarsely chopped
3 teaspoons crushed red pepper
1 can flat fillet anchovies
1 cup black olives, coarsely chopped
2 tablespoons capers
1 cup loosely packed Italian parsley, chopped
1 pound orzo or other small pasta cooked al dente
Salt and pepper

In a large saucepan, bring tomatoes to a boil over medium high heat. Lower heat, add basil leaves and simmer for 10-15 minutes. In a large sauté pan, add 3 tablespoons of olive oil. Sauté crushed pepper and garlic until the garlic is golden. Add anchovies and sauté for 2 minutes until they are dissolved. Then add the olives and capers and sauté. Add the chopped parsley and stir. Add the contents of the sauté pan to the tomatoes and simmer for 10 minutes more. Salt and pepper to taste.

Preheat an oven to 350° F. Rinse fish and pat dry. Put fish in a 9 x 13 inch baking dish and drizzle with the remaining 2 tablespoons of the olive oil. Bake for 30 minutes. After 30 minutes, spoon half of the sauce on top of the fish and bake for 15-20 minutes more depending on thickness of the fish. Use the remaining sauce to serve with the orzo. Add a crisp green salad and enjoy.

Snapper Vizcaya

JOEL HOFFMAN, Ph. D., EXECUTIVE DIRECTOR,
VIZCAYA MUSEUM AND GARDENS, RECIPE COURTESY OF GINA DOKKO

Built by agricultural industrialist James Deering in 1916, Vizcaya Museum and Gardens features a main house, ten acres of formal gardens, a hardwood hammock, and soon-to-be-restored historic village. In addition, Vizcaya is a lens through which to learn about art, interior design, architecture, landscape design, horticulture, and the environment, as well as the role of internationalism in the history of the United States and Miami.

Preheat an oven to 450° F. Cut 4 pieces (approximately 12 x 16 inch) of baking parchment paper or heavy duty aluminum foil, then fold each piece in half and open back up. If using foil, use non-stick or brush bottom half lightly with olive oil. If the fish has its skin, score the skin so the fish doesn't curl. Salt and pepper each fillet. Divide the fennel among the 4 packets; add a generous pinch of lemon zest, fish, tomato, thyme, lemon juice, and olive oil to each of the opened squares of paper or foil. If the fish fillets are too big for the packet, cut them in half. If you have a bottle of white wine open, you can add a splash to each packet as well. Fold the squares of paper or foil in half to make a loose packet. Seal the edges by folding them over twice. If using parchment, secure the edges by crimping them. Place on a baking sheet and bake for 20-25 minutes, turning the sheet halfway through to cook evenly. Check to see if the fish is fully cooked by opening one package; the snapper will be opaque when done. Serve the packets closed, allowing diners to open their own at the table. Serve with roasted potatoes and garlic. Cut 4-5 medium Yukon Gold potatoes into chunks about 1¹/2 inch in size. Place on a baking sheet with 10-15 cloves of peeled garlic. Toss this with about 2 tablespoons of olive oil and salt. You can also toss in 6-8 sprigs of thyme. You can roast this with the fish. Put them in 5-8 minutes before the fish and they'll be done about the same time.

SERVES 4

4 red snapper fillets (approximately 6 ounces each, scaled or skinned, smaller ocean perch fillets can be substituted, but you will need more of them)

1-2 medium fennel bulbs, sliced thin (about ⅛ inch slices)

2-3 large tomatoes, sliced in ¼ inch slices, totaling 8 slices

¼ cup freshly squeezed lemon juice (1-2 lemons)

Zest from 1-2 lemons

8-12 sprigs fresh thyme

4 teaspoons olive oil

Salt and pepper to taste

NOTE: *While your guests are waiting, I recommend a light and fresh Golden Dream Martini.*

GOLDEN DREAM MARTINI

Muddle fresh mint sprigs with a smattering of sugar in a small quantity of Chartreuse liqueur (1 part) and white grape juice (2 parts) Mix in vodka and shake, strain, and serve in a martini glass with a sugared rim.

Blackened Tuna Tacos
CHEF LOU CALLAHAN, JAKE'S BAR & GRILL

Jake's Bar and Grill opened its doors in 2001 and has become one of South Miami's top neighborhood hangouts. Unpretentious, eclectic, lively, aesthetically pleasing and palatably sophisticated, Jake's has truly become a "watering hole for grown-ups."

SERVES 4

20 ounces yellowfin (ahi) *tuna*

1 tablespoon olive oil

Cajun blackening spice (use commercial blend or see recipe)

2 ripe Hass avocados

½ pint salsa fresca *(use a jarred salsa or see recipe)*

8 ounce ancho *jam (see recipe)*

¼ head green cabbage, shredded

2 pints baby arugula

¾ pint sour cream

1 pint goat cheese

12 corn tortillas

ANCHO JAM INGREDIENTS

4 ancho chile peppers

1 teaspoon cinnamon

1 tablespoon honey

1 teaspoon ground oregano

1 teaspoon ground thyme

½ teaspoon coriander

2 tablespoons honey

Divide tuna into 4 5- ounce portions. Lightly rub the tuna with the olive oil and coat all over with the Cajun blackening spice. Heat a heavy dry skillet over high heat and quickly sear the tuna on all four sides. Set aside. Take the corn tortillas and warm them up in a warm oven. Spread the *ancho* jam on the warm tortillas. Add slices of avocado, shredded cabbage, arugula, and salsa. Take the tuna and slice it into 5 or 6 pieces per person. Add it to the taco. Top with the goat cheese and sour cream.

Ancho Jam:

Clean and remove all seeds from the *anchos*. Place the peppers and all of the other ingredients in a saucepan. Add water to cover and cook over low to medium heat until the *anchos* are soft. When done, let cool and blend the mixture with an immersion blender or regular blender until smooth.

Blackening Spice:

Combine all the ingredients and store in an airtight container.

Makes ½ cup

Salsa Fresca:

In a medium bowl, combine all of the ingredients together. Mix thoroughly.

Let stand 15 minutes before using.

BLACKENING SPICE INGREDIENTS

2 tablespoons sea salt

1 tablespoon granulated garlic

1 tablespoon onion powder

1 tablespoon dried thyme

1 tablespoon dried oregano

1 tablespoon hot paprika

2 teaspoons black pepper, freshly ground

2 teaspoons white pepper, freshly ground

1 teaspoon sweet paprika

SALSA FRESCA INGREDIENTS

4 ripe tomatoes, chopped

¼ red onion, chopped

1 jalapeño pepper, minced

8 cilantro sprigs, chopped

3 garlic cloves, minced

Juice of 1 lime

¼ cup olive oil

½ teaspoon salt

Ginger Salmon

OWNERS JoANN BASS AND STEPHEN SAWITZ,
JOE'S STONE CRAB

In 1913, Joe Weiss opened up a small lunch counter on Miami Beach. Back then, Miami Beach was just a quiet, backwater town. Folks stopped in to chat and for a top-notch fish sandwich and fries. This, of course, was only the beginning. For 96 years, no visit to Miami has been complete without stopping in at Joe's Stone Crab. From the beginning, it has always been the love of food, family, and friends that has brought in customers and kept them coming.

SERVES 4

4 6 to 8-ounce salmon fillets

2 tablespoons soy sauce

1 teaspoon sake or sherry

Pinch of cayenne pepper

1 teaspoon Tabasco sauce

1 teaspoon Worcestershire sauce

1 tablespoon dry white wine

1 teaspoon lemon juice, freshly squeezed

1 teaspoon fresh ginger, minced

½ teaspoon sugar

2 garlic cloves, minced

Rinse the salmon fillets and pat dry. Remove as many pin bones as possible. Cut two or three shallow slashes in each skin side, without slicing all the way through the fillet. Then make the marinade by combining the soy, sake or sherry, cayenne, Tabasco, Worcestershire, wine, lemon juice, ginger, sugar and garlic in a mixing bowl. Place the salmon, flesh side down, in a shallow nonaluminum dish. Pour in the marinade, cover with plastic wrap, and refrigerate for one to two hours, turning the salmon over once or twice. Preheat a broiler, with a rack about 5 inches from the heat.

Now make the sauce by first melting the butter in a small saucepan over medium heat. Then stir in the brown sugar. Add all of the remaining sauce ingredients and slowly cool until well mixed. Place the salmon in an ovenproof skillet; stir a tablespoon or two of water into the marinade and pour it around the fish. Place the skillet on a stovetop burner over medium heat. Cover the pan and bring to a simmer. Lower the heat and simmer gently for 2 minutes. Spoon the sauce mixture over the salmon; cover and simmer for 2 minutes longer. Now, uncover the pan and place it directly under the broiler. Broil for 2 to 3 minutes, or until the fish is glazed and just firm when touched gently with a fingertip. With a spatula, gently transfer the salmon fillets to warm serving plates. Pour a little of the pan juices over and around the fish and serve hot. Garnish with lime or lemon wedges.

156

Grilling Note:

Alternatively, to grill the salmon, prepare a hot charcoal fire or preheat a gas grill to a medium-high heat. Place the fish on a sheet of aluminum foil that is about 2 inches larger on all sides than the salmon. The aluminum foil should not cover the entire grill; the smoke should be able to come up and around it. You can do it this way, or place 4 individual portions on the foil. Place the foil on the grill. Pour any marinade left in the dish over the salmon. Cover the grill, leaving the vents open. Cook for 5 minutes. Uncover the grill and pour 1/4 cup of the sauce over the salmon. Cover and cook for 5 minutes. Repeat the process, using the remaining sauce. Cook for 2 minutes longer, or until salmon is just cooked through.

SAUCE INGREDIENTS

4 tablespoons unsalted butter

¼ cup brown sugar, packed

2 teaspoons lemon juice, freshly squeezed

2 teaspoons dry white wine

1 large garlic clove, minced

¼ teaspoon Tabasco sauce

⅓ cup onion, minced

Pinch of cayenne pepper

Lemon or lime wedges for garnish

Yellowtail Snapper Papillote
EXECUTIVE CHEF PIETRO ROTA,
La Marea at the Tides

La Marea at the Tides Hotel South Beach features the innovative Mediterranean cuisine of Executive Chef Pietro Rota, a new culinary star to South Florida. His formidable Italian influences are omnipresent; yet his penchant for the clean and basic techniques of the Mediterranean is evident in his carefully crafted menu. His signature dishes and menu selections reflect a simple, straightforward focus on quality and freshness.

SERVES 2

1½ pounds yellowtail snapper fillets

4 tomatoes, diced

4 baby carrots

4 baby fennel

2 garlic cloves

2 tablespoons white wine

2 basil leaves

Salt and pepper to taste

2 tablespoons olive oil

2 sheets of parchment paper

Preheat an oven to 350° F. Slice the fish into 2 fillets. Dice the tomatoes. Brush a sheet of parchment paper with the olive oil. Place one fillet each in the middle of the sheets of parchment paper. Cover the fish with the diced tomatoes, carrots, garlic, and fennel, a pinch of salt and pepper and sprinkle with the white wine. Wrap the fish in the parchment by folding it and secure it by crimping the edges all the way around the "envelope" of parchment paper. Place in the oven and cook for 7 minutes. Remove from the oven and serve the *papillote* on a dinner plate. Allow the diners to open the packets and they will be treated to the delights of the aromatic vegetables and steaming, moist seafood.

Photo Credit: José Molina

Shrimp Stir-Fry with Chinese Noodles
LINDA GASSENHEIMER

Linda Gassenheimer is a syndicated columnist, TV and Radio Personality and Award Winning author. Visit Linda for more recipes and to read her blog at www.DinnerInMinutes.com. Here's a quick and easy recipe from her latest book, The Portion Plan: How to Eat the Foods You Love and Still Lose Weight.

Shrimp Stir-Fry Method:

Heat a wok or skillet over high heat. Spray with vegetable oil spray. Add the onion and snow peas. Stir-fry for 2 minutes and add garlic, ginger and shrimp. Stir-fry 2 minutes more. Mix soy sauce and water together. Add and toss 1 minute. Remove from heat, add sesame oil and toss well.

Chinese Noodles Method:

Bring a large saucepan filled with water to a boil. Add 2 ounces steamed or fresh Chinese noodles. Bring back to a boil and then drain, reserving 1 tablespoon water. Toss noodles with water and sesame oil. Place on plate and serve shrimp stir-fry on top.

Vegetarian Suggestion:

Omit shrimp in stir-fry and substitute 6 ounces firm tofu cut into cubes.

© *The Portion Plan: How to Eat the Foods You Love and Still Lose Weight* by Linda Gassenheimer, DK Publishing. All Rights Reserved.

SERVES 1 (CAN BE DOUBLED OR TRIPLED AS NEEDED)
SHRIMP STIR-FRY INGREDIENTS

Vegetable oil spray

¼ pound trimmed fresh snow peas (about 2 cups)

½ cup onion, sliced

1 medium garlic clove, crushed

1 tablespoon fresh ginger, chopped (or ½ teaspoon ground ginger)

6 ounces shrimp, peeled

2 tablespoons low-sodium soy sauce

1 tablespoon water

2 teaspoons toasted sesame oil (or plain sesame oil)

CHINESE NOODLES INGREDIENTS

2 ounces steamed or fresh Chinese noodles (dried angel hair noodles can be substituted.)

1 teaspoon toasted sesame oil (or sesame oil)

Ginger Salmon
CHEF MARTIN PEREZ, OSTERIA DEL TEATRO

The award-winning Osteria del Teatro Ristorante Arte Deco Italiano, in the stylish South Beach, features succulent seafood, fresh al dente pasta, savory sauces and chewy just-baked bread. Superb Italian wines and stellar desserts complete the dining experience.

Chef Martin Perez has won many awards for his culinary artistry. He explains, "Osteria is a pioneer of fine food and Italian cuisine, and we're perfectionists."

Serves 2

1 piece salmon, 8 to 10-ounces

3 ounces fresh ginger, peeled and cut into julienne

1 tablespoon butter

1 ounce shallots, chopped

2 ounces brandy

3 tablespoons honey

1 cup balsamic vinegar

3 cups clam juice

Salt and pepper

Preheat an oven to 450° F. Bake the salmon in a sauté pan with the clam juice for about 12 minutes. In a separate sauté pan over medium heat, sauté the butter, ginger, and shallots. When the mixture is golden brown, pour in the brandy, slightly tilt the pan and let the mixture ignite. When the alcohol from the brandy is finished burning, add the honey and balsamic vinegar. Let it reduce until it gets a little thick, then add salt and pepper to taste. Place the salmon on a serving plate and pour the reduced sauce over the fish. Serve with salad or vegetables.

Grilled Shrimp Tamale
with Fava Beans, Roasted Poblano Chilies and Teardrop Tomato Vinairette
CHEFS & OWNERS ANDREA CURTO-RANDAZZO
& FRANK RANDAZZO, Talula Restaurant

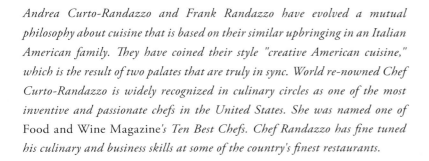

Andrea Curto-Randazzo and Frank Randazzo have evolved a mutual philosophy about cuisine that is based on their similar upbringing in an Italian American family. They have coined their style "creative American cuisine," which is the result of two palates that are truly in sync. World re-nowned Chef Curto-Randazzo is widely recognized in culinary circles as one of the most inventive and passionate chefs in the United States. She was named one of Food and Wine Magazine's *Ten Best Chefs. Chef Randazzo has fine tuned his culinary and business skills at some of the country's finest restaurants.*

To make the sauce, place the shallots, white peppercorns, lemon juice, white wine and bay leaf in a saucepan over medium heat and reduce by three quarters. Whisk in the butter cubes over high heat and emulsify. Strain the mixture through a *chinoise* or fine mesh strainer. Stir in the tomato paste, chopped chives, teardrop tomatoes and fava beans. Season with salt and white pepper. To make the *tamale*, season 12 whole shrimp and place on a charcoal or gas grill on high heat. Cook for 2 minutes on each side. Roughly chop the remaining 8 shrimp and place in a preheated sauté pan with a small amount of butter over medium heat. Add the corn and poblano chiles and sauté until the shrimp begin to cook and turn color. Add the cream and chicken stock, then reduce slightly. Add the *masa harina* and stir over low heat until well cooked, about two minutes. Season well with salt and pepper. Divide the cooked *tamale* into six corn husk "boats" on a serving plate. Garnish with 2 grilled shrimp each and 2 tablespoons of the sauce. Serve immediately.

*Note: A popular tomato cutie, the red teardrop tomato resembles its namesake: a tiny pear. Tender and thin-skinned, the juicy texture is much like that of a vine-ripened tomato. Its addicting flavor is sweet and rich. Also, *masa* is the traditional dough made from sun-dried or fire-dried corn kernels cooked in limewater. *Masa harina* (literally "dough flour") is flour made from dried *masa*.

SERVES 6
TAMALE INGREDIENTS
20 medium shrimp (16/20 size), marinated in chopped garlic and Italian parsley
1 poblano chile, roasted, peeled and diced small
1 cup fresh corn kernels
1 cup masa harina*
¾ cup chicken stock
1½ cups heavy cream
Salt and white pepper
6 corn husks

SAUCE INGREDIENTS
2 shallots, sliced
1 teaspoon white peppercorns
¼ cup lemon juice, freshly squeezed
½ cup white wine
1 bay leaf
1 pound butter, chilled & diced into ½ inch cubes
1 teaspoon tomato paste
2 tablespoons chives, chopped
½ cup teardrop tomatoes or*
large heirloom cherry tomatoes, cut in half
½ cup fava beans, blanched & peeled

161

Hazelnut Encrusted Chilean Sea Bass
With Truffles
EXECUTIVE CHEF TODD DAE KULPER, O ASIAN GRILL

Hidden on the historic Lincoln Road and tucked beyond the Noodle Shop doors is an unforgettable experience unique to South Beach. O Asian Grill & Lounge offers a distinct ambience and menu that caters to upscale, chic crowds. Our unparalleled menu created by prodigy chef, Todd Dae Kulper, boasts modern Japanese cooking fused with a European flair. "The goal to a successful dish is not how much you can add to it but how well you let the ingredients speak for themselves."- Todd Dae Kulper, Executive Chef

SERVES 4

4 fillets of Chilean sea bass (7-ounces each)

½ cup Ennis hazelnuts

1 tablespoon salt

1 tablespoon white pepper

1 tablespoon turbinado sugar or unrefined raw sugar

2 sprigs parsley

2 sprigs thyme

2 sprigs chives

1 teaspoon white truffle oil

1 fresh truffle

12 stalks asparagus

12 Shishito peppers

12 cherry tomatoes

½ cup tempura flour

2 ounces ice cubes

⅓ cup water

Vegetable oil for frying

1 clove garlic

1 small knob of ginger, peeled

⅓ cup soy sauce

1 cup sugar

Preheat an oven to 450° F. In a deep skillet, heat the vegetable oil to 350° F. Clean the *Shishito* peppers by running them under cold water and removing all of the dirt. Drain on paper towels until dry and then set aside in the refrigerator. Do the same with the cherry tomatoes, but once dry, skewer them with the skewers and set aside in the refrigerator. Clean the truffle by lightly brushing it with a clean cloth or toothbrush, taking care not to scratch the truffle but removing all of the particles of dirt logged within the creases. Wrap the cleaned truffle in a lightly dampened paper towel and set aside in the refrigerator. Wash the parsley and chives under cold water and set aside to dry. Remove all of the small leaves from the thyme by stripping the leaves with your fingers from the top of the sprig moving towards the bottom. Remove any larger stems and lightly chop the leaves. Finely chop the parsley and chives and add to the thyme. Place the herbs between dry paper towels and set aside in the refrigerator until needed. Blanch the asparagus by placing the asparagus in boiling salted water for 15 seconds and then plunge into ice water to stop the cooking. Drain and set aside in the refrigerator until ready to use. Toast the hazelnuts by placing in a stainless steel sauté pan and warming over medium to medium-high heat until the aroma is released and the hazelnuts have a lightly toasted color. Take care not to over toast or burn. Set them aside at room temperature until cool. Once cooled, place into a food processor and crush until there is approximately 2/3 finely ground

hazelnuts to 1/3 coarsely ground hazelnuts. Remove and place into a bowl and then add the reserved herbs with the salt, pepper, turbinado sugar, and herbs. Set out at room temperature until ready to use.

For the sauce, place the soy sauce and sugar into a saucepan and gently heat. The sugar should lightly thicken the sauce, but if not, add more sugar slowly until thickened but not syrupy. The sugar will also eliminate the saltiness from the soy sauce so if the soy sauce is still salty, add more sugar. Once the sugar and soy sauce mixture is lightly thickened and sweet, finely grate the garlic and ginger and add to the sauce. Set aside until ready to use. Mix the *tempura* batter by adding the water to the ice cubes then pouring the mixture into a bowl with the *tempura* flour. Mix until a smooth, velvety texture is achieved. Refrigerate until ready to use. Heat a nonstick sauté pan and a stainless steel pan over medium high heat. For the fish, press the top of the fish into the reserved hazelnut mixture, only coating one side. Place crust side down into the hot nonstick sauté pan and lightly brown so that the crust adheres to the fish. Flip the fish over and place into the oven for about 15 minutes or until just cooked. Remove and set aside to rest. In the other stainless steel pan, add the olive oil, butter, and asparagus. Season with salt and pepper. Finish with just a little truffle oil. Lightly batter the tomato skewer in the *tempura* batter and lightly fry until the batter becomes very crisp, about 1 minute. Lightly fry the *Shishito* peppers in the oil until cooked, about 10 seconds. Place the warm sweet ginger, garlic and soy sauce on the bottom of a serving plate. Place the warm truffled asparagus over the sauce, reserving the remaining truffle and butter sauce. Place the warm sea bass over the asparagus, crust side up, and pour a little of the truffle and butter sauce over the fish. Garnish with the *Shishito* peppers and tomato *tempura* skewer. Using a truffle shaver, thinly shave about 5 or 6 truffle slices over the sea bass and garnish the truffles with a nice grey sea or Malden salt.

INGREDIENTS CONTINUED

1 teaspoon butter
1 teaspoon olive oil
Vegetable oil for deep frying
Grey sea or Malden salt to garnish
4 Teppo Kushi *skewers, 3½ inches*

Red Snapper a la Veracruzana
OWNERS EDDIE & LETICIA BERRONES,
POBLANO COCINA MEXICANA

SERVES 6

3½ pounds whole red tomatoes

1 pound yellow onion, quartered

2 ounces garlic, peeled

Plus: 3½ pounds whole red tomatoes

1 pound yellow onion, quartered

1 cup water

Plus: 1 pound tomatoes, diced and seeded

8 ounces olive oil

4 bay leaves

1½ pounds onions, sliced

1 ounce garlic, finely chopped

12 ounces red bell peppers, seeded and sliced

12 ounces green bell peppers, seeded and sliced

10 ounces yellow bell peppers, seeded and sliced

1 cup dry white wine

4 ounces green olives

3 ounces capers

4 sprigs of fresh thyme

Salt and pepper

Fresh thyme for garnish

Whole pickled banana peppers for garnish

6 8-ounce skinless red snapper fillets

Fresh lime juice

Poblano Cocina Mexicana is an authentic Mexican restaurant mixing traditional Mexican cuisine with a gourmet flair. Every dish at Poblano Cocina Mexicana is prepared from scratch using only the freshest ingredients, including traditional sauces such as mole, adobo, *and* chile poblano. *The menu offers a wide variety of poultry, seafood, and beef dishes to please any palate, as well as homemade drinks such as* Limonada *and an impressive collection of traditional Mexican beer.*

Sprinkle the red snapper fillets with fresh squeezed lime juice and season with salt and pepper. Cover and refrigerate. Coat the bottom of a cast iron skillet with a little bit of oil and grill the 3 1/2 pounds of tomatoes, onion, and garlic until they have a charred exterior, then set aside. In a large saucepan, bring the remaining whole tomatoes, onion, and water to a boil, then set aside as well. Blend both the roasted and boiled ingredients in a food processor until well incorporated. You can add the boiled water if the sauce is too pasty. Strain the mixture to remove any seeds, then set aside. Heat a large skillet on medium heat and add olive oil. Add the bay leaves and sliced onions and cook until translucent. Add the bell peppers and chopped garlic and continue to cook until soft. Add the diced tomatoes and continue to cook for about 3 more minutes. Add the white wine, fresh thyme, olives, capers, and continue to cook over low heat for approximately 5 minutes. Add the tomato sauce to the mixture and bring to a boil. Cover and cook over low heat for approximately 8 minutes more. Season with salt and pepper and remove from the heat.

Coat the bottom of a large skillet with olive oil and place over medium high heat. Add the snapper fillets to the hot skillet, and quickly brown both sides until cooked through. Remove the fillets from pan and top with the *Veracruzana* sauce. Garnish with banana peppers and fresh thyme, then serve.

Fire Roasted Oysters on the Grill
With Sofrito, Chorizo and Queso Manchego
CHEF & OWNER DAVID BRACHA, THE RIVER OYSTER BAR

Since The River Oyster Bar's opening in 2003, Chef David Bracha has followed his passion and vision, pioneering a source of innovative, pleasing cuisine in an urbane, upscale-casual locale. As a result, The River Oyster Bar is a well orchestrated, unpretentious dining experience that never misses being "just right." Arriving daily from around the country, oysters are served raw with an assortment of exciting and pleasantly unpredictable sauces. They can also be enjoyed in an array of prepared dishes that impart a creative take on traditional favorites.

Remove the seeds and ribs from the *ancho* chile pepper. Place the heavy cream and *ancho* chile in a small saucepan over low to medium heat. Shuck the oysters, leave the meat on one side of the shell and refrigerate. Discard the other side of the oyster shell, take the natural juice from the oyster and add it to the *ancho* chile and cream mixture. Bring to a simmer and reduce by half.

To prepare the *sofrito* butter: remove the butter from the refrigerator for a half hour. In a food processor mix together the *poblano* and red peppers, onion, thyme, cilantro, garlic, tomatoes, hot paprika, black pepper and cumin. Blend the mixture until it is very finely chopped. If a food processor is not available, hand chop all of the ingredients very finely. Add the butter to the vegetable mixture and blend well. Place the butter in the refrigerator for 20 minutes until it becomes firm.

Peel and slice the *chorizo* very thinly. Remove the oysters from the refrigerator, drizzle a touch of reduced *ancho* cream on each oyster along with a dollop of *sofrito* butter, a slice of *chorizo*, and a bit of shredded *Manchego* cheese. Place on a charcoal grill for five minutes or till the *sofrito* butter begins to simmer and the cheese is melting. Serve immediately. *Bon Appetit!*

SERVES 5

10 each medium to large oysters, preferably a west coast oyster like Fanny Bay *or* Hama Hama, *although a fresh* Apalachicola *oyster will work just fine*

1 cup heavy cream

1 ancho *chile pepper*

½ poblano *chile pepper*

½ red bell pepper

¼ Spanish onion

3 sprigs fresh thyme, leaves stripped from the branches

6 sprigs fresh cilantro, leaves cut from the stems

2 garlic cloves

2 teaspoons cumin, ground

1 teaspoon hot paprika

2 teaspoons black pepper

2 Roma tomatoes, seeded

½ pound sofrito *butter*

2 links good quality Spanish chorizo

1 cup Manchego *cheese, shredded*

SERVES 4

6-8 red snapper fillets, approximately 2 pounds

1½ cups Gold Medal Wondra Instantized Flour

3 eggs, beaten

2 cups Panko breadcrumbs

Salt and pepper

Dr. Burke is a heart surgeon, software developer, author, and founder of The Congenital Heart Institute at Miami Children's Hospital in Miami, Florida and Arnold Palmer Hospital, in Orlando, Florida. He graduated Phi Beta Kappa from Stanford University, and then received his medical degree from Harvard. As an attending at Boston Children's Hospital, he performed the first pediatric Heart Lung Transplant in New England in 1992.

Dr. Burke has pioneered new surgical techniques, published over 60 articles in peer-reviewed medical journals, and lectures worldwide. Dr. Burke and his team have repaired thousands of children with complex heart defects. The Congenital Heart Institute's goal is to reach an unprecedented 100% survival rate in the treatment of children with congenital heart disease through the continued advancement of surgical and interventional catheterization skills, procedures and tools. These new advancements will not only minimize the significant cumulative therapeutic trauma these children undergo during the course of their lifetimes while undergoing the treatment for their respective conditions, but also improve the quality of life for these children and their families.

Get a fishing pole, preferably an Ugly Stick™ with a light tackle rig and a number 10 circle hook. Get some live shrimp for bait. I like Gordon's Bait Shop on 27th, they're excellent. Take your kids fishing, make them bait their own hooks, teach them that patience is a virtue and catch some legal snappers. Put the snappers on ice and high tail it for home while they're still fresh. Tell your wife you're cooking dinner and commandeer the entire kitchen counter. Get a dangerously sharp commando knife and fillet the snappers.

Cut the fillets into chunks the size of large ice cubes. Spread wax paper over the entire counter and line up the snapper chunks at one end, we'll be using the assembly line technique here. It's important to mess up as large an area as possible.

Take a large EZ lock plastic bag and fill the bottom quarter with Gold Medal Wondra Instantized Flour. Don't let your wife tell you that any flour will work. It has to be Wondra, and it has to come in the cardboard tube, not a paper bag. Put some peanut oil in a sauce pan and start heating it up, but don't burn it. To test the temperature and amuse your self, fling water on the oil until it snaps but doesn't explode all over the wall. Add some salt and pepper to the Wondra in the EZ lock bag. Drink some beer and yell at everyone to get out of your kitchen. Suggest to your wife that she prepare some vegetables, salad, drinks, and dessert to go with the dinner you are preparing. Ignore her smirking.

Dry off the snapper chunks using the paper towels, then put them in the EZ lock with the Wondra and roll them around in the flour until they are lightly dusted. On an open area of your counter pour out a huge pyramid shaped pile of *Panko* flakes. Violently crack three eggs in a bowl and mix them with a fork. Dip the flour dusted snapper chunks in the eggs, and then roll them in the *Panko* pyramid.

Drop the breaded snapper chunks into the peanut oil and turn them occasionally until they are golden brown. Pluck them out and put them in a basket with paper towels to suck up the oil. Triumphantly carry the *Panko* crusted snapper to the table and enjoy the cheers of your adoring family.

Printed with permission from Captain Dan Gauthier

Gnocchi with Rock Shrimp, Peas & Pancetta
CHEF & OWNER TIM ANDRIOLA, Timō Restaurant & Bar

SERVES 4

2 whole potatoes

2 egg yolks

2 tablespoons Parmesan cheese, grated

1 tablespoon salt

1 cup flour

3 tablespoons olive oil

2-3 cloves garlic

8 whole plum tomatoes

Splash of water

3-4 basil leaves

2 ounces pancetta, *diced*

4 ounces rock shrimp

2 ounces fresh shucked peas (blanched in salted water)

1 tablespoon basil, chopped

Salt and pepper to taste

Inspired food, carefully selected wine, attentive service, and beautiful decor combine to create a memorable dining experience at Timō. The emphasis is on freshness and purity of ingredients. Timō seeks to capture the highest level of flavors, highlighting the importance of its relationship with suppliers, from farmers to fishermen.

Chef Tim Andriola is a veteran of top restaurants. When it came to opening his own restaurant, he looked no further than his own backyard in Sunny Isles. While Timō may be slightly off the beaten path, his cooking always draws a packed house.

For the gnocchi, boil the potatoes in salted water with the skin on. Cook until fork tender. Drain, peel and pass through a food mill. Let cool. In a mixing bowl, add the egg yolks, Parmesan cheese and salt to the potatoes. Slowly fold in the flour until the dough is not sticky to the touch. Roll into 1 inch diameter logs and cut into 1/2 inch pieces. Boil in salted water until cooked (only a few minutes) and set aside.

For the tomato sauce, slowly heat 2 tablespoons of the olive oil and the garlic in a sauté pan over moderate heat, until the garlic starts to brown. Add the chopped tomatoes and the splash of water. Simmer over low heat for 15-20 minutes. Add 3 or 4 basil leaves and pass the sauce through a food mill. Season with salt and pepper. In a sauté pan over moderate heat, add 1 tablespoon of olive oil. Add the diced *pancetta* and render slightly. Add the tomato sauce to the pan. Bring to a simmer. Add the rock shrimp, the cooked gnocchi, basil, and blanched peas. Let simmer until the shrimp are cooked through. Adjust seasoning and serve.

Seafood Risotto
OWNER MAURIZIO FARINELLI, TRATTORIA SOLE

At this beloved Italian eatery, you'll be treated to fantastic Northern Italian cuisine whipped up with style. The kitchen wows regular customers with skilled preparations of Veal Marsala, *seafood fettuccine, and tender cannelloni. Even better, the pastas hold center stage. They're made from scratch everyday and cooked to perfection.*

In a large casserole, heat all of the fish broth, except for ¹/₂ cup, over medium heat. In a medium casserole heat 2 tablespoons of olive oil and one tablespoon of butter until it melts, being careful not to burn the butter. Add the onion and cook until the onions are translucent. Add the rice and mix for two minutes. Add one cup of white wine and stir, allowing it to evaporate over medium heat. Once the wine has evaporated, add 8 cups of fish broth and saffron and allow it to cook over medium heat for 10 minutes. While the rice is cooking, in a another large casserole, heat 2 to 3 tablespoons of olive oil and finely chopped garlic. Add the mussels and clams, mixing it well for 2 to 3 minutes. Add the remaining ¹/₂ cup of fish broth and 2 tablespoons of parsley and cook covered until the mussels and clams have opened. Lower the heat, being careful to keep the casserole warm. At this point, the rice should be ready. Mix the rice mixture well, being careful not to dry the rice. Add more liquid, if necessary. Add the remaining seafood and butter to the rice, leaving aside the mussels and clams and mix continuously, until the rice is creamy and *al dente*. Serve on a large dinner plate, adding the mussels, clams, and parsley.

SERVES 4

½ cup olive oil

3 cups Arborio or Camaroli rice

1 tablespoon butter

1 garlic clove

8 cups fish broth, ½ cup reserved

1½ cup white wine

½ cup fresh parsley, finely chopped

1 tablespoon onion, finely chopped

16 large shrimp, peeled and deveined

10 ounces calamari, cut into rings

16 mussels

16 clams

1 envelope or several threads saffron

Salt and pepper to taste

Linguini Malafemmina
CHEF GIUSEPPE ZUOCO, ANACAPRI ON PONCE

SERVES 4

2 pounds linguini pasta

1 dozen fresh small clams

4 (3 or 4-ounce) lobster tails

1 pound jumbo shrimp, clean and deveined

8 mussels, washed and scrubbed under cool running water

9 garlic cloves, sliced

¼ cup olive oil

1 cup bottled clam juice

½ cup dry white wine

Pinch of dry oregano

¼ teaspoon crushed red pepper

¼ cup Italian parsley, chopped

2 tablespoon seasoned breadcrumbs (see recipe below)

Salt to taste

ANACAPRI ORIGINAL BREADCRUMBS INGREDIENTS

3 cups plain breadcrumbs made from stale Italian bread

1 tablespoon garlic, minced

¼ cup Parmigiano *cheese, grated*

¼ cup Pecorino Romano *cheese, grated*

¼ cup Parmigiano-Reggiano *cheese, grated*

1 tablespoon fresh Italian parsley, chopped

¼ cup olive oil

1 tablespoon dry oregano

1 teaspoon paprika (not spicy)

Salt and pepper to taste

Even as modern, fusion cuisine and other more exotic dining options gain popularity, there will always be a place for traditional Italian-American restaurants like Anacapri. The menu is not anything fancy, but it is full of the kind of unforgettable, simple dishes that keep regulars coming back. The vivid red tomato sauce ensures that everything from the lasagna to the manicotti and the Veal Parmesan is full of flavor, and most dishes are topped with a generous portion of melted cheese. Fresh salads and a nice red wine list enhance the meal. Pasta with clams is very popular in Naples.

Heat the oil in a large saucepan over medium-high heat and sauté the garlic until it turns a light golden color. Add the clams, along with the wine and clam juice. Along with the clams, add the lobster tails, shrimp and mussels. Add the oregano, parsley, seasoned breadcrumbs, crushed red pepper and salt to taste. Cook until the wine evaporates and then cover the pan to steam the seafood. Check the clams and mussels often; when the shells are open, about 5 minutes, turn off the heat. Discard any unopened clams or mussels.

Meanwhile, in a large deep saucepan, cook the linguini, in boiling salted water until *al dente*, and drain. Return drained pasta to the pot over medium heat, and stir in the sauce. Toss together for a minute. Remove from heat and serve immediately in a large bowl. Enjoy!

Anacapri Original Breadcrumbs:

In a large salad bowl, mix all the dry ingredients. Add the olive oil into the mixture in a slow, steady stream. Work the mixture with the palms of your hands until you reach the desired texture. Keep covered and refrigerate until ready to use. Makes 1 quart

Fish Cakes with Tomato Sauce
JOHN MARTIN'S IRISH PUB & RESTAURANT

Long before the Chinese invented fireworks, many centuries before the discovery of the number "zero," long before their primitive British cousins were mysteriously erecting Stonehenge, the Irish were already world champs at the fine art of merrymaking. John Martin's is a stunning Gaelic food-fest of fine cuisine served and presented with incomparable Irish charm.

To make the tomato sauce, melt the margarine in a heavy saucepan over medium heat, add the bacon, onion, carrot, celery, bay leaves and thyme. Sauté until lightly browned. Add the flour and tomato paste and continue to cook for 5 minutes on a low heat. Then allow to cool slightly. Add the stock in stages, stirring constantly. Add the garlic and salt and pepper and cook slowly for 1 hour. Pass through a sieve before serving.

For the fish cakes, take a mixing bowl and combine the fish, potatoes, egg, green onions, tarragon, and salt and pepper. Divide into 4 equal portions and mold into rounded balls. Coat the balls with flour, dip in beaten egg, and roll in bread crumbs. Flatten the balls and shape into four cakes. In a skillet over medium high heat, add the vegetable oil and shallow fry the cakes in hot oil for 2 minutes per side until golden brown. Garnish with parsley and lemon and serve with the tomato sauce.

Reprinted with permission from *A Taste of the Market: A collection of recipes from Farmers Market at Merrick Park*, Coral Gables, Florida (January 1998)

SERVES 4

Cooked fish, such as cod or salmon, skin and bones removed, enough for 4 portions
8 ounces potatoes, mashed
1 egg
Salt & pepper to taste
1 green onion, chopped
2 tarragon branches, chopped
Parsley and lemon slices for garnish

BREADING INGREDIENTS

1 egg
2 ounces bread crumbs
1 ounce flour
Vegetable oil for frying

TOMATO SAUCE INGREDIENTS

1 ounces margarine
2 strips bacon, chopped
1 onion, chopped
1 carrot, chopped
2 stalks celery, chopped
2 bay and 2 thyme leaves
½ ounce flour
1 ounce tomato paste
½ quart vegetable stock
½ clove garlic, chopped
Salt & pepper to taste

MAIN DISHES
VEGETARIAN

FAIRCHILD TROPICAL GARDEN Photo Credit: Alina Balean

Pumpkin & Mascarpone Tortelloni
CHEF PAULA PIRICHINSKY, Balans Miami

SERVES 6

FRESH PASTA INGREDIENTS

3 ½ cups all-purpose flour plus extra for kneading

4 extra large eggs

½ teaspoon extra virgin olive oil

FILLING INGREDIENTS

1 large butternut squash (about 1½ pounds)

½ pound mascarpone cheese

1 ½ teaspoon salt

½ teaspoon pepper

1 teaspoon fresh thyme, chopped

2 tablespoons extra virgin olive oil

SAUCE INGREDIENTS

12 tablespoons butter

1 tablespoon garlic, minced

2 ½ cups heavy cream

2 pints cherry tomatoes, cut in halves

1 tablespoon fresh thyme

Salt and pepper to taste

Parmigiano-Reggiano cheese, grated for garnish

Balans Miami is located on Lincoln Road in South Beach and is set among the breezy palms of the historic Art Deco district. It is a groovy London import featuring "fresh and creative, light fare." Chef Paula, an Argentine native, sharpened her skills at some of the top restaurants on Plaza San Martín in Buenos Aires. As the Plaza's Florida Street is the most important pedestrian street in Buenos Aires, Pirichinsky, can find herself "at home" on Lincoln Road.

Mound 3 ½ cups of the flour in the center of a cutting board. Make a well in the middle of the flour and add the eggs and the olive oil, then begin to incorporate the flour, starting with the center of the well. The dough will come together when half of the flour has been incorporated. Start kneading the dough with the heels of your hands. When well-formed, remove it from the board and scrape and discard any leftovers bits. Re-flour the board and continue kneading for 6 minutes. The dough should be elastic and a little sticky. Wrap the dough in plastic and allow it to rest for 30 minutes at room temperature. Roll out the pasta using the thinnest setting on your pasta machine. Cut it into 4-inch circles and reserve. Preheat the oven to 350° F. Cut the squash in half, remove the seeds, drizzle with the olive oil and place on a baking sheet. Roast for 30 minutes or until the squash is very soft. Remove from the oven, let cool, then scoop out the flesh from the skin. In a large bowl combine squash, cheese, salt, pepper, and thyme. Stir well to combine. Place the circles of dough on a surface that has been lightly floured. Put 1 tablespoon of the filling in the center of each circle. Fold in half to form a half moon shape, pressing firmly to seal, then bring the two corners together in a ring and join the corners with firm finger pressure. Bring 6 quarts of salted water to a boil. Drop the tortelloni in the water and cook for 5 minutes or until tender. Drain the tortelloni. Meanwhile in a sauté pan, heat the butter over medium heat, add garlic, tomatoes and thyme and cook for 3 to 5 minutes, then add heavy cream and continue cooking for another 5 minutes. Add the tortelloni and toss very gently for 1 minute. Serve with Parmigiano-Reggiano grated on top.

Shai Vegetable Curry
HOUSE OF INDIA

"Indian food is as diverse as many ethnic and cultural groups in India. A typical Indian meal consists of starch, lentils or beans, and vegetable. At House of India, you can taste the best variety of Indian culinary creations with friends, since Indian food is designed to be eaten in groups." Voted Best Indian Restaurant ~ Miami Sun Post

Sauté the diced onion in oil in a large sauté pan or Dutch oven until lightly browned, then add the garlic and ginger and sauté with the onion. Add the bay leaves, cloves, cardamom seeds, and cinnamon sticks and combine well. Then add the salt, cumin, turmeric, coriander, and chili powder. Add the tomatoes and simmer until well blended. Add the potatoes and carrots and cook half-way, then add the remaining vegetables and simmer until done. Add a little water if the mixture becomes too dry.

Reprinted with permission from *A Taste of the Market: A collection of recipes from Farmers Market at Merrick Park*, Coral Gables, Florida (January 1998)

SERVES 4

1 cup cauliflower, cut into small pieces
1 cup eggplant, cut into small pieces
1 cup potato, cut into small pieces
1 cup green peas
1 cup chickpeas
1 teaspoon salt
1 teaspoon cumin powder
1 teaspoon turmeric
1 teaspoon coriander powder
1 teaspoon chili powder
2 bay leaves
2 or 3 cloves
2 cardamom seeds
2 cinnamon sticks
Vegetable oil
1 onion, diced
4 tomatoes, diced (or 1 small can of tomato paste)
1 inch piece of fresh ginger, sliced
4 or 5 garlic cloves, chopped

SERVES 4

GNOCCHI INGREDIENTS

3 large Yukon Gold potatoes

2 egg yolks, separated

¾ cup all-purpose flour, as needed

Salt and freshly ground black pepper

PESTO INGREDIENTS

1 bunch fresh mint

Extra virgin olive oil, as needed

2 garlic cloves, roasted

1 tablespoon capers

½ bunch fresh basil

Salt and pepper

¼ cup toasted walnuts

½ cup Parmesan cheese, grated

Sweet spring peas (you can substitute with frozen,
  if necessary)

Parmesan cheese, shaved from a block

The City Cellar Wine Bar and Grill was located in Coral Gables and is now located at City Place in downtown West Palm Beach where it overlooks the beautiful fountains in the courtyard. The City Cellar has a large and lavish dining room with high ceilings and a phenomenal view of the refrigerated wine cellar behind the bar that extends from floor to ceiling. Adjacent to the open kitchen in the rear is a brick oven. The City Cellar offers a menu with varying flavors and textures. Every entree is always beautifully presented and put together in a visual sense using the freshest of ingredients.

Boil the Yukon Gold potatoes with skin on until tender, but do not overcook. Remove from the water, let cool slightly and then peel the skins with a pairing knife or peeler. Put the potatoes through a ricer or a *chinoise*, or grate on the finest grating surface of a box grater.

Make a circle with the strained potato on a flat working surface and make a small well in the center. To this well add the beaten egg yolks; sprinkle half of the flour on top of potatoes and season with salt and pepper (Two teaspoons salt and one teaspoon pepper to start.). Bring the mixture together with your hands as you would when making dough for fresh pasta, taste for seasoning, adjusting the consistency with the reserved flour. Once the egg yolks are mixed in, bring the dough together, kneading gently until a ball is formed. Knead this gently for another few minutes until the ball is dry to touch. The dough should be able to be rolled without falling apart nor should it be too wet to be rolled. Roll the dough into several long "dowels" 1½ inches thick, then cut into 1 inch pieces, mark on the back with a fork and place on a floured sheet pan in the freezer.

Pesto:

For the pesto, combine all of the ingredients, except for the fresh peas in a blender or food processor and purée. Season to taste and adjust consistency, adding oil to your preference.

Boil the gnocchi in a pot of salted water until they float to the top. When they come to the surface, remove, strain and place in a large bowl or sauce pan. Add the pesto, fresh peas and shaved Parmesan. You need to use a peeler in order to shave off strips of the Parmesan. Mix the gnocchi and pesto together gently with a spoon, serve with a little Parmesan on top and a basil and mint leaf.

Harry and Susie Horgan's Shake-A-Leg Miami helps children and adults with physical, developmental, and economic challenges, liberating them from the realm of imagination into the realm of experience. It has successfully created an inspirational haven where people of all backgrounds and abilities find common ground. Susie Horgan is one of the first great photographers to grow out of and document the early punk scene in Washington D.C. in the early 80's. She now captures the literary scene in Miami with her personal and intimate photography.

SERVES 4

¼ cup olive oil

1 large sweet onion, diced

2 cloves garlic, chopped

2 cups crimini or small portabello mushrooms, sliced

2 cups firm tofu, cubed (herb flavored is best)

1 pound thin asparagus, chopped

½ cup dried cranberries

1½ cups brown rice

Salt and pepper

In a medium saucepan, prepare the brown rice. When the rice is almost done, take a large sauté pan, add the olive oil and sauté the large white sweet onion over medium heat until translucent. Add the chopped garlic and sliced crimini or portabello mushrooms. Cook until tender and then add the firm tofu. Cook over medium heat, stirring occasionally for 10 minutes. Then add the chopped asparagus and dried cranberries. Sauté together and stir occasionally until the asparagus slightly soften. Add salt and pepper to taste. To serve, place rice on a serving platter and top with the sauté mix. "Enjoy... the taste is so good you'll Shake-A-Leg!"

Stuffed Acorn Squash
LAURINDA SPEAR, FAIA, FOUNDING PRINCIPAL OF ARQUITECTONICA

As a founding principal of Arquitectonica, the architecture and interior design firm, Laurinda Spear has been a leading force in the design direction for many of the firm's landmark buildings and award-winning interiors. Ms. Spear also started the landscape architecture practice, ArquitectonicaGEO, focused on environmentally sensitive design. The firm explores the challenges of contemporary built and natural environments while developing design solutions with a modern aesthetic. In addition to many building, landscape, and interior designs, Laurinda Spear also designs products for highly regarded manufacturers including furniture, fashion accessories, objects for the home and office. Ms. Spear's designs have won countless awards and her work has been exhibited in numerous prominent museums.

Preheat an oven to 350° F. Cut the acorn squash into three to four rings and place the rings in a shallow baking pan with ¼ inch water for braising. Bake for 15-20 minutes or until tender. To prepare the stuffing while the squash is baking, sauté the onions, garlic, tomatoes and *seitan* in a sauté pan over medium high heat. Add 1 tablespoon of organic peanut butter to the cooked ingredients. Stuff the baked squash rings with the cooked mixture. Return the squash to the oven and heat the stuffed rings for a few additional minutes and serve. *Bon Appetit!*

SERVES 4

1 medium acorn squash
Salt and pepper to taste
¼ cup onions, chopped
1 teaspoon garlic, minced
1 box of seitan (a vegetarian meat substitute made from wheat gluten), cut into cubes
½ cup tomatoes, chopped
2 tablespoons coconut oil
1-2 tablespoons of organic peanut butter
Distilled water

MAIN DISHES
BREAKFAST

SOUTH BEACH Photo Credit: Miami Beach Chamber of Commerce

Guava Muffins

NORIS LEDESMA, Curator of Tropical Fruit at Fairchild Tropical Botanic Garden

Serves 12

2 cups all-purpose flour

3 tablespoons granulated sugar

½ teaspoon salt

¾ teaspoon cinnamon

1 tablespoon baking powder

2 large eggs, beaten

1 cup milk or buttermilk

4 tablespoons butter, melted

½ cup guava pulp, mashed

Guava is native to tropical America, but has been dispersed throughout all the equatorial regions. It is grown in subtropical Florida and California and the tree is a hearty one, producing large quantities of fruit each season. Guavas come in different shapes, sizes and colors, but generally they are oval and about two inches in diameter. The skin color of guava ranges from light yellow to dark purple. The flesh can be pink, white or red and the seeds are edible, although you may prefer to remove them. You can bite right into a ripe guava, which has a sweet yet delicate flavor. It is made into all sorts of food products from juice to jelly. Whole guavas are also canned and can be used to make pies, punch and ice cream. Guava is rich in Vitamin A and C, and high in fiber and antioxidants.

Preheat an oven to 400° F. Sift together the flour, sugar, salt, cinnamon and baking powder into a large mixing bowl and set aside. In a medium mixing bowl combine the eggs, milk, melted butter and guava pulp. Pour the wet mixture over the dry ingredients and mix until just blended together. Grease 12 regular size muffin cups and fill cups 2/3 full with the batter. Sprinkle the muffins with additional cinnamon and sugar. Bake the muffins for 20 minutes or until a cake tester or toothpick comes out clean. Cool 5 minutes on a wire rack before removing muffins from cups.

Palacsinta Teszta Pancakes

RENE MURAI, ESQ., FORMER CHAIRMAN,
BOARD OF DIRECTORS AT MIAMI CHILDREN'S HOSPITAL

Rene Murai was Chairman of the Board at Miami Children's Hospital from 2004 to 2008. He was also a member of the Board of Directors from 2000 to 2004. Currently, he is an attorney and a member of the firm of Murai, Wald, Biondo, Moreno, Brochin, P.A. in Coral Gables.

Beat together the milk, egg yolks, sugar, and flour in a mixing bowl until well blended. Beat the egg whites, until stiff but not dry, and fold them carefully into the batter.

Heat a heavy 8-inch skillet over medium heat and coat lightly with butter. Ladle about 1/3 cup of the batter into the hot pan while tilting the pan to distribute the batter evenly. If the batter is too thick to spread easily, stir in a small quantity of extra milk. Cook until lightly browned on the bottom; flip and brown the other side. The thinner the pancakes are, the better they taste. Continue making pancakes until all the batter is exhausted. Set the pancakes on a clean tea towel, or a wooden board. Spread with the apricot preserves, sprinkle with the sliced almonds and roll up into a "tube." Place the rolled pancakes in a buttered baking dish.

Preheat an oven to 325° F. Spoon the sour cream over the rolled pancakes and sprinkle with remaining almonds. Bake 10-15 minutes or until heated through. Serve sprinkled with confectioners' sugar, if desired.

YIELDS 12-15 PANCAKES

2 cups milk (approximately)
4 eggs, separated
1 tablespoon sugar
2 cups all-purpose flour
Softened butter
1 12-ounce jar apricot preserves
1½ cups sliced almonds
2 cups sour cream
Confectioners' (powdered) sugar (optional)

Serves 8

1 loaf challah *bread, whole, not sliced*

1 quart heavy cream

1 quart half-and-half

6 egg yolks

8 whole eggs

18 ounces sugar

1 teaspoon vanilla extract

2 teaspoons cinnamon powder

½ cup corn oil

Powdered sugar for dusting

Maple syrup (optional)

Apple and Mango Topping Ingredients

2 mangoes, peeled and cut into strips

2 apples, peeled, cored, and cut into strips

¼ cup brown sugar

4 tablespoons unsalted butter

¼ cup orange juice

Since it opened in May 2004, North One 10, the celebrated contemporary American restaurant owned and operated by husband and wife team Dewey & Dale LoSasso, has become a fine dining gem in South Florida. Located on the up-and-coming Biscayne Corridor, the restaurant has charmed diners and critics with its mix of casual sophistication, superb service and incredible food. With North One 10, the LoSassos, a pair of seasoned industry veterans, have created a culinary oasis that regularly draws diners from the haunts of Miami Beach and beyond. For North One 10, LoSasso, a founding member of the 1980's era "Mango Gang," has created what he calls "comfort food with an edge," a menu both familiar and evocative, infused with tropical ingredients from Florida's rich cornucopia and the subtle nuances of international haute cuisine.

Combine all of the ingredients, except the *challah*, in a bowl and whisk till smooth. Set aside. Cut the bread in 2-inch slices or about 5-6 slices. Place bread in a 4 inch deep container large enough so that the liquid will cover all of the sliced *challah*. Pour the reserved liquid over the sliced bread. Cover and let soak in the refrigerator for 3 hours. To sauté the French Toast, heat a 10-inch nonstick sauté pan over high heat and add some of the oil. Place the soaked bread slices in the pan and lower the heat to medium–high. Brown the slices of bread on each side. When golden brown, place the slices on a pre-greased cookie tray. Repeat until all the slices are browned. Preheat an oven to 350° F. Then bake the toast for 10-12 minutes. To serve, top with the sautéed mango and apples (see recipe) and dust with powdered sugar. Maple syrup is optional. Enjoy !!

Apple and Mango Topping:
Combine the orange juice, brown sugar and butter in a large saucepan over medium heat, then add the apples and mangoes. Cook, while stirring until the fruit is softened and the liquid has reduced. Remove from the heat and set aside to serve with the toast.

Toast with Peanut Butter, Seriously

DAVE BARRY, Columnist

Dave Barry is a humor columnist. For 25 years, he has been a syndicated columnist whose work appeared in more than 500 newspapers in the United States and abroad. In 1988 he won the Pulitzer Prize for Commentary. Many people are still trying to figure out how this happened.

Dave has also written a total of 30 books, although virtually none of them contains useful information.

Dave plays lead guitar in a literary rock band called the Rock Bottom Remainders, *whose other members include Stephen King, Amy Tan, Ridley Pearson, and Mitch Albom. They are not musically skilled, but they are extremely loud.*

Dave lives in Miami with his wife, Michelle, a sportswriter. He has a son, Rob, and a daughter, Sophie, neither of whom thinks he's funny.

This is a hearty snack that I generally enjoy 30 or 40 times per day when I'm supposed to be writing. You get yourself a slice of white bread, the kind with no fiber or vitamins or anything else healthy in it, and you put it in your toaster and push the lever down. I like my toast well-done, so I push the lever down three or four times, until the smoke detector is beeping. Then I get a spoon and smear a fist-size gob of Peter Pan brand peanut butter (creamy, NOT chunky!) on the toast and eat it.

HINT: If you're in a hurry, you can skip the toast and put the peanut butter straight into your mouth.

ADDITIONAL HINT: If you're in a REAL hurry, you can also skip the spoon.

Stuffed French Toast
SHANNON HORI, WFOR-TV/CBS4 ANCHOR

SERVES 4

16 slices of white bread

Jar of apricot jam (or your favorite flavor)

8 ounce package of cream cheese (reduced fat will work)

6 eggs

1 cup whole milk, or skim milk, if you're being good

Butter

Confectioners' sugar

Whipped cream

Maple syrup

Shannon Hori anchors CBS4's weekday newscasts with Antonio Mora. She came to CBS4 in June 2007 from KTVT/CBS 11/Dallas where she anchored the morning show. Prior to KTVT, Shannon worked for six years at WESH-TV, the NBC affiliate in Orlando, where she anchored the evening news and was nominated for two Emmy Awards. Some of the stories she covered while in Florida included the deadly Florida tornadoes of 1998, the Presidential election of 2000, and the Columbia Shuttle disaster, for which the station won a national Alfred I. DuPont-Columbia University Award. She also contributed reports to a series on home inspections that won a 2004 Peabody Award. Hori is on the board of Big Brothers Big Sisters of Greater Miami, a non-profit organization which matches children to mentors. She is also volunteering as a big sister herself (for the third time). She is very proud of the Neighbors 4 Neighbors program at CBS 4 and often contributes stories about what people are doing in the community to make a difference. In her spare time she loves doing anything outside and reading. She and her husband have a very well-trained black lab named Maddy Ann, who is a release dog from Canine Companions from Independence.

Sunday breakfast has always been one of my favorite rituals. For me it can never have too many calories - because I can always remind myself to start the healthy diet on Monday. This recipe is so easy and it's perfect when you have unexpected guests who are hungry and have a sweet tooth.

Beat the eggs and the milk together in a mixing bowl. Make sandwiches using the cream cheese and apricot jam spread on 2 pieces of bread like a peanut butter and jelly sandwich. Dip the sandwiches in the egg/milk mixture. In a buttered sauté pan cook the sandwiches until brown on both sides. Top with butter, confectioners' sugar, a dollop or two of whipped cream, and maple syrup.

SIDES

UNIVERSITY FOUNTAIN Photo Credit: University of Miami

Aloo, Matar, Tamatar
(Potatoes, Green Peas and Tomatoes)
EXECUTIVE CHEF & OWNER KAVITA KAMLANI, ISHQ

SERVES 6

3 russet potatoes, cut in ½ inch cubes

1 cup frozen green peas, defrosted

2½ cups tomatoes, chopped

2 tablespoons cilantro leaves, chopped

1 Serrano chile pepper, finely chopped

1 tablespoon garlic, chopped

1 tablespoon caraway seeds

1 tablespoon ground cumin

¼ tablespoon turmeric

3 tablespoons vegetable or canola oil

Salt to taste

Ishq *means love. At Ishq, you will discover the diversity, color, spice and excitement of contemporary Indian cuisine. India is an extremely diverse country, with hundreds of dialects and cultures that vary by region. The cuisine is equally diverse. In Northern India, breads are made with different wheat flours and the curries are more cream based, while rice is more prevalent in the South and curries get their richness from coconut milk. Naturally, since the South of India has an extensive coastline, seafood is more common, while Northern Indian cuisine showcases meat. Throughout the country, one common element of all of India's cuisine is spice. Spice is used to enhance the taste of meat, poultry, fish, vegetables, legumes and even the rice. A careful combination of spice is used to heighten the senses and to raise the intensity of the dining experience to a higher, yet pleasurable level.*

Heat the oil in a large sauté pan over low to medium heat. Add the caraway seeds and then the chopped garlic. Sauté the garlic until it is light brown and then add the turmeric and ground cumin, followed by the chopped tomatoes and the Serrano peppers. Add salt, cover the pan and let it simmer on medium heat. When the oil rises to the surface, add the potato cubes. Cook until potatoes are done. If the gravy gets too thick add 1/2 cup of water.

When you are ready to serve, add the defrosted green peas and chopped cilantro leaves. Cook a few minutes more until the peas and the vegetables are heated through.

Savory Mushroom Brioche Bread Pudding

MRS. JODI DICKINSON, Philanthropist, wife of BOB DICKINSON, CEO, Carnival Cruise Line

Jodi Dickinson is an active supporter of several charitable organizations, Kristi House, United Way and Camillus House among them. She is a gourmet cook whose sought-after, multi-course dinners are auctioned to raise funds for charitable causes. Her husband Bob, CEO of Carnival Cruise Lines, pairs wines from his world-class collection with Jodi's extraordinary fare.

Serve with seared foie gras.

Preheat an oven to 350° F. Lightly spray 10 small ramekins with vegetable or olive oil, or brush with olive oil. In a large saucepan bring the milk and cream just to a boil over medium high heat. Remove from the heat quickly. Set aside. In a separate sauté pan, melt the 2 tablespoons of butter. Add the mushrooms and the shallots and sauté until cooked. Place the cubed bread in a large bowl, whip all the eggs and yolks together and pour this, along with the milk mixture, over the bread, then gently combine until well mixed. Then add the mushroom and shallot mixture and combine well. Add the sea salt and pepper to taste.

Fill a large roasting pan (either a glass or metal one) with about 4 cups of simmering water. Fill each ramekin to the top with the bread mixture. Place the ramekins in the pan with simmering water. Bake for approximately 25 minutes, or until the custards set. Allow them to cool 5 minutes before unmolding.

Note: These can be cooked in advance and refrigerated in their mold, and reheated at 325° F for approximately 10 minutes.

SERVES 10

5 stale croissants or 1 small brioche loaf, cubed into 1-inch chunks

3 cups heavy cream

3 cups milk

3 8-ounce or small package white button mushrooms, sliced

1 cup shallots, diced

2 tablespoons butter

Sea salt and pepper to season

4 large eggs

4 egg yolks

Canistel Vegetable Rice

NORIS LEDESMA, CURATOR OF TROPICAL FRUIT
AT FAIRCHILD TROPICAL BOTANIC GARDEN

The skin of the canistel is thin, waxy, and smooth. It is green when immature and bright yellow to bright orange when ripe. The pulp is relatively firm, smooth, creamy, sweet, and also bright yellow to orange when ripe. Some cooks have compared canistel to persimmons.

SERVES 6

1 cup rice

3 cups water

1 cup canistel, mashed

¼ cup red peppers, chopped

¼ cup orange peppers, chopped

¼ green bell peppers, chopped

½ cup carrot, chopped

½ cup onion, chopped

½ cup chickpeas (garbanzo beans)

Salt to taste

2 tablespoons olive oil, plus olive oil to taste

2 teaspoons garlic powder

Parsley, chives or paprika for garnish (optional)

Sauté onion, garlic powder and carrots in a medium sauté pan or skillet over medium heat, add the peppers and chickpeas. Then, in a separate pot, toast the rice over medium heat with 2 tablespoons olive oil for 10 minutes, stirring constantly. Add the mashed canistel and the 3 cups of water with salt and oil to taste. Lower the temperature and cover; cook for 15 minutes and serve warm. For variation, you can add chopped, cooked chicken, pork or steak to the rice. You can also garnish the dish with parsley, chives or paprika.

Consommé Rice
ALVAH H. CHAPMAN, JR.

Alvah H. Chapman, Jr. was CEO and chairman of The Miami Herald *publisher Knight-Ridder. Fifteen years into his retirement, Chapman, continues his civic involvement with the Community Partnership for Homeless Inc., a not-for-profit of which he was the Founding Chairman. He remains one of the region's most influential, and certainly one of its most storied, corporate citizens.*

Preheat an oven to 350° F. Combine rice in skillet with melted butter until rice is coated with butter. Then put in the beef consommé and water, the Worcestershire, bay leaves, and salt and pepper to taste. Put the rice mixture in a casserole and cover. Bake for about an hour or until the liquid is absorbed by the rice. This is delicious served with steak, barbecued chicken or any meat that does not require gravy. A real family favorite!

SERVES 6-8

1⅓ stick of butter

2 cups long-grain white rice, washed and drained

2 cans beef consommé

2 cans water

4 tablespoons Worcestershire sauce

6 bay leaves

Salt and pepper

Nana Rose's Noodle Kugel
FLORIDA STATE SENATOR GWEN MARGOLIS

SERVES 6

½ pound medium egg noodles
  (Mueller's is a long-time favorite)

½ cup sugar

6 eggs

1 can (14-ounces) evaporated milk

1 jar pineapple preserves

1 glass (14-ounces) whole milk

⅓ stick butter, melted

White raisins

Cinnamon for top

Senator Gwen Margolis began her business career in real estate development, but soon found her true interest in public service. After serving six years in the Florida House of Representatives, she moved on and was elected to the Florida Senate where she served for twelve years, culminating as president of the Florida Senate, the first woman to serve in this capacity. She also served as chairperson of the Miami-Dade County Commission. She presently serves as a Senator, representing the 35th District and is the proud mother of four children and seven grandchildren.

My mother's prize-winning recipe has been passed down from generation to generation and I am proud to pass it on to future generations to enjoy!

Cook the egg noodles in a large pot, drain when done and set aside to cool. Preheat an oven to 350° F. In a large mixing bowl, combine the sugar with cooked, drained and cooled noodles. Add the eggs and remaining ingredients and mix well. Place in a 9 x 13 inch pan and generously, sprinkle the top with cinnamon. Bake until browned on top, approximately 50-60 minutes.

Humberto's Black Beans

HUMBERTO CALZADA, Artist

Humberto Calzada was born in Cuba in 1944 and has lived in the United States since 1960. He began painting in 1972 and since 1976 has dedicated his time exclusively to painting. His work has been said to carry on the classical Latin American artistic tradition: dreamlike realism, tension created by the contrast between calm and conflict, and the use of timeless symbols as a universal language. Throughout his career, he has applied these themes through architectural imagery. He depicts harmony through the use of natural elements, and he depicts conflict through the opposition of the ephemeral movement of light and water against the static force of stone and glass.

Note: All ingredients (especially the salt, sugar and vinegar) will have to be adjusted during cooking. The amounts are all starting amounts. The recipe can be doubled and can also be frozen. The black beans taste better the second day so, if possible, cook ahead.

Use a pot that is wider than it is tall (in a tall pot, the heavy beans sink to the bottom and burn, while all the liquid rises to the top). Combine all the ingredients except for the black beans in the pot and cook over medium heat in the olive oil until soft. Add cans of black beans and soup, and then the bay leaves, wine, vinegar and sugar and stir. Cook at medium low for about 1 hour, stirring often and making sure nothing is sticking to bottom. Adjust the seasoning, especially the balance between vinegar and sugar. If it gets too thick add either water or more *vino seco* (careful, this affects the salt).

SERVES 6 AS A SOUP
SERVES 8-10 AS SIDE DISH OVER RICE

4 cans black beans (I usually use Iberia)

1 can condensed black bean soup (I prefer Knorr)

½ cup extra virgin olive oil

2 cups onions, chopped (can be chopped in the food processor)

1 cup green bell pepper, chopped into smallish cubes

1 cup red bell pepper, chopped into smallish cubes

1 tablespoon garlic, finely chopped

1 teaspoon plus of ground oregano

½ teaspoon plus of ground cumin

½ teaspoon ground black pepper

½ teaspoon sea salt (if you use iodized, slightly less to start)

2 good sized bay leaves

1 cup Edmundo-brand cooking wine (vino seco Edmundo)

⅓ cup white vinegar

3 tablespoons sugar

SERVES 4

1 cup Italian Arborio *rice (risotto rice)*

2 tablespoon butter, either salted or unsalted

Olive oil

Garlic cloves, finely chopped, to your taste

Mushroom mix; can include shiitake, crimini, *oyster and button mushrooms; your choice*

Broth, choose either chicken, vegetable, beef or, my favorite, champagne, depending on the type of dish you are serving alongside the risotto

1 medium white onion, finely chopped

Parmigiano-Reggiano cheese

Salt and pepper to taste

The Historical Museum of Southern Florida tells the stories of South Florida and the Caribbean. The museum promotes understanding of the past in order to inform the present and create a better quality of life. The Historical Museum is one of the largest private, regional history museums in the country, recognized for excellence in programming and management by the Florida Department of State and national museum services organizations.

This is an interesting recipe, because it can be tailored to fit any other fish, fowl or meat dishes being served.

In a heavy saucepan, sauté the onion in enough olive oil and butter to cover the bottom of the pan. Add the mushrooms and continue to sauté. Add the garlic just before finishing the sautéing and set aside in a bowl. In the same saucepan, sauté the Italian *Arborio* rice in olive oil and butter until very lightly browned. Add ½ cup of the broth (or champagne). Stir constantly on medium low heat until the liquid is absorbed, about 25 minutes, and add additional broth, stirring until the rice becomes almost cooked. Preheat an oven to 350° F. Add the mushroom mixture to the rice and mix well. In an ovenproof dish, add the rice and mushroom mixture and top with the grated *Parmigiano-Reggiano* cheese. Bake for 20-30 minutes. Serve as a main dish with salad and crispy bread, or as a complement to meat or fish.

Awesome Asparagus!
LISA PETRILLO, WFOR-TV, CBS 4 NEWS,
ENTERTAINMENT AND LIFESTYLE REPORTER

As the Emmy-Winning Entertainment Reporter for CBS4, Lisa Petrillo makes it her business to mingle with the rich and famous. During her years as South Florida's premier entertainment reporter, Lisa had the opportunity to interview some of today's most spectacular stars, among them Paul McCartney, Sting, Tom Cruise, Oprah Winfrey, Jennifer Lopez, Arnold Schwarzenneger, Elton John, Julio Iglesias, Warren Beatty and the late Audrey Hepburn. It's this part of the job that appeals to her most, namely "meeting incredibly interesting and talented people, then creating stories about their lives and careers."

SERVES 4-6

1 bunch asparagus, the thin stalks are best
Vegetable or olive oil cooking spray
2 tablespoons butter or margarine
1 tablespoon soy sauce
1 teaspoon Balsamic vinegar

Preheat oven to 425° F. Take the asparagus stalks and trim about a half-inch off the stems. Arrange them in a single layer in a large sauté or roasting pan. Spray the asparagus with a thin coat of vegetable or olive oil cooking spray. Bake the asparagus for 10-12 minutes. In the meantime, heat the butter or margarine, soy sauce and balsamic vinegar in a microwave oven for about 20 seconds, until the butter or margarine melts. When the asparagus look roasted, remove and place on a decorative plate. Pour the sauce over the asparagus and enjoy!

Piononos (Ripe Plantain Wheels, Stuffed with Picadillo)
LATIN GRAMMY WINNER NESTOR TORRES AND HIS MOTHER, PROVI F. TORRES

SERVES 6-8

4 ripe yellow plantains

2 cups ground beef

1 cup ground pork

2 eggs, beaten

3 slices of American cheese (or any cheese of choice)

Vegetable oil

SEASONING INGREDIENTS FOR *PICADILLO* (GROUND MEAT)

1 small onion

1 Italian pepper

3 garlic cloves, minced

1 tablespoon fresh cilantro, crushed

1 tablespoon fresh oregano, crushed

1 tablespoon capers

1 tablespoon olives with pimiento, minced

Flautist and Latin Grammy Award winner Nestor Torres has been captivating audiences with his distinctive mix of Latin, Jazz and Pop sounds for more than two decades. By transforming the flute's role in the contemporary musical landscape, this remarkable virtuoso has earned a devoted following, and has practically established a new genre of popular music. Throughout this time he also performed and recorded with a variety of Latin Pop & Jazz luminaries, including Gloria Estefan, Jon Secada, Herbie Hancock, and Wayne Shorter. In 2001, Nestor Torres won a Latin Grammy for his CD, This Side of Paradise.

In a large mixing bowl, combine the ground beef and the ground pork. Season the ground meat with onion, pepper, garlic, cilantro, oregano, capers and olives, making sure to combine well with the ground meat. Place one tablespoon of the vegetable oil into a large sauté pan and cook the *picadillo* to your liking. When done, set aside. Beat the eggs until you get a nice full batter. Cut cheese into 16 small 2 x 2 inch slices. Peel the plantains and cut lengthwise into long, broad ribbons. Heat one cup of the vegetable oil in a medium sauté pan and place 2 or 3 slices of the plantain into the pan and fry until the plantains are golden on both sides. Place the fried plantains on the plate with paper towels to drain the excess oil. Repeat until all the plantain are fried. Renew paper towels as needed. Once all of the slices of plantains are fried, take each slice and wrap into a hollow wheel and secure with a toothpick so that it stays in the form of a wheel. Slightly fill a soup spoon with beaten egg. Carefully place the plantain wheel on the egg batter filled soup spoon and stuff it (fill the hole of the wheel) with the cooked *picadillo*. Place it back in the pan with hot oil and fry at low heat. While frying, place a slice of cheese over the *picadillo* and pour another soup spoon of egg batter over each wheel to seal the wheel. Once the plantain wheels are sealed and the cheese is just melted, remove and keep warm. Repeat until all of your *Piononos* are cooked. Remove from oven and serve. *Buen Provecho!*

Potato au Gratin
CORPORATE CHEF TINDARO LOSURDO,
PRIME BLUE GRILLE

Prime Blue Grille is an innovative steak and seafood restaurant, which embraces a modern approach to the traditional steakhouse fare and décor and is the first national restaurant company to serve only all natural, corn-fed, hormone-free, premium beef. And while aged prime steaks are at the core of the menu, Prime Blue Grille is more than just a steakhouse. Just as much focus is on our seafood and shellfish choices, fresh from the market daily.

In a medium saucepan, bring the heavy cream just to a boil with ½ cup Parmesan cheese. Remove from the heat and set aside. Bake 6 large Idaho potatoes until almost done but still a little firm. Peel them and slice thin. Julienne the proscuitto.

Preheat an oven to 350° F. In a buttered casserole layer the potatoes and the Parmesan-cream, sprinkling in the proscuitto. Top with the shredded fontina cheese and the 2 tablespoons of grated Parmesan. Bake for 30-45 minutes or until potatoes are soft and the cheese is browned slightly on top. The Parmesan cream will be boiling so be careful when you remove it from the oven.

SERVES 6-8

3½ cups heavy cream
½ cup plus 2 tablespoons Parmesan cheese, grated
6 large Idaho potatoes
1 cup proscuitto, julienned
1 cup of fontina cheese, shredded

Broccoli "O" Gratin

EXECUTIVE CHEF LUIS LOPEZ, Soyka's Restaurant Café & Bar

A converted railway station that's now a bustling, hip eatery just north of Miami's downtown area, Soyka was founded by Mark Soyka who gave us the News Café and Van Dyke's. His trademark is outdoor dining perfectly suited to the tropical heat of Miami.

SERVES 1 AS ENTRÉE
SERVES 2-3 AS SIDE DISH

8 ounces Red Bliss potatoes, sliced

4 ounces broccoli florets, steamed

1½ ounces heavy cream

½ teaspoon garlic, finely minced

2 ounces Parmigiano-Reggiano *cheese, grated*

2 ounces Gorgonzola cheese, crumbled

Pinch each of salt and black pepper

Preheat an oven to 400° F. In a medium sized mixing bowl, toss the steamed broccoli with the garlic, cream, salt and pepper. Line a 20-ounce or 8 x 8 inch ovenproof dish with one half of the sliced potatoes topped with one half of the *Parmigiano-Reggiano* and Gorgonzola cheese. Top the cheese with the broccoli mixture. Top the broccoli with the remaining potatoes and finish with a layer of the remaining cheese. Bake for 15 minutes in a conventional oven or 10 minutes in a convection oven. This dish is wonderful with a medium bodied California red wine.

Tropical Fruit Relish

EXECUTIVE CHEF SEBASTIEN LAYEN, Two Sisters Restaurant

The Two Sisters Restaurant is one of Coral Gables' premier fine dining landmarks with French influenced Mediterranean Cuisine and featuring the exquisite, award-winning culinary creations of Executive Chef Sebastien Layen.

Dice fruit to your preference. Add the kiwis, mango and papaya to a mixing bowl, toss and then add the cilantro, onion, and orange sections. Lastly, add the lemon and lime juice. Mix well. Cover and let stand for one hour in the refrigerator. Remove the relish from the refrigerator and add the tomato and serve. The fruit relish is good with meat, poultry, or fish. Large dice make for an excellent summer salad on it's own.

Reprinted with permission from *A Taste of the Market: A collection of recipes from Farmer's Market at Merrick Park*, Coral Gables, Florida (January 1998).

SERVES 8

2 kiwis, peeled
½ mango, peeled
½ papaya, peeled & seeded
½ ounce cilantro, diced
1 small red onion, diced small
1 orange, sectioned
Juice of one lemon
Juice of one lime
1 medium tomato, diced small

Jackfruit Casserole
NORIS LEDESMA, CURATOR OF TROPICAL FRUIT
AT FAIRCHILD TROPICAL BOTANIC GARDEN

SERVES 4

2 small green jackfruits (makes about 2 cups)

2 eggs

1 cup mayonnaise

1 can cream of mushroom soup

1 cup cheddar cheese, grated

1 teaspoon white onion, minced

Jackfruit is commonly used in Southeast Asian cuisines. It can be eaten unripe (young) or ripe, and cooked or uncooked. The seeds can also be eaten cooked or baked like beans; they taste similar to chestnuts. Unripe, young jackfruit can also be eaten whole. Young jackfruit has a mild flavor and distinctive texture. The cuisines of India, Bangladesh, Sri Lanka, Indonesia, and Vietnam use cooked young jackfruit. In many cultures, jackfruit is boiled and used in curries as a food staple

Peel and chop the jackfruits, removing the seeds. Boil for 30 minutes and change the water. Boil one more time for 30 minutes, drain. Preheat an oven to 450° F. In a medium bowl, beat the eggs. Blend in mayonnaise and cream of mushroom soup. Stir in the cheese, minced onion and jackfruit. Turn into a two-quart casserole. Bake for 45 minutes.

Pomodoro Sauce
OWNER STEVE PERRICONE,
PERRICONE'S MARKETPLACE & CAFE

The last thing you expect to discover on the outskirts of downtown Miami is a cozy New England barn sitting in a quiet park surrounded by lush vegetation. But that's exactly what you find at Perricone's Marketplace and Cafe. Its resistance to rampant modernity is a welcome surprise in the shadows of skyscraping banks that line the famous Brickell Avenue along Biscayne Bay.

The refreshing simplicity of the taste of fresh tomatoes has made this sauce an enduring favorite at Perricone's. Serve with your favorite pasta and a beautiful salad and never be disappointed.

In a large sauté pan, heat the garlic in olive oil at medium high for a minute, then add tomatoes and simmer for 5 minutes. Add the herbs, wine and marinara sauce. Season with salt and pepper and serve over your favorite pasta.

SERVES 6-8

2 tablespoons virgin olive oil

1 tablespoon garlic, minced

1 cup ripe tomatoes, diced

1 tablespoon fresh parsley, chopped

2 tablespoons fresh basil, chopped

½ cup dry white wine

1 cup marinara sauce

Salt and freshly ground black pepper

Pigeon Peas & Rice
CHEF RICARDO GIRDWOOD, JUMBO'S RESTAURANT

Family owned for over 50 years, Jumbo's was one of the first Miami restaurants to integrate in 1966 and was the first white-owned restaurant in the city to hire black front of the house workers. Known for its luscious fried shrimp, Jumbo's also serves soul food favorites like oxtails and rice, chicken fried steak, and specialties named after local schools and sports teams. The neon sign that welcomes diners (24 hours a day) sums up the Jumbo's experience with the words "a nice place for nice people." Jumbo's was awarded the James Beard Award for "An American Classic" in 2008.

"There are many pigeon peas recipes, but this is the best, our favorite!"

SERVES 8

2 ounces vegetable oil

2 ounces garlic, finely chopped

4 ounces green peppers, finely chopped

4 ounces yellow onion, finely chopped

1 can (15-ounces) of pigeon peas, drained

1 can (13½-ounces) of coconut milk

2 or 3 sprigs fresh thyme

1 teaspoon black pepper

1½ tablespoon salt or to taste

2 cups washed rice (I prefer Mahatma Rice)

In a large skillet or heavy casserole, heat the oil over medium heat and sauté the garlic, green peppers and onion. Then add the pigeon peas, rice, thyme, coconut milk, and salt and black pepper to the sauté. There should be 1½ inches of liquid above this mixture. If not, add about ½ cup water to make it so. Let it simmer on medium, then turn it down to low and cover. Stir only once or twice until all the liquid is absorbed. Do not over stir—let it steam.

Harriette's Aunt's Squash Soufflé
JUDGE WILLIAM M. HOEVELER

Senior U.S. District Judge William M. Hoeveler of the Southern District of Florida is the recipient of the prestigious Judicial Recognition Award from the National Association of Criminal Defense Lawyers. Hoeveler was appointed to the Federal Bench in Miami by then-President Jimmy Carter in April 1977. The recipient of many honors and recognitions over the years, Judge Hoeveler also has at least two professional awards named after him: the Florida Bar's William M. Hoeveler Judicial Award and the University of Miami Law School's William M. Hoeveler Ethics and Public Service Award.

SERVES 4

2 cups squash, mashed (acorn, butternut or other large squash will do)
1 cup milk
3 egg yolks
3 egg whites
2 tablespoons butter
2½ tablespoons flour
2 teaspoons onion, chopped
1 tablespoon sugar

Preheat an oven to 350° F. Cut the squash in two and place on a baking sheet. Bake in the oven for 45 minutes. Remove, let cool, remove the seeds and then scrape the flesh into a mixing bowl. Mash the squash until you have 2 cups of smooth squash. Set aside. Melt the butter in saucepan over medium heat. Add the onion and sauté until it is soft and translucent. Add the flour, stirring to make a *roux*. In a mixing bowl, beat the egg yolks lightly with milk and sugar, then add slowly to the *roux*. Cook over medium heat until it reaches a creamy consistency. Combine this sauce with 2 cups mashed squash. Beat the egg whites with a mixer until they form soft peaks. Gently fold the mixture into the beaten egg whites. Add salt and pepper to taste. Pour the mixture into a baking dish and bake for 45 minutes. Serve immediately.

DESSERTS

ARSHT CENTER Photo Credit: Robin Hill

Mango Mousse

CHEF & OWNER ALLEN SUSSER, Chef Allen's Restaurant

SERVES 6

3 tablespoons Myer's Rum

2 tablespoons unflavored gelatin

6 large egg yolks

⅔ cup confectioners' sugar

3 tablespoons lime juice, freshly squeezed

1 cup mango, freshly puréed

1 cup heavy cream, whipped

1 ripe mango, sliced for garnish

Chef Allen's Restaurant has won accolades from local and national food writers. Food and Wine Magazine *named Allen Susser as one of the "Top 10 New Chefs in America" in 1991.* TIME Magazine *called Allen's cuisine "a New World marvel."* The New York Times *named Allen Susser "the Ponce de Leon of New Floridian cooking."* Chef Allen's dramatic translation of the bounty of South Florida's foodstuffs has become known as New World Cuisine, an innovative signature and important contribution to American culinary craftsmanship.

To prepare the mousse, sprinkle the gelatin over the rum in a small bowl. Let this soak for 5 minutes. In a stainless steel bowl, beat the egg yolks and lime with the confectioners' sugar over a warm water bath until it starts to thicken. It is thick enough when the batter can coat the back of a spoon. Remove from the heat, and beat until cool. Finally, to complete the mousse, melt the gelatin over the warm water bath. Fold the mango purée in to the egg mixture, followed by the softened gelatin and then fold in the whipped cream. To serve, pour into 6 tall parfait glasses and chill for 2 hours in the refrigerator. Garnish each serving with the fresh mango slices.

Mom's Sweet Potato Pie

ALONZO MOURNING, MIAMI HEAT PLAYER & FOUNDER OF ALONZO MOURNING CHARITIES & HIS MOTHER, JULIA HADNOT

Alonzo Mourning is founder of Alonzo Mourning Charities, a public fundraising foundation, created to encourage the educational development of youth by developing programs and youth enrichment centers that promote positive change in low socioeconomic communities. Since 1997, Mourning has raised more than $6.5 million for various programs that aid in the development of children and their families. With the help of donors, Mourning opened the first center in 2003 in the historic area of Overtown.

Mourning was drafted as the number two pick, of the first round, by the Charlotte Hornets in the 1992 National Basketball Association's (NBA) draft. After three successful years with the Hornets, Mourning moved on in 1995 to spend seven years with the Miami Heat leading the team to several Eastern division titles. Diagnosed with a degenerative kidney ailment at the start of the 2000-2001 season, Mourning led a campaign and raised $2 million for research, education, and testing. He returned to the court after undergoing a kidney transplant in that same season. In 2005 he was an integral part in leading the team to their first NBA Championship in the 2005-06 season. Mourning is a seven-time NBA All-Star and two-time Defensive Player of the Year (1999 and 2000). He is currently among the league's leaders in blocked shots, field goal percentages and rebounds per game.

MAKES 2 PIES

2 9-inch pie crusts, normally available in the frozen foods section of your grocer

3 medium size sweet potatoes, boiled until soft, peeled

1 cup butter or margarine

2 cups sugar

Dash salt

6 eggs

2 tablespoons vanilla extract

¾ tablespoon cinnamon

¼ teaspoon nutmeg

½ large can (12-ounces) evaporated milk

Preheat an oven to 350° F. Place potatoes and butter into a mixing bowl and mix on medium speed with a hand or stand mixer until combined. Remove any potato strings from the mix. Mix in the remaining ingredients on medium speed until the mixture is smooth. Divide mixture into two (2) nine-inch pie crusts. Bake for approximately one hour, or until heated throughout and golden brown on top.

Café Con Leche with Crème Anglaise

EXECUTIVE CHEF MICHAEL GILLIGAN, ATRIO

Conrad Miami's signature restaurant Atrio welcomes diners into a heightened sense of elegance and style. From the spectacularly designed ambiance and décor, to the progressive, global fare by acclaimed Executive Chef Michael Gilligan, Atrio embodies Conrad's sense of luxury and flair.

"This dessert is a firm favorite at Atrio. The tradition of an after dinner cup of joe has taken on a new meaning here as we use espresso beans covered in chocolate, ground Oreo cookies to resemble ground coffee beans and a dessert that tastes like a creamier version of the classic café con leche*. What is a* café con leche*? Well, let's put it this way.* Café con leche *is to the Cuban child what a triple-shot, double-vanilla non-fat mocha latte dark is to a member of corporate America. Why do we put these things together in one dish? Because a day without love, laughter or dessert is a wasted day." – Chef Michael Gilligan*

SERVES 12

4 eggs

4 ounces sugar

4 tablespoons instant coffee

7 ounces flour

1 pound butter, softened

1 pound white chocolate chips

12 4-ounce soufflé ramekins or aluminum soufflé cups

A little butter and flour to coat the cups

CRÈME ANGLAISE INGREDIENTS

6 egg yolks

½ cup sugar

½ quart heavy cream

2 vanilla pods, split open and deseeded

Preheat an oven to 350° F. In a stand mixer with the whip attachment, whisk the eggs and the sugar until "fluffy" and doubled in size. Dissolve the instant coffee granules in a little hot water and allow to cool. Add the flour and coffee to the egg mixture and incorporate well until there are no lumps of flour. In a mixing bowl over a pot of boiling water, melt the chocolate first, then fold in the softened butter. Incorporate the chocolate mixture into the egg mixture and blend well. Line the soufflé cups with a little butter and then dust with flour. Spoon about 3 ounces of the mixture into each cup. Bake for 9 minutes. Serve with ice cream, (We use Cookies and Cream Ice Cream at Atrio), *Crème Anglaise* or a Raspberry Coulis. (See recipes)

Crème Anglaise:

Place a medium bowl into a larger bowl filled with ice water. Place a fine mesh strainer inside the empty bowl. Set aside. Place the cream in a medium-sized saucepan. Split the vanilla bean down the center with the tip of a paring knife and scrape out as many of the seeds as possible. Place the seeds

and entire vanilla pod into the cream mixture. Bring mixture just to a boil. Remove the pan from the heat. Allow the mixture to stand for at least 30 minutes allowing the vanilla bean flavor to infuse into the cream. Set aside. In a stainless steel bowl suspended over a saucepan of simmering water beat the yolks and sugar together until the mixture has thickened and is a pale yellow color. Remove the vanilla bean pod from the cream mixture and bring the cream mixture just back to a boil. Add approximately 1/2 cup of hot cream mixture to the egg mixture to temper the yolks, mixing while adding the hot milk. Then, while stirring constantly with a heat resistant spatula, add the egg mixture back into the pan with the remaining cream mixture. Stir the mixture constantly over medium-low heat until the mixture is the consistency of heavy cream or until you can draw a line with your finger along the back of the spoon and have the mixture leave a trail. If the mixture stays separated and leaves a distinct path without the two sides running together the cream is finished. Immediately strain the finished cream through a fine mesh strainer into the iced bowl. Stir occasionally until cooled. Store, tightly covered, for up to 2 days in the refrigerator.

Raspberry Coulis:

Combine the sugar and water in a medium heavy pot and bring to a boil over high heat. Reduce the heat to medium low and simmer until the sugar dissolves, about 2 minutes. Add the raspberries and cook, stirring occasionally, until the syrup thickens and reduces by 3/4 in volume, about 5 minutes. Transfer to a blender or food processor, and purée on high speed. Strain through a fine mesh strainer, pressing down with a rubber spatula to extract as much juice as possible. If too thick, add water a teaspoon at a time to reach the desired consistency. Cover and refrigerate until ready to use. The coulis can be refrigerated in an airtight container for up to 3 days. Yields 2/3 cup.

RASPBERRY COULIS INGREDIENTS
1/4 cup sugar
1/4 cup water
2 cups fresh raspberries, rinsed and picked over

When it comes to style and spectacle, event Impresario Barton G. Weiss - Barton G. - has mastered the art of environmental transformations. With Barton G., The Restaurant, the event virtuoso brings his signature sophisticated aesthetic flair and culinary artistry to Miami's dining landscape. Barton G. has reincarnated one of Miami's landmark dining venues. A popular spot for some of America's most famous (and infamous!) when it first opened in 1925 as Gatti's, it later played a significant role in the SoBe Renaissance as Starfish. Today, the restaurant evokes the timeless elegance of its predecessors while offering a relaxed ambience for a new generation of diners.

MAKES 18 CUPCAKES

CUPCAKE INGREDIENTS

2 large eggs

4½ ounces sugar

4½ ounces vegetable oil

4½ ounces all-purpose flour

½ teaspoon baking powder

2 pinches of salt

BUTTER CREAM ICING INGREDIENTS

8 ounces butter

11 ounces confectioners' sugar

1 egg white

Vanilla extract to taste

Cocoa powder to taste

Peanut butter to taste

Marzipan for modeling (optional)

For the butter cream icing, cream the butter in a bowl on a stand mixer, add the confectioners' sugar and the egg white. When creamy, divide the batter into two equal parts. Flavor one part with peanut butter and the other with the cocoa powder or another flavor of your choosing.

Preheat an oven between 320° F to 340° F (depending on your oven). For the cupcakes, put all the flour, baking powder and salt in a mixing bowl. Mix the eggs and the vegetable oil together in a separate bowl and add to the dry mixture. Stir with a spatula and add the cocoa powder to taste. Bake in a 18-cup muffin pan for 25 minutes. Remove from the oven and allow the cupcakes to cool and then fill each with the peanut butter cream. Ice the top with the chocolate butter cream icing using a small spatula.

For the modeling, use marzipan for the ears, trunks and any other features you'd like. You can create colors with food coloring; you can ether paint or mix the colors on or with the marzipan. Candy or cookies may also be used to create the features.

Nannie's Southern Pound Cake
With Chocolate Frosting
BECKY ROPER MATKOV, EXECUTIVE DIRECTOR, DADE HERITAGE TRUST

Dade Heritage Trust is the leading voice for historic preservation in Miami-Dade County. Founded in 1972, Dade Heritage Trust works to preserve the architectural, cultural and environmental heritage of South Florida through advocacy, education and restoration. Dade Heritage Trust works to save historic properties and revitalize historic neighborhoods. Efforts include restoring landmarks, working with the media and community leaders, publishing books and magazines, and presenting tours and historic programs for schools and the general public.

My dear grandmother in Alabama – who lived to 100!—made this for us when I was a little girl visiting for Christmas and summers.

To prepare the cake, cream the butter and shortening in a mixing bowl. Then add sugar gradually. Beat in eggs one at a time. Add a little milk, then a little flour, alternating until all is beaten in smoothly. Stir in the vanilla and lemon extracts.

Preheat an oven to 350° F. Grease and flour a large tube pan. Pour in the cake batter and bake approximately one-and-a-half hours. Remove from the oven and cool upside down and then turn onto a cake platter. Honestly, it is delicious served plain! Especially with eggnog! Or topped with frosting. To prepare a chocolate frosting, I like the included recipe.

Chocolate Frosting:
Stir together the ingredients in a saucepan over medium heat. Bring to a boil and cook for 2 minutes, stirring. Remove from the heat and beat until cooled then immediately frost cake.

SERVES 8
CAKE INGREDIENTS
½ pound butter (2 sticks)
½ cup solid shortening (Crisco)
3 cups sugar
½ teaspoon baking powder
3 cups cake flour, sifted
1 cup whole milk
5 eggs
1½ teaspoons vanilla extract
½ teaspoon lemon extract

CHOCOLATE FROSTING INGREDIENTS
2 cups sugar
¼ cup cocoa
½ cup solid shortening (Crisco)
⅔ cup whole milk
2 teaspoons vanilla

Photo Credit: Gio Alma

South Florida Tropical Carrot Cake
With Toffee Sauce

CHEF TOM AZAR, EMERIL'S MIAMI BEACH

Chef Emeril Lagasse brings his high energy, bold exciting flavors and an unforgettable dining experience to Miami's South Beach. Like Lagasse's flagship restaurant, Emeril's in New Orleans, the menu features what Lagasse calls "new" New Orleans cuisine, which includes the history and richness of Creole cuisine with the addition of progressive, cultural and seasonal influences. Emeril's Miami Beach is in the hands of talented chef Tom Azar.

Preheat an oven to 325° F. To prepare the cake, sift all of the dry ingredients together in a bowl. Then mix the pineapple, coconut, and raisins into the dry ingredients and toss to coat well. This is important as it keeps them from sinking to the bottom of the cake. In a food processor, purée the carrots with the vegetable oil until the mixture is ground fine. Add the eggs and vanilla to the carrot mixture. Mix together the dry ingredients and the carrot mix and add the nuts. Spread the batter evenly on a greased bundt pan. Bake for approximately 25 minutes or until a toothpick stuck in center of the cake comes out clean.

To prepare the Toffee Sauce, combine the sugar and butter and melt in a saucepan over medium heat. Whisk together well when it comes to a boil and the butter and the sugar are combined. Then remove from the heat and whisk in the heavy cream and rum. When smooth and dark, pour the toffee sauce over the carrot cake and place in the oven for 2-3 minutes.

SERVES 8
CAKE INGREDIENTS

8½ ounces all-purpose flour

2 teaspoons baking powder

1 teaspoon baking soda

1 teaspoon cinnamon

¼ teaspoon salt

⅛ teaspoon nutmeg

¼ teaspoon ginger

9¾ ounces sugar

1 cup vegetable oil

6 ounces eggs

½ cup raisins*

5 ounces carrots, shredded

½ cup walnuts*

1 teaspoon vanilla extract

1 cup pineapple, diced small*

½ cup shredded coconut

*Optional ingredients, but makes the cake tropical

TOFFEE SAUCE INGREDIENTS

4 ounces butter

6 ounces brown sugar

4 ounces heavy cream

⅛ cup Myer's Rum

Florida Key Lime Pie
GOVERNOR CHARLIE CRIST

Charlie Crist now serves as Florida's 44th Governor. He vows to work as "The People's Governor" because he is working for the people of Florida—the people he calls his Boss. Today, he is ready to lead Florida onward, to new opportunities and to Florida's brightest future ever.

Preheat an oven to 325° F. If you'd like, you can use a ready made graham cracker pie crust. For the filling whisk the egg yolks and lime zest together in a mixing bowl until it turns a light green. This should take about 2 minutes. Then beat in the milk and the juice and set aside until it thickens. In a food processor, pulse the graham crackers. Mix the graham cracker crumbs and sugar in another bowl. Add the butter and stir with a fork until well blended. Bake the pie crust on the center rack in the oven for about 15 minutes until the crust is light brown. Remove from the oven and allow to cool to room temperature. Pour the lime filling into the crust, spread evenly, and then bake for 15 minutes until the center sets but still wiggles when shaken. Remove from the oven and cool to room temperature. Refrigerate until thoroughly chilled and enjoy.

"No-Bake" Version:
In large bowl combine the lime juice with the grated lime zest. Stir in the sweetened condensed milk. Allow the mixture to sit about 10 minutes. Fold in the whipped topping thoroughly. Pour the mixture in the graham cracker pie crust and refrigerate at least 3 hours or until thoroughly chilled. Enjoy!

SERVES 8

½ cup Key lime juice, freshly squeezed (you can use any fresh lime juice, if necessary)
4 teaspoons lime zest, grated
4 egg yolks, separated
1 can (14-ounce) sweetened condensed milk
11 graham crackers
3 tablespoons granulated sugar
5 tablespoons unsalted butter, melted

"NO-BAKE" INGREDIENTS

½ cup Key lime juice, freshly squeezed (you can use any fresh lime juice if necessary)
4 teaspoons lime zest, grated
1 can (14-ounce) sweetened condensed milk
1 container (14-ounce) whipped topping
1 ready-made graham cracker pie crust

Chocolate Mousse Cake
DEBORAH SPIEGELMAN, EXECUTIVE DIRECTOR, MIAMI CHILDREN'S MUSEUM

SERVES 8

1 12-ounce bag of chocolate chips

9 eggs, separated

¾ cup sugar, less 3 tablespoons

1½ sticks butter

3 tablespoons instant coffee, dissolved in a
 small amount of hot water

2 half pints heavy cream, whipped

Founded in 1983, the Miami Children's Museum is located on Watson Island and opened its new building to the public in September 2003. Visitors of all ages are encouraged to play together, learn, imagine and create. The Miami Children's Museum is dedicated to enriching the lives of all children by fostering a love of learning and enabling children to realize their highest potential. The museum offers interactive exhibits, programs, and learning materials related to arts, culture, community and communication.

Preheat an oven to 350° F. Melt the butter, chocolate chips and coffee in the top of a double boiler. Stir until smooth. Cool slightly. In a bowl, beat the egg yolks and sugar together. Add this to the chocolate mixture. With an electric stand or hand mixer, beat the egg whites until stiff, then fold into the chocolate mixture. Pour half of the batter into a greased springform pan. Bake for 30 minutes. Remove from the oven and let cool. Fold one half pint whipped cream into the remaining batter. Then pour into the baked shell and freeze. Before serving, place in the refrigerator for about 3-4 hours. Serve with the remaining whipped cream.

"The Secret To A Man's Heart Is Through His Stomach"

Sour Cream Cheesecake

EVELYN LANGLIEB GREER, ESQ.,
MIAMI DADE COUNTY PUBLIC SCHOOL BOARD MEMBER

Evelyn Langlieb Greer was elected to the School Board in 2004. Ms. Greer was the co-founder and first mayor of the Village of Pinecrest from 1996 to 2004. She is president, founder and CEO of Greer Properties, Inc., a diversified real estate developer. She is also an attorney with Hogan, Greer & Shapiro, P.A., a commercial law practice. Ms. Greer has been a member of the Miami-Dade County Superintendent Search Committee, the Joint Task Force on School Overcrowding, and is a current member of Our Kids, a state authorized foster care privatization effort.

This rich and creamy cheesecake is a guilty pleasure and a great crowd pleaser. It is easy to make although not a last minute dish as you have to do it over time in a few steps. You may substitute low fat cream cheese and sour cream without sacrificing taste. Then you can tell everyone that it is good for them!

To make the crust for the cheesecake, first, take the graham crackers, zwieback or ginger snaps and process them in a blender, until very fine. Add the melted butter, confectioners' sugar and the cinnamon until well blended. Pat the mixture into a 9-inch springform pan to an even thickness. Chill the crust well, but do not bake it.

Preheat an oven to 375° F. In a mixing bowl, combine the beaten eggs, soft cream cheese, 1/2 cup sugar and lemon juice or vanilla. Mix well, then pour into the chilled crust. Bake for about 20 minutes. Remove from the oven and dust the top with the cinnamon. Let the cake cool to room temperature. Then heat the oven to 425° F. In a bowl, mix together the sour cream, 2 tablespoons sugar, the vanilla and salt. When well mixed, pour over the cooled cake. Bake in the oven for about 5 minutes to glaze the cheesecake. Remove from the oven and allow to cool. Then refrigerate for 6 to 12 hours before serving.

SERVES 10-12
CRUST INGREDIENTS

1½ cups graham crackers, zwieback or ginger snaps

¼ cup sifted confectioners' sugar

6 tablespoons butter, melted

1 teaspoon cinnamon (optional)

CHEESECAKE INGREDIENTS

2 eggs, well beaten

4 packages soft cream cheese (¾ pound)

½ cup sugar

1 teaspoon lemon juice or ½ teaspoon vanilla

1½ cups thick cultured sour cream

2 tablespoons sugar

½ teaspoon vanilla

⅛ teaspoon salt

Cinnamon to dust

217

Canistel Pie

NORIS LEDESMA, CURATOR OF TROPICAL FRUIT AT FAIRCHILD TROPICAL BOTANIC GARDEN

SERVES 6

3 eggs

1 cup milk

1 cup ripe canistel, peeled and mashed

1 teaspoon ground cinnamon

½ teaspoon ground cloves

1 teaspoon vanilla

1 cup sugar

1 unbaked deep-dish pie shell

Canistel is an orange-yellow fruit whose flesh is sweet, with a texture often compared to that of a cooked egg yolk, hence its colloquial name of "eggfruit." The flavor is sweet and somewhat like that of a baked sweet potato or cooked pumpkin. It is delicious when mixed with milk products, because it doesn't sour the milk like many fruits do.

Preheat an oven to 450° F. Mix eggs and milk together and gradually add the remaining ingredients. Pour into an unbaked pie shell and bake for 15 minutes. Lower temperature to 350° F and bake for 10 minutes more. Let cool before serving.

Pound Cake *With Light Caramel Icing*

BERTA BLECKE, CHILD ADVOCATE, OUR KIDS

Berta, Miami's life-long community volunteer extraordinaire, was instrumental in founding CHARLEE Programs; the Guardian Ad Litem Program; the Haitian Neighborhood Center, Sant La, Inc., Our Kids of Miami-Dade and Monroe Counties; and, of course, Kristi House. She has continued to guide Kristi House and many other organizations as a board member, advocate and generous volunteer.

In a mixing bowl, cream the butter and sugar. Add the eggs one at a time, alternating with flour. Mix well after each addition and then add the vanilla. Start the cake in a cold oven. Bake in a greased and floured bundt pan at 350° F for 1 hour. For the light caramel icing, cook the sugar and milk in a heavy saucepan over medium heat until it forms a soft ball when dropped in water. Remove from the heat and add the butter and vanilla. Stir until creamy and cool. Pour over the cooled pound cake.

SERVES 8
CAKE INGREDIENTS
2 sticks butter (8 ounces)
1¾ cups sugar
6 eggs
2 cups sifted all-purpose flour
1 teaspoon vanilla

CARAMEL ICING INGREDIENTS
3 cups sugar
1 cup milk or light cream
1 cup butter
1 teaspoon vanilla

Walnut Praline Cake
CHEF DAVID BOULEY, Evolution Restaurant

David Bouley, whose other restaurants include Bouley, Danube and Bouley Bakery in New York City, brought his focus on natural flavors to this Miami Beach restaurant at the Ritz Carlton. David Bouley was born and raised near Storrs, Connecticut. From early on he was strongly influenced by life on his grandparent's farm, drawing upon their French heritage and instilling a love of the land, an appreciation for fresh products, care in their preparation, and the inspiration to cook and enjoy healthful meals.

Makes one 10-inch cake, Serves 8

1 cup plus 3 tablespoons sugar

1 cup walnut halves, toasted

2 tablespoons unsalted butter

4 large eggs, separated

⅓ cup plus 2 tablespoons confectioners' sugar

2 ounces milk chocolate, melted and cooled

Pinch of salt

Preheat an oven to 325° F. Butter a 10-inch round cake pan. Line a baking sheet with buttered parchment paper. To prepare the praline, sprinkle ¼ cup of the sugar in an even layer in a heavy skillet. Cook over medium heat, without stirring, until it melts and turns into an amber caramel (swirl the pan if it colors unevenly), for about 5 minutes. Remove the pan from the heat and add the walnuts and butter (stand back, the caramel may sputter), stirring with a wooden spoon. Continue to cook until any hard bits of the caramel melt. Spread the nuts onto the prepared baking sheet to cool. Then transfer the nuts to a food processor and pulse until coarsely ground. Set the nuts aside. Whisk the egg yolks and the confectioners' sugar together in a bowl and stir in the melted chocolate. Set it aside. Place the egg whites in a clean bowl of an electric stand mixer fitted with the whisk attachment, and beat at medium speed until foamy. Sprinkle ½ cup of the remaining sugar and the salt over the egg whites, and beat on high speed until soft peaks form. Gradually sprinkle in the remaining 7 tablespoons of the sugar and beat until stiff, glossy peaks form. Whisk a little of the egg white mixture into the chocolate mixture. Then gently fold the remaining whites into the chocolate. Fold in the walnuts. Scrape the batter into the prepared cake pan and bake until the cake is golden brown on top but still moist inside, about 45 minutes. Let it cool in the pan.

Black Sapote Pudding
NORIS LEDESMA, CURATOR OF TROPICAL FRUIT AT FAIRCHILD TROPICAL BOTANIC GARDEN

A member of the persimmon family, the black sapote is native to both coasts of Mexico. Outside Mexico, it is cultivated in the Philippines, the Dominican Republic, Cuba, Hawaii and Florida. The black sapote, or "Chocolate Fruit", is round and flattened like a tomato. The flesh is dark brown and has a sweet flavor which many people compare to chocolate pudding. Another amazing tropical fruit, it is low in fat and healthy to eat. Most black sapote in South Florida ripen from December through March, a time when we have few other tropical fruits to enjoy. The fruit is picked when full size but unripe (olive-green in color). It will ripen in 10 days at room temperature and is soft when fully ripe. The fruit can be used fresh or frozen. Ripe fruit will store for 3 or 4 days at room temperature. For longer storage, (up to 6 months) pulp should be removed from the fruit and stored in an airtight plastic bag in the freezer. Black sapote is rich in Vitamin A and Vitamin C, and has a relatively high amount of potassium and small amounts of other vitamins and minerals.

SERVES 4

1 cup black sapote, mashed
2 tablespoons coffee flavored brandy
Ladyfingers or other plain cake
10 ounces whipped cream

Mix the black sapote with the brandy and let sit for 15 minutes. Line a deep glass dish with ladyfingers or two layers of thinly cut sponge or plain cake to form a shell about half an inch thick. Spread the brandied black sapote on top of the cake. Chill for 5 hours in the refrigerator.

Flan de Leche *(Traditional Cuban Custard)*
JON SECADA, Singer & Songwriter

SERVES 8

½ cup sugar

½ cup water

1 cup evaporated milk

1 can sweetened condensed milk

1 whole egg

4 egg yolks

2-3 drops vanilla extract

Jon Secada is not only blessed with a soulful voice, but also with an artistry to create, write and produce music. Born in Havana, Cuba, Secada arrived in the United States at the age of nine. In the late 1980's he joined Gloria Estefan as a background singer and co-wrote "Coming Out of the Dark", Gloria's number one hit from her 1991 album, Into the Light. *His self-titled solo debut album sold six million plus copies worldwide and was certified triple platinum in the U.S., where it reached No.15 among Billboard Pop albums. Jon has amassed a career sales total of more than 20 million albums worldwide and he has won three Grammy Awards. Apart from his dedication to music, Jon devotes himself to various charitable endeavors. His commitment to education and helping others led him to create the Jon Secada Music Scholarship at the University of Miami. He also raises funds in Washington, D.C. for the NARAS national "Keeping Music in Schools" and is a supporter of many initiatives including the Pediatric AIDS Unit at Jackson Memorial Hospital, the Lifebeat Concert to benefit AIDS, Amigos Together for Kids, Make-A-Wish Foundation and the Boys and Girls Club, among a host of other charitable organizations.*

Preheat an oven to 350° F. Stir the sugar and water over medium heat in the bottom of a round baking pan until caramelized. Remove from the heat, wait a minute and place the pan in the freezer so that the glaze hardens. In a medium mixing bowl, blend the milks, the egg and yolks, and vanilla. Beat with a whisk or electric mixer until whipped.

Pour the mixture into the baking pan from the freezer. Bake in a water bath for 1 hour. Remove from the oven and let cool for 30 minutes before refrigerating for 4 hours or overnight. Invert onto a serving platter. Serve cold out of the refrigerator.

Pascal's Cookies
MICHAEL B. JACOBS, GRASS RESTAURANT & LOUNGE

The ambiance of Grass invokes dinner in paradise with cushy white banquettes, plush sofas and a full bar illuminated by a wall of apothecary jars brimming with colorful flora. A carpet of thick grass borders the dining room; bonsai plants, bamboo trees and climbing vines cast lovely shadows on the walls. The innovative dinner menu perfectly complements the design, deftly uniting fresh American and Asian ingredients to create light yet satisfying contemporary dishes using light sauces and delicate spicing so as to enhance rather than overshadow the natural flavors. We have created an innovative menu that perfectly fuses contemporary American and Asian ingredients to create light yet satisfying dishes that sing.

SERVES 6-8

2 cups all-purpose flour
1 teaspoon baking powder
8 ounces butter or margarine, softened
6 ounces sugar
7 ounces brown sugar
1½ teaspoon salt
1 whole egg
½ vanilla bean
1 12-ounce package of mini chocolate chips

Preheat an oven to 360° F. Combine the flour, baking powder, salt, sugar, brown sugar, and the butter or margarine in a stand mixer on medium speed. Add the eggs and vanilla mix. Keep mixing until the color starts to change. Add mini chocolate chips and mix on medium high until they are completely incorporated. Divide cookie dough into equal portions and roll into a small thin log, no bigger than a half dollar size. Wrap in baker's paper or plastic wrap and put in the freezer to firm up. To make the cookies, remove the cookie dough from freezer, and cut into ¼ inch thick pieces. Line them up on a cookie sheet lined with baking paper or a silicon pad. Bake for 7-8 minutes. Place on a rack and cool. Serve with a nice cup of hot coffee, espresso, or cappuccino.

Mrs. Russell's Key Lime Sublime

JAMES GRIPPANDO, TRIAL LAWYER-TURNED-BESTSELLING AUTHOR AND HIS MOTHER-IN-LAW, MRS. RUSSELL

*"My dad was a stripper. Okay, now I've got your attention. Actually, he was a printer for almost thirty years, and the technical term for his skill was—I kid you not—'stripper.' My mother was a teacher and later a published author. With that combination, perhaps writing was in my genes. I write thrillers, and it's no accident that thirteen of my fourteen novels—including one for young adults-- are legal thrillers. After all, twelve years as a trial lawyer taught me a thing or two about telling stories. (I said telling stories, not making them up, wiseguy.)"
– James Grippando.*

This recipe is called "Mrs. Russell's Key Lime Sublime." It won a Miami Herald contest for the best Key lime pie in Miami. Mrs. Russell is James Grippando's mother-in-law.

SERVES 8

PIE SHELL INGREDIENTS

2 cups all purpose flour

¼ teaspoon salt

1¾ cups sugar

3½ sticks (14-ounces) unsalted butter

1 egg, lightly beaten

1 tablespoon lime juice, freshly squeezed

3 tablespoon lime zest

FILLING INGREDIENTS

1 cup Key lime juice, freshly squeezed

11 egg yolks, separated and lightly beaten

4 ounces softened cream cheese

1 cup heavy whipping cream

¼ cup superfine (10X) sugar

Preheat an oven to 375° F. In a food processor combine the flour, salt and ½ cup of the sugar. Then add 1½ sticks of the unsalted butter until the mixture resembles coarse corn meal. Add the lightly beaten egg, the lime juice and a tablespoon of the lime zest and pulse until the mixture comes together. Roll the dough out on a floured surface. Carefully place into an 11-inch tart pan with removable sides and crimp the edges. Refrigerate until well chilled. When chilled, remove from the refrigerator and bake for about 20 minutes, cool. In a large saucepan over medium low heat, combine the 2 sticks of butter, 1¼ cups sugar, the cup of Key lime juice and the egg yolks. Bring the mixture to a boil, stirring constantly. Gently boil for about 5 minutes. Don't stop stirring and don't overcook or let the mixture curdle. Remove from the heat and pour ⅓ of the mixture into the pie crust and refrigerate until set, or about 2 hours. Then, in the food processor, mix ½ of the remaining mixture with the softened cream cheese until the mixture is smooth. Then carefully spoon over the chilled pie. Finally, in a mixing bowl, beat 1 cup of heavy whipping cream with ¼ cup superfine sugar until peaks hold their shape. Gently fold in the remaining lime mixture. Spread on top of the chilled pie and sprinkle with grated lime zest.

Avocado Ice Cream
NORIS LEDESMA, CURATOR OF TROPICAL FRUIT
AT FAIRCHILD TROPICAL BOTANIC GARDEN

"Four or five tortillas (corn cakes), an avocado, and a cup of coffee—this is a good meal," proclaimed Wilson Popenoe, one of the foremost avocado explorers. He spent years in the wilds of Central America hunting for the best avocados, surviving on scarcely more than corn and avocado. Avocado is a very healthy fruit; it is relatively low in calories, high in Vitamin A and potassium, and contains no cholesterol. Avocados are great with lemon juice and salt. They can be mashed for guacamole, but are also delicious sliced and served with vegetables, or as an avocado salad with crab, tuna or chicken. Avocados are good in sandwiches and on hamburgers. In Brazil, Vietnam, the Philippines and Indonesia, it is looked on more as a dessert fruit and made into a delicious mousse or ice cream.

MAKES 1 QUART

3 avocados (2 cups)
¼ cup lime juice
1 cup sugar
1 large can sweetened condensed milk
2 cups whipping cream

Process the avocado pulp, lime juice and sugar in blender or food processor. Pour the avocado mixture in an ice cream maker and add the whipping cream and the condensed milk, following the manufacturer's instructions. Freeze and churn until ready.

Favorite Chocolate Meringue Cookies
LAURIE JENNINGS, WPLG-TV Local 10 Anchor

MAKES 24 COOKIES

2 egg whites

½ cup granulated sugar

¼ teaspoon salt

1 small bag semi-sweet chocolate chips

1 teaspoon vanilla

1½ cup flaked coconut

½ cup nuts, walnuts preferred

Laurie Jennings is a two-time Emmy award-winning reporter and the main anchor on the Local 10 News. You can catch her every weeknight at 6 and 11, and often hosting charity or community events in between the evening newscasts. She started her career reporting and anchoring in Youngstown, Ohio at WKBN (CBS), and then in Cleveland at WJW (CBS). From there, it was off to Boston's WHDH (NBC) as their morning anchor, and then to Miami to become the main anchor at WSVN (FOX). After five years at WSVN, she followed her dream of anchoring at the network level when she moved to New York City to anchor for MSNBC. She hosted from two to four hours of breaking news daily, and served as substitute anchor on CNBC with Brian Williams and The Lester Holt Show. South Florida and Local 10 ended up drawing her back — to work and to start her family here. She is the proud mother of identical twin boys, Luke and Jake.

Preheat an oven to 350° F. In a small bowl, melt the chocolate chips over a pan of hot water. In a mixing bowl, use an electric stand or hand mixer to beat the egg whites until stiff and then slowly add the sugar and salt. Combine the two mixtures by folding in the chocolate, being careful not to stir the beaten egg whites. Add the remaining ingredients and mix lightly. Drop spoonfuls of the batter on greased cookie sheets, or on parchment paper-lined baking sheets, and bake for 15 minutes. Enjoy!

Tarte Tatin

FRANCE INGRAHAM AND CHEF CHRISTIAN ANTONIOTTI, Le Provençal

Le Provençal provides all the extravagance and flavor that has made French cooking so famous without a heavy reliance on copious amounts of butter and cream. Instead, you will find an artistic use of herbs and savory vegetables to flavor many traditional French favorites. For example, it is hard to resist the Bouillabaisse, a seafood soup made with various fish and shellfish, served with toasted rounds of French bread. Simple, aromatic and delicious!

Preheat an oven to 375° F. To make the *pâte brisée*, sift the flour, salt, and sugar into a mixing bowl. Cut the butter into small pieces. Using your fingertips, rub the butter into the flour until it is the size of peas. Stir the water and the 2 egg yolks together. Add this to the flour mixture until the dough is supple and free from cracks. Chill in the refrigerator for 30 minutes.

Peel and cut the apples in eighths. Take a round baking dish or flameproof baking dish if you want to start on the stove. Add the sugar and 3 teaspoons of water. Place in the preheated oven or on the stove at moderate heat until you have a nice caramel color. Add the apples and butter to the pan. Put the pan back in the oven for at least 25 minutes. Then cover with a round piece of rolled out short pastry crust. Return it to the oven for about 15 minutes more, or until the crust is golden. Remove from the oven and immediately invert the pan onto a serving platter. The *Tarte Tatin* should release from the pan. Cool slightly. Serve warm *à la mode* with vanilla ice cream.

SERVES 8
FILLING INGREDIENTS
8 Red Delicious apples, peeled and cut in eighths
¾ cup sugar
2 teaspoons butter
3 teaspoons water

SHORT CRUST PASTRY (*PÂTE BRISÉE*) INGREDIENTS
2 cups flour
3 teaspoons sugar
½ teaspoons salt
½ cup butter
2 egg yolks
¼ cup water
NOTE: *Makes ½ pound*

227

Icebox Key Lime Pie
LEE BRIAN SCHRAGER, DIRECTOR,
FOOD NETWORK SOUTH BEACH WINE & FOOD FESTIVAL

MAKES ONE 9-INCH PIE

1½ cups Oreo cookie crumbs

1¼ cups sugar

4 tablespoons butter (½ stick), melted

2 cans (14-ounces each) sweetened condensed milk

1 cup Key lime juice, freshly squeezed

2 large egg yolks

6 large egg whites

Key lime slices for garnish

"No one else does or has ever done what Mr. Schrager does in the food world. As Bill Graham was to booking rock 'n' roll acts from the 1960s through the 1980s and Swifty Lazar was to closing Hollywood deals during the studio era, Mr. Schrager is to wrangling celebrity chefs. They know him, they love him, they cross oceans for him. As the charismatic director of the South Beach Wine & Food Festival, he has in seven years transformed what was originally a one-day wine tasting event on the campus of Florida International University for a few hundred people into a four-day extravaganza on the sand attracting tens of thousands of visitors, and, this year, a live broadcast on the Today *show."*
– New York Times

Preheat an oven to 350° F. In a medium bowl, mix together the Oreo crumbs, 1/2 cup of the sugar, and the melted butter until the mixture resembles wet sand. With clean hands, firmly press the mixture evenly across the bottom and up the sides of a 9-inch pie pan. Place the pie pan in the oven and bake until the crust is firm, about 15 minutes. When done, remove the pie crust from the oven and let cool completely on a wire rack before filling.

In a separate bowl, whisk together the condensed milk, Key lime juice, and egg yolks. Pour into the cooled pie shell. Place the pie in the oven and bake until set, about 15 minutes. Remove from the oven and transfer to a wire rack to cool. While the pie is baking, make the meringue by placing the 6 egg whites in a large clean bowl and beating them with an electric hand mixer until soft peaks start to form. Slowly add the remaining 3/4 cup of sugar while beating constantly. Beat until stiff, glossy peaks form. Be careful not to overbeat the meringue, as it will appear grainy or clumpy instead of smooth and glossy and will be difficult to spread. Using a rubber spatula, spread the meringue evenly over the warm pie filling, smoothing out to the edges so the meringue won't pucker or get runny during baking. With a dull knife, make decorative peaks in

the meringue.

Position the baking rack in the upper third of oven and preheat the broiler. Place the pie under the broiler and cook until the meringue is golden brown, about 1 minute. Make sure to keep an eye on this, it will brown quickly! Very carefully remove the pie from under the broiler. Refrigerate until thoroughly chilled, at least 2 hours. Serve garnished with a Key lime slice if desired.

Lucy's Mom's Bread Pudding
LUCY MORILLO, ESQ., PRESIDENT,
MIAMI CHILDREN'S HOSPITAL FOUNDATION

SERVES 16

1 pound sliced white bread

3½ cups milk

4 tablespoons melted butter

1¼ cups sugar

¼ teaspoon salt

2 teaspoons vanilla

1 tablespoon cinnamon

½ cup seedless raisins

3 lightly beaten eggs

Lucy Morillo, the president of the Miami Children's Hospital Foundation, brings knowledge, enthusiasm and energy to her mission of letting out the secret that Miami Children's Hospital, recognized as one of the best children's hospitals in the country, is right here in our own backyard. Lucy, an attorney bar certified to practice law in Florida, comes to Miami Children's Hospital Foundation with extensive experience in fundraising, previously as the Executive Director of Estate and Gift Planning for the University of Miami.

Preheat an oven to 350° F. Trim off the bread crusts and soak the bread in the milk until soft, then mash or purée. Add the melted butter and blend well. Add the sugar, salt, vanilla, cinnamon and raisins. Mix well. Add the eggs, mix well, and pour into a buttered 9 x 9 x 2 inch baking dish. Bake for 1 1/2 hours or until a toothpick or cake tester inserted near the center comes out clean. If it is browning too fast, reduce the heat to 325° F. When done, remove from the oven and let cool in the baking dish.

Mississippi Mud
LYNN MARTINEZ, WSVN-TV CHANNEL 7 NEWS ANCHOR, DECO DRIVE CO-HOST

Martinez came to WSVN in 1991 as a co-anchor of Today in Florida, *and general assignment reporter. One of a trio of anchors in the morning, Martinez quickly rose through the ranks and was promoted to weekend anchor. Two years later, she moved to her current assignment on the weeknight news. In 1998, she began co-hosting* Deco Drive, *the half-hour news magazine show known for celebrity news and the latest on the South Florida entertainment circuit. For* Deco Drive, *Martinez has also interviewed numerous celebrities, among them Gloria and Emilio Estefan, Julio Iglesias, Cameron Diaz, Andy Garcia and Keanu Reeves. Martinez won an award for a series on organ donation called "Dying for an Organ," and was nominated for an Emmy for her coverage of Hurricane Andrew.*

"This is a recipe I remember from my childhood. My granny is from the south and used to make this for us in the summer. It's super simple and decadent and perfect for kids."

Preheat an oven to 350° F. In a mixing bowl, cream the butter, sugar and 4 teaspoons of the cocoa. Then add the eggs and a teaspoon of the vanilla. Mix well and add the flour, coconut and nuts. Beat for 2 minutes. Spread the batter on a greased cookie sheet and bake for 30-40 minutes. Remove from the oven and spread the marshmallow cream on top and let cool. To make the frosting, mix the stick of butter, a teaspoon of the vanilla and 2 tablespoons of cocoa with the splash of milk. Add the powdered sugar as needed to get a smooth and spreadable consistency. Spread the chocolate frosting over the top. Serve with a glass of milk!

SERVES 12
2 sticks butter
2 cups sugar
4 eggs
1 teaspoon vanilla
1½ cups all-purpose flour
4 teaspoons cocoa
1⅓ cups shredded coconut
1½ cups nuts
1 jar marshmallow cream

FROSTING INGREDIENTS
1 stick butter
1 teaspoon vanilla
2 tablespoons cocoa
Splash of milk
Powdered sugar, as needed

Grannies' Apple Cake

TRUDY NOVICKI, EXECUTIVE DIRECTOR OF KRISTI HOUSE, INC

Kristi House provides a healing environment for all child victims of sexual abuse and their families, regardless of income, through prevention, treatment and coordination of services with our community partners. Kristi House strives to end the epidemic of child sexual abuse in Miami-Dade County by healing those who have been victims and breaking the cycle of abuse for future generations. Kristi House is dedicated to respecting, protecting, and healing the children and families that pass through its doors.

SERVES 8

CAKE INGREDIENTS

3½ cups tart apples, peeled and diced

2 cups sugar

1 cup butter, melted

2 eggs

3 cups flour

2 tablespoons baking soda

½ tablespoon each salt, cinnamon, allspice, nutmeg, and cloves

1 cup English walnuts

GLAZE INGREDIENTS

1 stick of margarine, melted

2 tablespoons hot water

1½ cups confectioners' sugar, sifted

Preheat an oven to 375° F. In a large bowl, combine the sugar with the apples and let stand while sifting all of the dry ingredients together in a separate bowl. Stir a little of the dry mixture into the chopped walnuts. Next, add the melted butter to the sugar and apple mixture and then beat in the eggs. Blend in the dry ingredients and, lastly, the walnuts. Turn the batter into a well greased 9-inch tube pan and bake for 1 hour. Remove from the oven and let cool for 5 minutes before removing from the pan. Turn out onto a cake plate and cool to lukewarm.

Glaze:

To make the glaze, beat together the margarine, hot water and the sifted confectioners' sugar in a bowl. Spread the glaze on the warm cake and serve.

Note: Mix the cake by hand because an electric mixer will destroy the texture of the apples.

Christmas Pie

MARY CAGEL, FORMER CEO OF CHARLEE HOUSE

Over the past 25 years, CHARLEE of Dade County, Inc. has cared for the hardest to serve foster children, who have been abandoned, abused or neglected by their biological families. CHARLEE, which stands for Children Have All Rights: Legal, Educational, and Emotional, was incorporated in Miami in 1983 through the coordinated efforts of the Junior League of Miami, the National Council of Jewish Women, and the Episcopal Diocese of Southeast Florida. Since its inception, CHARLEE has helped thousands of children in the foster care system begin a new life and today, CHARLEE serves approximately 1,000 children and their families annually.

Mix the envelope of unflavored gelatin and 1/4 cup of cold water in a small bowl to soften the gelatin. In a saucepan, mix together the sugar, flour and salt. Then gradually stir in the 1 1/2 cups of milk. Put the saucepan over medium low heat until it boils and allow it to boil for 1 minute. Remove from the heat and stir in the softened gelatin and then allow to cool. When it's partially set, beat until smooth. Then blend in the vanilla and almond extracts. Fold in the 1/2 cup whipped cream. In a separate mixing bowl, make a meringue by beating the egg whites and cream of tartar until the mixture becomes frothy. Gradually add 1/2 cup of the sugar and continue beating until the mixture becomes stiff and glossy. Then fold 1 cup of the angel flake coconut into the mixture and fold the meringue into the whip cream batter. Pour the combined mixtures into the pie shell. Sprinkle the remaining 1/2 cup coconut on top. Chill in the refrigerator, until set, for about 2 hours.

SERVES 8

1 envelope unflavored gelatin

1/4 cup cold water

1/2 cup sugar

4 tablespoons flour

1/2 teaspoon of salt

1 1/2 cups milk

3/4 teaspoon of vanilla

1/4 teaspoon almond extract

1/2 cup whipped cream

3 large egg whites

1/4 teaspoon of cream tartar

1/2 cup sugar

1 1/2 cup angel flake coconut

1 cooled baked pie crust,

(or pre-made pie shell from the grocer)

Rosa Wolfson's Pound Cake
MICHELE OKA DONER & MITCHELL WOLFSON, JR., AUTHORS

SERVES 8

2 cups butter

2 teaspoons vanilla

3 cups sugar

2 teaspoons almond flavoring

8 eggs, separated

2 jiggers (6 tablespoons) bourbon

3 cups flour

½ cup, or more pecans, finely chopped

Mary Randolph's 1824 cookbook, The Virginia Housewife, *was the first collection of what were considered to be American recipes and included a recipe for pound cake. The book establishes a provenance for what has been a favorite dessert for American families for almost two centuries. Her recipes attempted to standardize classics, and pound cake has as many variations as the cook's palate or the location's peculiar ingredients. Mrs. Wolfson's family pound cake increased the sugar and decreased the flour. This was a departure from the original pound cake recipe, which earned its name from a uniform measurement of ingredients: a pound of butter, a pound of sugar, and a pound of flour. The incorporation of pecans adds a southern touch appropriate for the great-granddaughter of a soldier who fought for the Confederacy. Mitchell Wolfson also fondly recalled his mother Rosa's pound cake. Rosa used cashews instead of pecans. The African influence on American cooking is noteworthy, and one wonders if this influence is responsible for the introduction of nuts into pound cakes from southern kitchens. It is within the realm of possibility to take this already perfect pound cake a little bit further. The vanilla vine, a member of the orchid family, grows in Dade County. The vine crawls freely over trees, clinging with its tenacious roots. If you can find these or more readily available* Vanilla planifolia, *take the fresh vanilla bean, enclose it in a jar of sugar, and seal it tight. Within a week, the perfumed sugar is ready to be added to the pound cake.*

Preheat an oven to 350° F. Cream the butter, gradually adding sugar and beat until fluffy. Then add egg yolks one at a time, continuing to beat until very light and fluffy. Be sure not to under-beat. Add the vanilla and almond flavoring, along with the bourbon, to the mixture. Then add the flour. Beat the egg whites until they form stiff peaks. Carefully fold the stiffly beaten egg whites into the batter. Grease a tube pan. Line with wax paper and in the bottom of the pan spread a layer of finely chopped pecans. This layer should be about one-quarter inch thick. Carefully pour in the batter and bake for an hour-and-a-half. When a toothpick inserted into the cake comes out clean, remove from the oven and set aside to cool.

Reprinted with permission from *Miami Beach: Blueprint of an Eden: Lives Seen through the Prism of Family and Place.* Feierabend Unique Books.

Grandma Sarah's 7-Layer Cake

PAMELA KATZ ZAKHEIM, M. ED., FOUNDER, THE WELLNESS COMMUNITY OF GREATER MIAMI AND OF BOSTON

The Wellness Community provides psychosocial support services free of charge to those affected by cancer.

This yellow cake with mocha frosting never ceases to impress my guests, but it's actually very easy to make and it's delicious. I don't know where my Hungarian grandmother got the recipe from originally, but she would literally throw this cake together for special occasions, always using her hands as measuring cups. When I was a child this was my favorite cake, (still is actually), so one day I got the recipe from her by taking her handfuls of each ingredient, putting them into measuring cups and then writing each measurement down in my childish handwriting.

Preheat an oven to 350° F. Butter and flour seven 9-inch cake pans. In a bowl on an electric stand mixer, beat the eggs for about 15 minutes or until thick and and light yellow. Add the sugar and salt and beat until well blended. Sift the flour with the baking powder and add this to the egg mixture. The batter will be very thick at this point. Mix the vanilla and water together and add slowly to the batter. Spoon about 1 soup ladle (or about 8 ounces) of batter into each of the 7 prepared layer pans. The batter should cover the bottom of each pan evenly. Bake each pan for about 15 minutes, or until the center springs back to your touch (I put three in one oven and four in another). When ready, remove from the oven and turn out onto a rack and to cool.

To prepare the icing, beat the butter until fluffy and add the melted chocolate and coffee. Add the powdered sugar and mix until smooth. Taste to see if it has enough coffee flavor, if not add some more espresso. If frosting becomes too soft, refrigerate it for a short time before frosting the cake. It should be soft enough to spread easily, but not so soft it runs. Frost each layer and when finished stack the next layer on top of it. It will be a very tall cake! When the full cake is assembled place in refrigerator. To serve, remove from the refrigerator and serve at either room temperature or cooled. Enjoy!

SERVES 10

CAKE INGREDIENTS

6 extra large eggs

2 cups sugar

1 dash salt

2 cups cake or all-purpose flour

2 teaspoons baking powder

⅔ cup water

2 teaspoons vanilla

ICING INGREDIENTS

3 sticks butter, softened

3 ounces unsweetened chocolate, melted (I think Bakers™ brand chocolate is best)

1 box powdered sugar, sifted

4 tablespoons instant Espresso coffee, dissolved in hot water or hot coffee—you want to end up with very strong espresso and you'll use about 3 tablespoons for flavoring the frosting.

235

Hot Apple Walnut Upside Down Pie
GENERAL MANAGER PETER KNEZEVIC,
The Rusty Pelican Restaurant

The Rusty Pelican is the most sought after restaurant with a view in South Florida. With the sun setting on Biscayne Bay against the backdrop of the alluring Miami skyline, The Rusty Pelican is the perfect spot for a romantic interlude or that special occasion. Located on Key Biscayne, The Rusty Pelican has a breathtaking view of the City of Miami while offering superb cuisine and service. The fresh seafood changes with the season, deliciously enhanced with island-influenced salsas and flavors.

Makes one pie

7 ounces butter, melted

10 ounces light brown sugar

7 ounces walnuts, coarsely chopped

Parchment or baking paper

½ ounce butter spray or vegetable oil spray

2 refrigerated pie pastries, to make 9⅝-inch pie

1½ pounds fresh apples, peeled and cut into wedges

Egg wash (1 egg beaten with 1 teaspoon water)

½ ounce butter to butter pie pan

Cinnamon Mix Ingredients

1 ounce ground cinnamon

½ teaspoon grated nutmeg

Pinch of salt

¼ cup flour

1 pound sugar

Prepare cinnamon mix by combining all ingredients together in a bowl and set aside.

Preheat an oven to 325° F. Heat the butter in a heavy round brazier or large sauté pan and add the sugar, stirring until the sugar dissolves. Then stir in the walnut pieces. Blend well, cool and set aside. To make the pie, line the bottom of the pie pan with baking paper. Spray the baking paper with the butter spray. Spread the butter-nut mix over the bottom of the baking paper and about 3/4 inch up the sides of the pie pan. Lay the bottom pie crust over the butter-nut mix, stretching it slightly to fit. Lay the apples on top of the pie crust. Dab the butter, broken into small pieces over the top of the apples. Place on top of this the second pie pastry. Crimp it together. Flute the edge removing any trace of the original crimp. Cut 4 "V's" in the crust for the pie to breathe. Brush the pie with egg wash and sprinkle it with the cinnamon mix. Bake for about 1 hour and 15 minutes. Cool it on a baking rack for 2 hours before serving. Serve with cinnamon ice cream.

Chocolate Lava Cake

ROBERT M. HEUER, GENERAL DIRECTOR, FLORIDA GRAND OPERA

Florida Grand Opera, celebrating its 68th anniversary season of continuous performances, stands as one of the oldest performing arts organizations in Florida. Florida Grand Opera is one of the four resident companies of The Adrienne Arsht Center for the Performing Arts of Miami-Dade County, making its home the Sanford and Dolores Ziff Ballet Opera House. Florida Grand Opera was formed in June 1994 by the merger of Greater Miami Opera, founded in 1941, and The Opera Guild Inc. of Fort Lauderdale, founded in 1945. Florida Grand Opera presents five main-stage productions annually at The Adrienne Arsht Center for the Performing Arts of Miami-Dade County, and at the Broward Center for the Performing Arts in Fort Lauderdale.

"This rich warm chocolate cake can be prepared ahead of time and only requires 6-7 minutes in the oven to serve. The outside is cake-like and the center will ooze like lava. This is the easiest desert I have ever made and very impressive to serve to guests."

SERVES 4

¾ cup butter (1½ sticks), additional butter for the molds

6 ounces bittersweet chocolate, such as Valrhona

3 whole eggs

3 egg yolks

⅓ cup sugar

1 teaspoon vanilla

3 teaspoons flour, additional for dusting the molds

Confectioners' sugar

Preheat an oven to 400° F. Heat the butter and chocolate in the top of a double boiler or in a bowl over a pot of hot water, until melted. While the butter and chocolate are melting, beat the whole eggs, egg yolks and sugar until light and thick. Then beat the melted chocolate and butter and add to the egg mixture. Add vanilla and then the flour quickly and mix lightly. Butter and flour six (4-ounce) star shaped or similar molds or ramekins. Be sure to tap out the excess flour. Pour the batter into the molds. The molds can now be stored in the refrigerator until you are ready to bake them. Remove molds from the refrigerator several hours before baking to return them to room temperature. Place the molds on a cookie sheet and bake for 6-7 minutes. The outside should be firm and the inside very soft. Invert each mold onto a dessert plate and lift the mold off. If necessary, tap the mold a couple of times and the cake with fall onto the plate. Sprinkle with the confectioners' sugar and serve immediately. You can also serve with fresh berries or caramel ice cream.

Mango Cake
ROBERT & TRACEY MOEHLING,
ROBERT IS HERE FRUIT STAND & FARM

SERVES 8-10

CAKE INGREDIENTS

4 eggs

1½ cups sugar

½ cup vegetable oil

1 cup honey

2 cups flour

2 teaspoons baking powder

2 teaspoons cinnamon

1½ teaspoons baking soda

1 teaspoon nutmeg

2 cups mango, diced

½ orange rind, grated

½ lime rind, grated

1 cup chopped walnuts or pecans

½ cup raisins

GLAZE INGREDIENTS

1 cup sifted powdered sugar

1 tablespoon orange juice

Robert Is Here Fruit Stand was established by Robert in 1959. At that time, six-year-old Robert was set on a street corner with some of his father's cucumber crop and told to "Sell 'em!" Robert sat all day on that Saturday and no one even stopped. That evening, Robert's father decided "there can't be that many people who don't like cucumbers; they must not see this little boy standing here on the corner." The next day Robert's father placed a sign on each side of the table proclaiming in big red letters "Robert Is Here". By noon Robert had sold all of the cucumbers and walked home.

As a farmer specializing in tropical fruits, Robert has been featured on NBC's Today Show, *on* World News Tonight, *and in newspapers and magazines across the country. But don't bet on leaving his fruit stand empty-handed; you'd have a hard time resisting the wonderful aromas of fresh fruits and vegetables. Fruits like* Monstera deliciosa, *which looks like a giant green ear of corn but tastes like banana and pineapple; Carambola, or "Star Fruit"; Mamey; Lychee; Atemoya; Papaya; and in summer Robert's pride and joy—MANGOES!*

Preheat an oven to 350° F. In a large mixing bowl, beat the eggs until fluffy, then beat in the sugar, then the oil and gradually add honey. In another bowl, combine the flour, baking powder, cinnamon, baking soda and nutmeg. Mix well and add to the wet mixture gradually in four parts. Next, stir in the mango, grated rinds, nuts and raisins. Bake in a lightly oiled and floured large bundt pan for 40-45 minutes or until the edges of the cake separate from the pan. To make the glaze for the cake, mix together the powdered sugar and orange juice and pour the glaze over the cake after the cake is cold.

Ginger Scented Dark Chocolate Torte
EXECUTIVE CHEF MARK ZEITOUNI,
LIDO RESTAURANT & BAYSIDE GRILL

The Lido Restaurant & Bayside Grill at The Standard Miami are inspired by the traditional Mediterranean diet and lifestyle; healthy, sun-kissed, wholesome and natural. Executive Chef Mark Zeitouni meticulously executes the menu with an emphasis on high quality and organic meats and fish, olive oil, fresh herbs, unprocessed foods, grill cooking with organic and bio-dynamic wines. The philosophy of living and eating well is an integral part of Mediterranean culture from Turkey to Greece, Italy and the South of France.

Preheat an oven to 350° F. Line a 9 x 13 inch cake pan with wax paper and lightly grease.

Place a small saucepan half filled with water on the stove on medium-low heat and place a bowl with the chopped chocolate on top of the saucepan. Carefully melt the chocolate and remove when all of the chocolate is fully melted. Then mix the 1/2 cup water, ginger juice, and sugar in a saucepan over medium heat, until the sugar is dissolved. Lightly mix the 6 whole eggs in a separate bowl.

Add the ginger, water, and sugar mixture to the chocolate, then add the eggs. Mix carefully. Pour the batter into the cake pan and bake for 23 minutes.

SERVES 6

16 ounces dark chocolate, chopped
½ cup fresh ginger juice
½ cup water
½ cup granulated sugar
6 whole eggs
4 ounces butter
180 grams (or roughly 6⅓ ounces) fresh brewed coffee

Warm Apple Cake with Crème Anglaise
LOUIS AGUIRRE, WSVN-TV CHANNEL 7 DECO DRIVE CO-HOST

Award- winning journalist Louis Aguirre began his television career at Telemundo in 1989 as a reporter, where he received an Emmy for a series chronicling the AIDS Crisis in America. In 1990, Aguirre joined WPLG as a reporter later becoming weekend anchor. In 1994, Aguirre left South Florida to become a correspondent for EXTRA!, *a nationally syndicated entertainment show. Later, Aguirre served as correspondent on* A Current Affair *and hosted the FOX morning news show,* FOX and FRIENDS. *Aguirre then decided to pursue a career in entertainment. He served as guest star on hit shows such as* Sex And The City, Days of Our Lives *and* JAG. *He returned to South Florida in 2003 as WSVN's entertainment reporter and fill-in anchor for* Deco Drive, *the station's wildly popular entertainment show. He is now the permanent co-host of* Deco Drive.

First, you need to prepare the *crème anglaise*, which can be made the day before and refrigerated until ready to use. In a medium mixing bowl, whisk the egg yolks and 2/3 cup sugar until well blended. Pour the half-and-half into a medium saucepan. Slice open the vanilla bean and using the back edge of a paring knife, scrape the seeds from the vanilla bean into the half-and-half in the saucepan. Then add the vanilla bean husk. Bring the mixture to a simmer over medium heat. Remove from the heat and very gradually whisk the hot half-and-half mixture into the egg mixture. Note that you must do this very slowly or the eggs will curdle! Return the mixture to the saucepan and stir over medium low heat for about 12 minutes or until the custard thickens slightly and leaves a coating on the back of the spoon. Discard the vanilla bean. Cover and refrigerate until well chilled.

To prepare the cake, preheat an oven to 350° F and coat an 8-inch spring form pan with vegetable cooking spray. Core and cut the apples into 1-inch chunks and set aside. In a mixing bowl, combine the sugar, margarine, cream cheese, and vanilla. Beat at low speed with a electric stand or hand mixer for

SERVES 8
CAKE INGREDIENTS

3 cups Rome or Golden Delicious apples, cut into 1-inch chunks

2 eggs

½ cup margarine

6 ounces cream cheese (you can use low-fat but not non-fat)

1½ cups sugar

1 teaspoon plus pure vanilla extract

1½ cups unbleached flour

1½ teaspoons baking powder

¼ teaspoon salt

TOPPING INGREDIENTS

¼ cup sugar

2 teaspoons cinnamon

CRÈME ANGLAISE INGREDIENTS

6 egg yolks

⅔ cup of sugar

2 cups whole milk or half-and-half

1 vanilla bean

Strawberries for garnish

240

Photo Credit: Paul Greco

about 4 minutes or until creamy. Add the eggs one at a time. In a separate bowl, sift together the flour, baking powder and salt. Slowly add the dry ingredients to the wet mixture, while mixing on low speed until completely blended. In another bowl, combine the 2 teaspoons cinnamon and 1/4 cup sugar for the topping and mix together well. Add 2 tablespoons of the cinnamon sugar mixture to the chopped apples and stir to coat well. Add the apples to the cake batter and mix. Pour the batter into the prepared spring form pan. Sprinkle the remaining cinnamon sugar topping over the batter and bake until a toothpick or knife comes out clean. This should take about 45 to 75 minutes, depending on your oven. When done, remove from the oven and let cool for 1 hour. Slice and serve over the *crème anglaise*. Garnish with strawberries.

Key Lime Pie
OWNERS JoANN BASS AND STEPHEN SAWITZ,
JOE'S STONE CRAB

The recipe for Joe's Stone Crab's world-famous Key Lime Pie has been a closely held family secret for decades. Now you can make this south Florida classic in your own kitchen!

MAKES ONE 9-INCH PIE

INGREDIENTS FOR THE CRUST

1 wax paper-wrapped package graham crackers

(⅓ of a 1 pound box) or

1 cup and 2½ tablespoon graham cracker crumbs

5 tablespoons unsalted butter, melted

⅓ cup sugar

INGREDIENTS FOR THE FILLING

3 egg yolks

1½ teaspoon grated zest of 2 limes

1 14-ounce can sweetened condensed milk

⅔ cup lime juice, freshly squeezed

INGREDIENTS FOR THE TOPPING

1 cup heavy or whipped cream, chilled

1 tablespoon confectioners' sugar

To make the graham cracker crust, preheat an oven to 350° F. Butter a 9-inch pie pan. Break up the graham crackers and place in a food processor and process to crumbs. If you don't have a food processor, place the crackers in a large plastic bag, seal it, and then crush the crackers with a rolling pin. Add the melted butter and sugar and pulse or stir until combined. Press the mixture into the bottom and sides of the pie pan, forming a neat border around the edge. Bake the crust until set and golden, about 8 minutes. Set aside on a wire rack and leave the oven on.

Meanwhile, to make the filling, beat the egg yolks and lime zest at high speed in a mixing bowl using an electric stand mixer with the wire whisk attachment until they are very fluffy, about 5 minutes. Gradually add the condensed milk and continue to beat until thick, 3 or 4 minutes longer. Lower the mixer speed and slowly add the lime juice, mixing just until combined, no longer. Pour the mixture into the crust. Bake for 10 minutes or until the filling has just set. Cool on a wire rack, then refrigerate. Freeze for 15 to 20 minutes before serving.

Finally, to make the topping, whip the cream and the confectioners' sugar until nearly stiff. Cut the pie in wedges and serve very cold, topping each wedge with a large dollop of whipped cream.

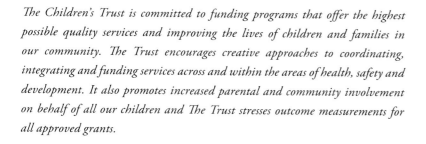

Bobbi & Aunt Ceil's Chocolate Chip Bundt Cake

DAVID LAWRENCE, JR., CHAIRMAN, THE CHILDREN'S TRUST

The Children's Trust is committed to funding programs that offer the highest possible quality services and improving the lives of children and families in our community. The Trust encourages creative approaches to coordinating, integrating and funding services across and within the areas of health, safety and development. It also promotes increased parental and community involvement on behalf of all our children and The Trust stresses outcome measurements for all approved grants.

Preheat the oven to 350º F. Butter and flour a bundt pan. In a mixing bowl, combine the eggs, vegetable oil and water and mix together. Add the cake mix and instant pudding. Using a hand or stand mixer, mix for 5 minutes. Grate the German chocolate into the cake mix and then fold the German chocolate and chocolate chips through the cake mixture. Pour the mixture evenly into the bundt pan. Bake for approximately 60 minutes, or until the cake springs back when touched. Remove the cake from the oven, cool for 10 minutes and then turn onto a cake rack. Sprinkle with confectioners' sugar and allow cooling before cutting and serving.

SERVES 6-8

1 box yellow cake mix (I prefer Duncan Hines brand)
1 small box instant vanilla pudding
(I prefer Jell-O brand)
½ bar Baker's German sweet chocolate
1 small package chocolate chips (I prefer Nestlé brand)
4 whole eggs
½ cup vegetable oil (I prefer Crisco brand)
1 cup water
Confectioners' sugar

In 1977 Elizabeth Plater-Zyberk was a co-founder of the architectural firm Arquitectonica. In 1979 she began teaching at the University of Miami School of Architecture at which she is now the Dean for the department. Dean Plater-Zyberk is a founder and emeritus board member of the Congress for the New Urbanism, which was established in 1993. She has been awarded many honorary doctorate degrees and awards. Her recent publications include "The New Civic Art" and "Suburban Nation: The Rise of Sprawl and The Decline of the American Dream".

SERVES 4-6

THIN PASTRY CRUST INGREDIENTS

1¼ cup flour

½ teaspoon salt

¼ cup ice water (or more, if needed)

¼ cup (½ stick) salted butter

FILLING INGREDIENTS

6-7 yellow skin apples

Pinch of cinnamon

Walnuts

Raisins

TOPPING INGREDIENTS

2 tablespoons flour

3 or 4 tablespoons sugar

2 tablespoons butter

Allspice

Sift flour and salt; cut in butter, flake with fingers. When the flour is mealy, add ice water. Work mixture into a ball with your hands. Roll the pastry in a ball and wrap in waxed paper. Refrigerate 30 minutes. Roll the chilled pastry out on a floured surface, turning several times. Place in a pie pan, then flute the edges.

Combine topping ingredients together in a bowl and set aside.

Preheat an oven to 350° F. Core the apples (do not peel), then cube the apples and put in the crust. Sprinkle with cinnamon, walnuts and raisins. Cover with the topping mix. Bake for 45 minutes. Cool, slice and enjoy!

Recipe used with permission of Bob Davis.

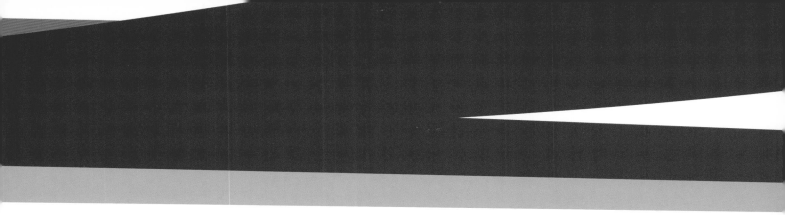

RESTAURANT LIST

1 Bleu Restaurant
10295 Collins Avenue
Bal Harbour, Florida 33154
305-455-5400

A Fish Called Avalon Seafood Grille
700 Ocean Drive
Miami Beach, Florida 33139
305-532-1727

Alta Cocina
5837 Sunset Drive
South Miami, Florida 33143
305-662-7435

AltaMar Restaurant
1223 Lincoln Road
Miami Beach, Florida 33139
305-532-3061

Anacapri On Ponce
2530 Ponce de Leon Boulevard
Coral Gables, Florida 33134
305-443-8388

Andú Restaurant & Lounge
141 SW 7th Street
Miami, Florida 33130
786-871-7005

Atrio
Conrad Miami
1395 Brickell Avenue
Miami, Florida 33131
305-503-6529

Azul
Mandarin Oriental Miami
500 Brickell Key Drive
Miami, Florida 33131
305-913-8358

Balans Restaurant
1022 Lincoln Road
Miami Beach, Florida 33139
305-534-9191

Barton G. The Restaurant
1427 West Avenue
Miami Beach, Florida 33139
305-672-8821

Berries in the Grove
2884 SW 27th Avenue
Coconut Grove, Florida 33133
305-448-2111

Blue Door Restaurant
Delano Hotel
1685 Collins Avenue
Miami Beach, Florida 33139
1-800-697-1791

Cacao Restaurant
141 Giralda Avenue
Coral Gables, Florida 33134
305-445-1001

Café Pastis
7310 Red Road (SW 57th Avenue)
South Miami, Florida 33143

Caffè Abbracci
318 Aragon Avenue
Coral Gables, Florida 33134
305-441-0700

Casa Juancho
2436 SW 8th Street
Miami, Florida 33135
305-642-2452

Casa Tua
1700 James Avenue
Miami Beach, Florida 33139
305-673-1010

Casablanca Seafood Bar & Grill
400 NW North River Drive
Miami, Florida 33128
305-371-4107

Cefalo's Wine Cellar in the Grove
3540 Main Highway
Coconut Grove, Florida 33133
305-971-2400

Chef Allen's
19088 NE 29th Avenue
Aventura, Florida 33180
305-935-2900

Chispa Restaurant & Bar
11500 NW 41st Street
Doral, Florida 33178
305-591-7166

CHOCOLATE, FINE ARGENTINEAN CUISINE
2093 Coral Way
Miami, Florida 33145
305-858-1787

CITY CELLAR WINE BAR & GRILL
Coral Gables Location CLOSED
700 South Rosemary Avenue
City Place
West Palm Beach, Florida 33401

DOLORES BUT YOU CAN CALL ME LOLITA RESTAURANT & LOUNGE
1000 South Miami Avenue
at the Fire Station #4
Miami, Florida 33130
305-403-3103

EMERIL'S MIAMI BEACH
Loews Miami Beach Hotel
1601 Collins Avenue
Miami Beach, Florida 33139
305-695-4550

ESCOPAZZO ORGANIC ITALIAN RESTAURANT
1311 Washington Avenue
Miami Beach, Florida 33139
305-674-9450

EVOLUTION RESTAURANT
CLOSED

FRANCESCO RESTAURANT
325 Alcazar Avenue
Coral Gables, Florida 33134
305-446-1600

GARCIA'S SEAFOOD GRILLE & FISH MARKET
398 NW North River Drive
Miami, Florida 33129
305-375-0765

GOURMET CREATIONS
9529 SW 72nd Street
Miami, Florida 33173
305-598-3240

GRASS RESTAURANT & LOUNGE
28 NE 40th Street
Miami, Florida 33137
305-573-3355

HOUSE OF INDIA
22 Merrick Way
Coral Gables, Florida 33134
305-444-2348

HY VONG VIETNAMESE CUISINE
3458 SW 8th Street
Miami, Florida 33135
305-446-3674

ISHQ
530 Ocean Drive
Miami Beach, Florida 33139
305-532-4747

JAKE'S BAR & GRILL
6901 Red Road (SW 57th Avenue)
South Miami, Florida 33143
305-662-8632

JOE'S STONE CRAB
11 Washington Avenue
Miami Beach, Florida 33139
1-800-780-CRAB (2722)

JOHN MARTIN'S IRISH PUB AND RESTAURANT
253 Miracle Mile
Coral Gables, Florida 33134
305-445-3777

JUMBO'S RESTAURANT
7501 NW 7th Avenue
Miami, Florida 33150
305-751-1127

KARU & Y
Restaurant CLOSED at time of printing
Will re-open late 2008
71 NW 14th Street
Miami, Florida 33136
305-403-7850

LA COFRADIA
160 Andalusia Avenue
Coral Gables, Florida 33134
305-914-1300

La Marea at the Tides
1220 Ocean Drive
Miami Beach, Florida 33139
305-604-5070

La Palma Ristorante
116 Alhambra Circle
Coral Gables, Florida 33134
305-445-8777

Lan Pan Asian Café
8332 South Dixie Highway
Miami, Florida 33143
305-661-8141

Le Croisic French Bistro
180 Crandon Boulevard
Suite 117
Key Biscayne, Florida 33149
305-361-5888

Le Provencal Restaurant
382 Miracle Mile
Coral Gables, Florida 33134
305-448-8984

Lido Restaurant & Bayside Grill
The Standard Hotel Miami
40 Island Avenue
Miami Beach, Florida 33139
305-673-1717

Lotus Garden
318 Miracle Mile
Coral Gables, Florida 33134
305-446-2360

Mark's South Beach
The Nash Hotel
1120 Collins Avenue
Miami Beach, Florida 33139
305-604-9050

Maroosh Mediterranean Restaurant
223 Valencia Avenue
Coral Gables, Florida 33134
305-476-9800

Michael's Genuine Food & Drink
Atlas Plaza, Miami Design District
130 NE 40th Street
Miami, Florida 33137
305-573-5550

Michy's
6927 Biscayne Boulevard
Miami, Florida 33138
305-759-2001

North One 10 Restaurant
11052 Biscayne Boulevard
North Miami, Florida 33161
305-893-4211

Novecento Restaurant
1414 Brickell Avenue
Miami, Florida 33131
305-403-0900

O Asian Grill
330 Lincoln Road
Miami Beach, Florida 33139
305-531-2811

Oriente at Cardozo
Cardozo Hotel
1300 Ocean Drive
Miami Beach, Florida 33139
305-695-2822

Ortanique on the Mile
278 Miracle Mile
Coral Gables, Florida 33134
305-446-7710

Osteria del Teatro
1443 Washington Avenue
Miami Beach, Florida 33139
305-538-7850

Palme d'Or
The Biltmore Coral Gables
1200 Anastasia Avenue
Coral Gables, Florida 33134
305-913-3201

Pascal's on Ponce
2611 Ponce de Leon Boulevard
Coral Gables, Florida 33134
305-444-2024

Perricone's Marketplace & Cafe
15 SE 10th Street
Miami, Florida 33131
305-374-9449

Poblano Cocina Mexicana
5850-B Sunset Drive
South Miami, Florida 33143
305-740-9087

Prime Blue Grille
315 South Biscayne Boulevard
Miami, Florida 33131
305-358-5900

Shula's Steakhouse
The Alexander Hotel
5225 Collins Avenue
Miami Beach, Florida 33140
305-341-6565

Soyka's Restaurant Café & Bar
5582 NE 4th Court
Miami, Florida 33137
305-759-3117

Table 8
1458 Ocean Drive
Miami Beach, Florida 33139
305-695-4114

Talula Restaurant
210 23rd Street
Miami Beach, Florida 33139
305-672-0778

The Café at Books & Books
265 Aragon Avenue
Coral Gables, Florida 33134
305-442-4408

The Captain's Tavern Restaurant
9621 South Dixie Highway
Pinecrest, Florida 33156
305-666-5979

The Oceanaire Seafood Room
900 South Miami Avenue
Suite 111
Miami, Florida 33130
305-372-8862

The River Oyster Bar
650 South Miami Avenue
Miami, Florida 33130
305-530-1915

The Rusty Pelican
3201 Rickenbacker Causeway
Key Biscayne, Florida 33149
305-361-3818

Timō Restaurant & Bar
17624 Collins Avenue
Sunny Isles, Florida 33160
305-936-1008

Touch Catering
860 NE 79th Street
Miami, Florida 33138
305-758-7191

Trattoria Sole
5894 Sunset Drive
South Miami, Florida 33143
305-666-9392

Tutto Pasta Ristorante
1751 SW 3rd Avenue
Miami, Florida 33129
305-857-0709

Two Chefs
8287 South Dixie Highway
South Miami, Florida 33143
305-663-2100

Two Sisters Restaurant
Hyatt Regency Coral Gables
50 Alhambra Plaza
Coral Gables, Florida 33134
305-441-1234

Versailles Restaurant
3555 SW 8th Street
Miami, Florida 33135
305-444-0240

Yuga Restaurant
357 Alcazar Avenue
Coral Gables, Florida 33134
305-442-8600

INDEX

༺༚༻

The index for Miami Flavors was written
by Donna Drialo, a professional indexer.

It was a privilege to write the index for
this book, to be able to give back to the
community of children's hospitals in this
small way.

My husband and I have four daughters
by adoption. Over the years, our
children have received exemplary care
for their growth issues, cleft lip and
palate and congenital heart defects at
children's hospitals in Russia, India and
the United States. We are enthusiastic
supporters of all children's hospitals
and we wish this one, Miami Children's
Hospital, all our best as they continue in
their special mission to serve the most
precious lives on our planet.

Donna Drialo